The Journey Continues

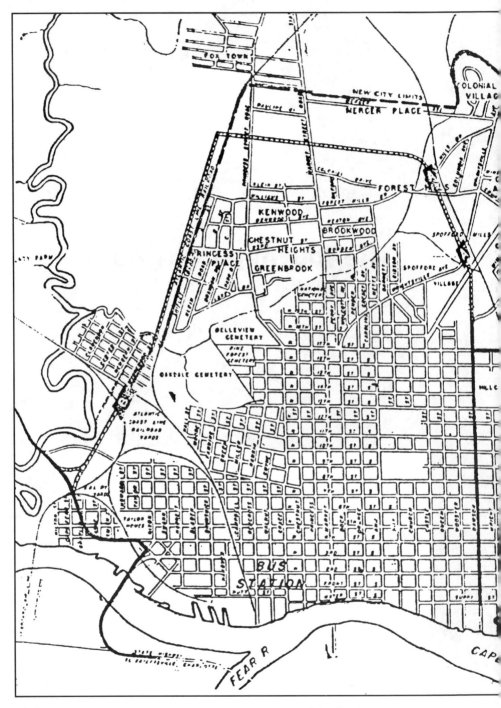

Wilmington, N.C., 1946, following postwar extension of city limits

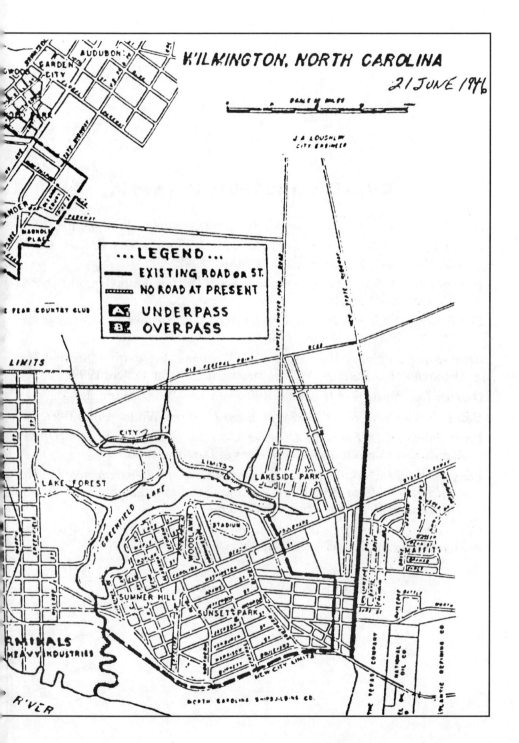

Wilmington Morning Star, June 21, 1946

Other Books by Wilbur D. Jones, Jr.

A Sentimental Journey: Memoirs of a Wartime Boomtown. White Mane, 2003.

Forget That You Have Been Hitler Soldiers: A Youth's Service to the Reich, with Hermann O. Pfrengle. White Mane, 2002.

Hawaii Goes to War: The Aftermath of Pearl Harbor, with Carroll Robbins Jones. White Mane, 2001.

Condemned to Live: A Panzer Artilleryman's Five-Front War, with Franz A. P. Frisch. White Mane, 2000.

Arming the Eagle: A History of U.S. Weapons Acquisition Since 1775. Department of Defense, and Government Printing Office, 1999.

Gyrene: The World War II United States Marine. White Mane, 1998.

Giants in the Cornfield: The 27th Indiana Infantry. White Mane, 1997.

From Packard to Perry: A Quarter Century of Service to the Defense Acquisition Community. Department of Defense, 1996.

Congressional Involvement and Relations: A Guide for Department of Defense Acquisition Managers, Four Editions. Department of Defense and Government Printing Office, 1986–1996.

Glossary: Defense Acquisition Acronyms and Terms, Two Editions. Department of Defense, 1987–1990.

Visit his website: *www.wilburjones.com*

The Journey Continues

The World War II Home Front

By
Wilbur D. Jones, Jr.

Foreword by Hugh Morton

WHITE MANE BOOKS
SHIPPENSBURG, PENNSYLVANIA

This White Mane Books publication
was printed by
Beidel Printing House, Inc.
63 West Burd Street
Shippensburg, PA 17257-0708 USA

The acid-free paper used in this book meets the guidelines for permanence and durability of the Committee on Production Guidelines for Book Longevity of the Council on Library Resources.

For a complete list of available publications
please write
White Mane Books
Division of White Mane Publishing Company, Inc.
P.O. Box 708
Shippensburg, PA 17257-0708 USA

Library of Congress Cataloging-in-Publication Data

Jones, Wilbur D.
    The journey continues : the World War II home front / by Wilbur D. Jones, Jr., with a foreword by Hugh Morton.
        p. cm.
    Includes bibliographical references and index.
    ISBN 1-57249-365-8 (alk. paper)
    1. World War, 1939-1945--North Carolina-Wilmington. 2. World War, 1939-1945--War work-North Carolina-Wilmington. 3. Wilmington (N.C.)--Social conditions. 4. Wilmington (N.C.)--Biography. 5. Wilmington (N.C.)--History. I. Title.

D769.85.N81W554 2005
940.53'75627--dc22

2005042247

PRINTED IN THE UNITED STATES OF AMERICA

This book is dedicated to my parents, Wilbur D. and Viola M. Jones, my sister, Elizabeth Jones Garniss, and the countless numbers of local people whose exceptionally hard work on the home front contributed mightily to the national war effort, and helped make Wilmington America's unique wartime boomtown.

AND

To the people of Southeastern North Carolina who also contributed to the area's war effort through defense work, civic activities, government and business service, and maintained the home front so we children could grow up as normal as possible.

Contents

Illustrations

ix

Foreword

Wilbur D. Jones, Jr., has produced a meticulously researched history of the Wilmington area and its residents during the time I was growing up. I treasure his tales involving many of our townspeople that he and I knew. Louis T. Moore, revered predecessor Wilmington historian to Wilbur, surely is looking down from heaven on him with an approving smile for authoring *The Journey Continues*.

Sometimes when a person is referred to as a "name-dropper," the term may not be considered altogether favorable, except when we decide that author Jones is one. We give him that name-dropper title in the most favorable possible sense. All of us who love the Port City owe him for this extremely industrious and interesting literary work.

By quoting chapter and verse via notes at the end of the book, credibility is provided that adds immensely to the value of this history of the Wilmington area in the period during and following World War II. About that war, it delights me that Wilmington is the site of the USS North Carolina Battleship Memorial. On that great ship, listed county by county, are the names of the more than 10,000 North Carolinians from all the military services who died in WWII.

My grandfather, Hugh MacRae, has been described by many people as being "fifty years ahead of his time." He is quoted in Chapter 4 of this book just four days after Pearl Harbor as saying: "Visioning victory—what does this mean to Wilmington, North Carolina? It means we awaken to the opportunity, and we will, that Wilmington will become a city of not less than 200,000 inhabitants." Every time I am exposed to the traffic on Market Street, College Road, and Oleander Drive I have the impression that Hugh MacRae's forecast more than 60 years ago was very close to correct.

The wars the United States has fought since WWII have not generated the same intensity of patriotism nationwide that seemed to prevail then. Nearly everyone in the country had a job directly or indirectly involving them in the war effort. This book emphasizes that point time and again. The able-bodied who were young enough were in the military, and everyone else was in war-related industries or volunteer work.

Wilbur scoured the pages of the *Wilmington Star-News* for months to come up with his notes on the numerous wartime weddings. Many of them were in Wilmington churches, but I am astounded how many were in far-away places like Belfast, Ireland; West Point, New York; London, England, and so on. This book has expanded my knowledge of what was going on in New Hanover County while I was in the army overseas. I was extremely interested in knowing we had hundreds of German prisoners of war in the Wilmington area, and that some had been good workers in Otto Leeuwenburg's dairy and in fertilizer plants.

The war was fought all over the globe, and scanning the names of countries and regions in which Wilmingtonians served in uniform makes this book a geography lesson. Our people were stationed literally everywhere. I have always been a proud booster of Wilmington, and *The Journey Continues* arms me to do an even better job now. Wilmingtonians on the moon may come later.

The local breakdown in 1944 between Democrats and Republicans is another item that particularly caught my eye. There were 13,841 registered Democrats and 410 Republicans. That same year Democrat Franklin D. Roosevelt topped Thomas E. Dewey 9,431 to 1,820 in the race for president. A few months later Roosevelt died.

Many Wilmingtonians who read *The Journey Continues* will find a mention of their kin or good friends, or familiar names. It may be in the cases heard in the New Hanover courthouse by Judge H. Winfield Smith, or may be lucky like me. My sister, Agnes Morton, is reported in *The Hanoverian* yearbook to have won the Athletic Superlative for the New Hanover High School class of 1943. Aggie played the No. 3 spot on the six-member school boys golf team. Later she was four times women's golf champion of the two Carolinas. My mother, Mrs. Julian Morton, made the wartime Wilmington book too, because of her tough volunteer job working for the Office of Price Administration's rationing board.

This is a great book, and every family living in Southeastern North Carolina should have a copy. My main disappointment is that Wilbur did not find a way to make the last chapter a happy one. It is titled "What if They Had All Come Home?" This may be the most meaningful chapter of all, however, and contains important information that I am glad to have.

Hugh Morton
Grandfather Mountain
Linville, N.C.

Author's note: *Former Wilmingtonian and University of North Carolina graduate Hugh Morton was an army combat newsreel cameraman in World War II in the Pacific, receiving the Bronze Star and Purple Heart. Among his lifetime of statewide and community civic contributions, he served in 1948 as the first president of the North Carolina Azalea Festival in Wilmington, and is largely credited with bringing the Battleship North Carolina Memorial to Wilmington in 1961.*

A nationally renowned photographer, journalist, author and businessman, his numerous awards and other recognition give testimony to his well-deserved reputation and esteem as North Carolina's most respected and prominent citizen.

Preface

For those who have not read *A Sentimental Journey: Memoirs of a Wartime Boomtown*, my "volume one" about the Wilmington and Southeastern North Carolina home front during World War II, a brief introduction is necessary. Because of its mighty contributions to the war effort, Wilmington rightfully earned the title "The Defense Capital of the State." It was undoubtedly America's unique wartime boomtown.

The Journey Continues further explores in greater depth the area's culture, social life, families, and their sons and daughters in uniform. Mindfully, some of the Preface and Introduction will be familiar or repetitive.

A Sentimental Journey has been in national distribution since 2003, receiving favorable reviews and the North Carolina Society of Historians 2003 Willie Parker Peace Book Award.

* * *

Over the years on visits to Wilmington I had driven through my boyhood neighborhood, past my house at 102 Colonial Drive, my Forest Hills grammar school, and the backyards and used-to-be woods and fields, the railroad tracks and creek, where we boys had played Marine and soldier growing up during wartime. (Without us, I often tell my Marine veteran friends with tongue-in-cheek, they would not have won the Pacific War.)

My school-days pals and I reminisced about crowds coming and going at the train station, war bond stamp drives, army truck convoys monopolizing city streets, air raid blackout drills, German army prisoners encamped across from Williston School, P-47s roaring overhead, new kids moving into town, no meat, ships torpedoed off the beaches, the horde of shipyard workers and GIs on Front Street on weekends, and long lines at the picture shows.

In 1995 after attending the V-J Day commemoration on the Battleship North Carolina Memorial in Wilmington that ended the war's 50th Anniversary, a passionate need compelled me to write the wartime history of my community, my people, my childhood—my sentimental journey, a sentimental journey home.

Most books on the WWII home front are generic or universal subject-specific. These two volumes are geographical-area specific, a personal exploration of a community encased within a unique regional war effort—a subject not undertaken to any extent by historians.

This book fuses memoirs of varying perspectives: a city, a county, their natives, wartime visitors, husbands and children in uniform, and of course mine. It is also the memoir of the *Wilmington Star-News*. My remembrances link and interpret these perspectives.

The Journey Continues is a snapshot study, but is neither a chronological nor an all-inclusive history. Although my Wilmington background influences my contributions, impartiality and objectivity prevail. Most of my observations will please readers, others will not, but all will inform. The record shows this area had both a decided upside and a downside.

Approximately 90 percent of the research is original primary source material from my more than 220 personal interviews, wartime letters, author's surveys, news items collected from the microfilm records of virtually every daily *Morning Star* and *Sunday Star-News* from early December 1941 through December 1946, and the American Legion Post 10 wartime scrapbooks kept by my mother, Viola M. Jones, auxiliary president in 1943.

Some editorial notes are in order. (To reflect the record of the times, this book cannot be "politically correct" by today's definitions.)

- To be as historically accurate as possible, and add a "down home" flavor, when appropriate I wrote in certain vernacular of the day. Examples: I used the term Negro(es) for the current African American(s), or black(s), and Negress to indicate a female. I used "girl" when applying to women past high-school age, which it did except for one's mother's age, and "boy" for all men in uniform.

- To show proper respect of the time, when referring to adults I used the title I knew them by then.

- For the names of females who were unmarried then I used their maiden names. That's how I knew them, and in many cases how they're still referred to by classmates and friends. Example: in the text my female classmate Willie Stanford is by that name. Later she married classmate Louis Leiner. When cited in the Notes, the full maiden-married names are used for women who subsequently married—and which are known to me: Willie Stanford Leiner. In the Bibliography she is listed as Leiner, Willie Stanford (her current name). In the Index she is listed under her maiden name: Stanford, Willie (Leiner). Okay, it may be a bit confusing, but you'll get the drift.

- The *Wilmington Star-News* did not use the titles "Mr.," "Mrs," or "Miss" in referring to Negro males and females, usually only their first name, married or not. The newspaper referred to white females by title, either by their husband's entire name or with their own first name: Mrs. H. M. Roland, or Perida Roland. Women are "Miss" unless identified as "Mrs."

• While WWII Negro remembrances and activities are adequately covered, my original intent was to report more details. My repeated efforts by advertising in the *Journal*, spreading the word, and trying to establish contacts with Williston Industrial School alumni brought limited success. Why is beyond me. *Star-News* coverage of Negro persons and events was sparse and excluded Negro photographs. Negroes were identified accordingly. Otherwise, the person was assumed to be white. Wilmington had virtually no other minorities except for a few Chinese Americans.

Errata from a *Sentimental Journey:* *Memoirs of a Wartime Boomtown*

Preface, pg. xvii—The British female service personnel would likely be "WAAFs," members of the Women's Auxiliary Air Force, Royal Air Force (not "Wrens," their Royal Navy counterpart).

Chapter 1, pg. 3—Dr. R. T. "Tom" Sinclair, Jr., was on army active duty at Fort Benning, Ga., on December 7, 1941 (not on Mimosa Place).

Chapter 2, pg. 24—"Five men from within a couple of blocks..." should read "Six men from within a couple of blocks...." Ensign Herman John Gerdes, Jr., U.S. Navy, submarine USS *Rabalo* (SS-273), failed to return from mission near Philippines in August 1944; parents lived at 114 Keaton Avenue.

Chapter 2, pg. 25—Captain John Richard "Dick" Garrabrant was killed in action near Montebourg, France (not near St. Lô). His daughter is Margey Garrabrant (not Marjorie).

Where appearing, name spelling correction: Evenson, Janet Rabunsky (not Everson).

Acknowledgments

Like *A Sentimental Journey*, this book was possible only because of the hundreds of present or former Wilmington and Southeastern North Carolina residents who remembered World War II here, and provided me with tons of interesting material. For this enthusiasm and cooperation, I am forever grateful. Folks supported the value of this project because they wished to record and preserve this rich period in our local history.

I sincerely appreciated those who answered my requests, particularly New Hanover High School alumni. I respect those Wilmingtonians who shared their painful remembrances of personal or family tragedies when loved ones in uniform died. No matter of time or circumstance has removed those memories, only dimmed them slightly.

For aiding in specific research, I thank these fine people: Jerry Parnell and the staff of the William Madison Randall Library, University of North Carolina at Wilmington; Beverly Tetterton of the New Hanover County Public Library; Margaret Sampson Rogers; Linda Pearce; the late George Norman and Bill Childs; Vince Lindenschmidt; Harold Fussell; David Stallman; John J. Burney, Jr. (perhaps my most enthusiastic supporter who firmly believed in my goals); Herman Alberti; Philip Jones; E. L. Mathews, Jr.; Julie Wilsey; Bill Humphrey; Ronnie Phelps; the Lower Cape Fear Historical Society and Cathy Myerow Boettcher; Dr. Chris Fonvielle; and Dr. Everard H. Smith.

As with *Journey*, this "volume two" is possible because of the professional cooperation and support of Harold Collier of White Mane Publishing Company, Inc., and the staffs of White Mane and Beidel Printing House, particularly Vicki Stouffer, Marianne Zinn, Michele Fritz, and Angela Guyer.

My family agreed I should take on this two-book effort, and strongly encouraged and motivated me. My wife, Carroll, my best and most serious editorial critic on whose judgment and sharp eyes I rely heavily, believed this project's link to my roots was not only historically necessary, but good for my peace of mind after returning to my hometown to live.

With this tremendous help, I believe I have made a serious contribution to the history of Wilmington, Southeastern North Carolina, the state, and WWII.

Introduction

Southeastern North Carolina, with its population, economic, social, and cultural hub in Wilmington in New Hanover County, contributed heavily to the nation's war effort in World War II. For numerous reasons it was America's unique wartime boomtown. Each of the armed forces was stationed here in numbers, its strategic location made it vulnerable to enemy attack, its shipyard was a massive producer of cargo vessels, its key port shipped vital war materials, farms and other defense industries produced at capacity, and the area dispatched thousands to fight. One hundred and ninety-one boys from New Hanover County did not return.

The county more than doubled from its pre-war population of 43,000 with the heavy influx of military personnel and war workers and their families. Quiet Wilmington, only 50 years earlier the state's largest city, creeping along for decades afflicted by geographical isolation, suddenly found itself by location an exploding national center of military life and defense production at the edge of the Atlantic conflict.

No other U.S. city matched the magnitude of the area's diverse activities and its complete absorption by the war. How the area managed the social, civic, jurisdictional, and governmental complexities in its economic boom amazes me six decades later.

The Journey Continues, therefore, has vast national appeal to any reader interested in WWII, particularly the home front, and American social and cultural history.

With several exceptions the area was totally unprepared for such an onslaught of people, activities, and responsibilities beginning in early 1941. Immediately after the Japanese attack on Pearl Harbor, Hawaii, on December 7, the area's defense requirements multiplied. Infrastructure and support services pushed past the limits and almost burst with ever-increasing demands for goods and services. These demands included housing (the most serious problem); food products and eating establishments; clothing, gasoline, tires and other strictly rationed items; school classrooms; social services; public transportation; and entertainment facilities.

The community constantly struggled to operate within frequently changing edicts from capitals in Washington and Raleigh, and its own pressures to serve the war effort, administer to citizens, manage huge construction projects, cope with civic stress and the racial chasm, combat the black market and a zooming crime scene, and apply equal justice. Elected and public leadership was generally adequate, and if inexperienced with managing a crisis of this proportion, valiantly adjusted through trial-and-error.

Meanwhile, a generally patriotic populace took pride in its war role, made forward strides, enjoyed a temporary increase in stature (an airy haughtiness diminished a subliminal chip-on-the-shoulder), and projected optimism in planning for the unknown postwar future.

Daily editions of the "voice of conscience," the *Wilmington Star-News*, exhorted women to volunteer for aircraft recognition and hospital work, men to buy more bonds, common sense from the Office of Price Administration, housewives to save cooking fats, and downtown jaywalking to cease.* But "the conscience" essentially ignored the rising tide of murders, prostitution, robberies, accidents, and petty crimes—readily identifying those committed by Negroes (perhaps two-thirds of its news items about Negroes were negative).

Its coastal location and war effort required Wilmington to mount a massive civilian defense program. Washington and local military officials bombarded the populace with fears of possible enemy attacks by sea and air, issuing through 1943 a drumbeat awareness of proper preparations. German U-boats ravaged offshore during that time, sinking ships off the coast, which belched their debris upon favorite bathing spots.

Home front efforts included: Inland Waterway patrols; airplane spotters, air raid wardens, drills, lighting dimouts, and total blackouts; no bathing suits at the beaches after dark; auxiliary police and firemen; rolling bandages for military hospitals—a hundred ways for involving volunteers. Some civilian defense jobs were kept manned, others were not. Most were subject to the availability of caring citizens. Occasionally positions were short but none were in jeopardy. I heard of conscientious people who worked at several such jobs or in civic service, and many others who lifted no finger.

Even as the casualty lists grew,† social life generally proceeded at the country club and beach clubs, as did school activities, sports events, and big

---

* The journalist-patriot publisher R. B. Page cast the newspaper in the war effort. "Our chief aim—to aid in every way the prosecution of the war to complete victory." [*Wilmington Morning Star*, January 7, 1943]

† Perhaps every block had at least one boy in uniform. Downtown Wilmington had a Gold Star mother on nearly every street. In my neighborhood, a boy from every other home served; most were officers; many flew fighters and bombers. Their exploits and visits home created quite a stir for us boys seeking to emulate them. My heroes still, not all returned alive, including at least four right down the street and six overall in my neighborhood.

band appearances—except when gasoline shortages prohibited "pleasure driving." Wrightsville Beach's Lumina pavilion, the area's premiere nightlife attraction, flourished from patronage by soldiers and their girls. Romance ruled. Everyone of an age fell in love, if only for a moment. Multitudes of area girls became engaged to or married visiting GIs.* For many teenage girls and young "spinsters," the war admittedly was the most exciting time of their life.

The major activities in the area's war effort included:

- North Carolina Shipbuilding Company (Wilmington)—built 243 Liberty, C-2, and AKA-type vessels for the navy, Maritime Commission, and private lines; the largest employer in the state with a peak of 23,000 in 1943

- Camp Davis, Holly Ridge (Pender and Onslow Counties)—army coast artillery and antiaircraft artillery training base; a peak of some 50,000 trained there; one hour north by vehicle†

- Fort Fisher, Kure Beach (New Hanover County)—army antiaircraft artillery advanced training base; one hour south

- Camp Lejeune, Jacksonville (Onslow County)—Marine Corps training base, the largest on the East Coast; 1½ hours north

- Bluethenthal Field Army Air Base (Wilmington)—army air forces P-40 and P-47 fighter training field, earlier a B-24 antisubmarine patrol base

- Fort Caswell Naval Station, Fort Caswell (Brunswick County)—navy inshore-warfare patrol (antisubmarine) base; two hours southeast on Cape Fear River

- Coast Guard and Coast Guard Auxiliary patrol and rescue bases at Wrightsville Beach (New Hanover County), ½ hour east, and Wilmington

- Port of Wilmington, Cape Fear River—shipped Lend-Lease materials to Europe and other war materials, and imported petroleum, 18 miles upstream from ocean

- Atlantic Coast Line Railroad headquarters (Wilmington)—a workhorse in moving troops, equipment, material, and passengers

---

* In 1943 my sister Elizabeth met Camp Davis officer candidate George Garniss at our home, became engaged, and married him after his service in India. So typical.

† All highways out of Wilmington were narrow and two lanes. Travel time depended on vehicle volume and weather.

- Ethyl-Dow Chemical Company (Kure's Beach,[*] New Hanover County)—only East Coast plant manufacturing ethlyene bromide high-octane additive for military aviation gasoline[†]

Ethyl-Dow Chemical Company, which made bromine out of seawater for use in aviation gasoline, near Kure's Beach. On the night of July 24–25, 1943, a German submarine surfaced and fired at least three shells at the plant. They hit in the river instead. This action may have been the only German attack on America.

Randall Library, UNC Wilmington

- Other war industries around Wilmington included small ship and craft repair facilities, truck farms, fertilizer plants, clothing manufacturers, pulpwood producers, floating drydocks construction, and more

---

[*] After the war the name became just Kure Beach.

[†] Whether a German U-boat actually fired on the Ethyl-Dow plant on the night of July 24–25, 1943, has been debated locally ever since. The answer is in *A Sentimental Journey*.

- Three German prisoner of war camps (Wilmington)—in 1945 held a peak of some 550 *Afrika Korps* soldiers, a subject of community fascination, who worked on farms and dairies and in local industries

- The combat deeds of Wilmington area men are legion. Hundreds were decorated for valor and service. Overseas duty molded and hardened those who would return to lead Wilmington's eventual postwar transformation. *The Journey Continues* engages the reader with some of these deeds and experiences.

- Two Medal of Honor recipients graduated from New Hanover High School, to my knowledge the only high school with that distinction for WWII. They were army Lieutenant Charles P. Murray, Jr. ('38), awarded for valor in France in December 1944, and navy corpsman William David Halyburton, Jr. ('43), awarded posthumously for valor on Okinawa in May 1945.[*]

- Three Wilmingtonians were decorated heroes at the Battle of Midway. Two were rightful, the other not. For sinking the Japanese carrier *Kaga*, USS *Enterprise* (CV-6) carrier pilots Carl David Peiffer (NHHS '34) and Clarence Earle Dickinson (NHHS '32) received the Navy Cross, Peiffer posthumously. Army air forces B-17 formation leader Brooke E. Allen (NHHS '29) received the Distinguished Service Cross (the army equivalent to the foregoing navy's highest award), but his bombs hit no targets. Dickinson also received a Navy Cross for sinking a submarine four days after Pearl Harbor, three Navy Crosses all told.

- New Hanover County's 191 dead and missing in action during service in the armed forces and merchant marine were augmented in numbers by another 57 dead with a direct county connection.[†] Local boys died in Tunisia, Italy, France, Belgium, Luxembourg, and Germany, and Cape Gloucester, Saipan, Peleliu, New Guinea, and the Philippines, and in the skies above and waters around them, or in other service-related situations.

---

[*] On October 11, 2003, the City of Wilmington and the World War II Wilmington Home Front Heritage Coalition dedicated a sign to the future new William D. Halyburton, Jr., Memorial Park. This ended 58 years of neglect by the community in officially recognizing Halyburton. At the same time, the NHHS Class of 1943, Wilmington-Cape Fear Homebuilders Association, and Coalition dedicated a new memorial with plaque to Halyburton and Murray in front of NHHS. Halyburton Park opened one year later.

[†] The connections included prior residency, schooling, or employment, or having families living here during the war.

Three sailors died during the attack on Pearl Harbor, one while fighting on the USS *Arizona* (BB-39). Two Negro sailors were among those killed during the huge 1944 ammunition depot explosion at Port Chicago, California. Two families lost two sons each, one losing both within several weeks after the Normandy D-Day invasion. Like Peiffer, two NHHS graduate fighter pilots killed in action—First Lieutenants Robert Aaron Goldberg, Jr., and James Borden Lynch II— were from leading families, extremely popular, heads of their classes, and considered bound for unlimited success.

- Local men fought on other storied battlegrounds including Normandy, the Bulge, Colmar Pocket, Arnhem Bridge, Siegfried Line, Burma, Sicily, Coral Sea, Guadalcanal, and Iwo Jima. They served in ships, submarines, bombers, tanks, and field hospitals, and in the infantry, artillery, and support services.

- One family sent six sons into the nation's service, and several sent four into the armed forces. All survived.

* * *

Wilmington, of course, was the South. So were my Forest Hills neighborhood and my roots. I was born in Wilmington's James Walker Memorial Hospital on July 9, 1934, to Wilbur David and Viola Murrell Jones. I graduated from Forest Hills School in '47 (skipping the first grade), NHHS in '51, and the University of North Carolina in '55.

My father, born in 1892 and raised in a large family of tenant farmers on the border of poor Onslow and Jones Counties, served during World War I as a navy hospital corpsman with the 6th Marines in the Caribbean. In 44 years with Carolina Savings and Loan Association here, he advanced his sixth-grade education into becoming its chief executive. My mother, born here in 1903, was educated through eight grades. Her divorced mother, Hattie Murrell, kept the downtown women's public restroom to support her three children, while my mother took

Must be a Sunday School project I'm beaming over, late 1941.

Author's collection

care of a younger brother. Mother never had a paid job outside the home but excelled in volunteer civic work during and after the war. Sweethearts during WWI when she was 14, they married here in 1921. He died here in 1967, she in 1973. Both are buried in Wilmington's Oakdale Cemetery.

My sister, Elizabeth "Lib" Jones Garniss, born here in 1922, an alumna of NHHS ('39) and Agnes Scott College ('43), and former social worker and bank employee, has lived in the Seattle, Washington, area for more than 30 years.

(While working on these books I am continually mindful of my parents, where they came from, what they made of themselves, and what they raised me to become—and reflected on what tremendous strains and stresses parents and community leaders endured during the war. Somehow, my parents maintained their family lives and work, volunteer and personal, in rational balance. How, I will never know, because as a natural boy I got into natural mischief.)

For my friends and me, war dominated but did not totally preoccupy our lives, including play time. Proper growing-up came first. My parents saw to my learning, thought, and doing the right things as groundwork for a full, productive, and virtuous life. For their examples and inspirations, I am eternally grateful.

My generation, those born in the Great Depression, or between the years 1932–40, are sometimes called the "forgotten generation." History's most fearsome war radically blurred our childhood. Now mostly retired, by default we are the bridge generation between those who won WWII and their offspring, the Baby Boomers, whose indelible traits have been protest against traditions and authority their parents had built.

I further beg the reader understand the difficulties in comparing current city and county governments with those of wartime Wilmington. Various similarities exist, such as with the Board of Education, but in those days the city dominated political, economic, civic, and social activities because of its population and resources center.

Draw a box. The county jurisdiction (hard to visualize now) roughly began at 17th Street to the east, Greenfield Lake to the south, Hilton Park to the north, and the Cape Fear River to the west. The county was mainly rural farming country with few modern roads, in some places lacking electricity and running water, and isolated largely from urban intercourse. "Going down town" from the beaches or sounds or Castle Hayne was a *real big deal*, because only a handful of retail, dining, and entertainment establishments such as mom-and-pop grocery stores, fish houses, and filling stations existed outside the box. County law enforcement and fire protection was less in numbers and unpredictable.

All county residents had city mailing addresses, but county folks (like today) paid no city taxes. Several "suburbs" like the Oleander and Forest Hills developments contained many of the area's leading citizens, and living outside the limits never deterred broad participation in activities or the war effort. To residents like my parents, the jurisdictions were the same.

In the time line of history for the Wilmington area, WWII will always appear as an abruptly peaking and then equally descending bell curve. But for our purpose here, it witnessed the rise and fall of America's unique wartime boomtown.

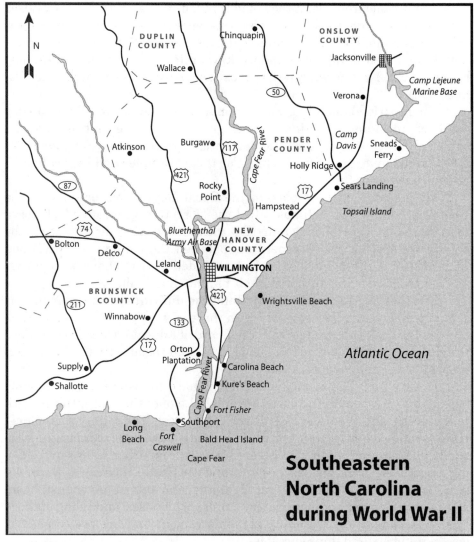

Southeastern North Carolina during World War II

Map prepared by author, drawn by Jim Robinson

Chapter 1

The Senses of Nostalgia

Did you ever stick your nose in the bloom of an open gardenia, or feel a tickle in the fragrance of a wispy orange and yellow mimosa blossom, or jump back from a jealous bee while sniffing in the midst of bunches of crepe myrtle? Wasn't it all the more delightful to the senses after a sudden summer rain? Didn't the pavement of the street you lived on lightly sizzle and puff steam at the first drops, while the fresh cleansing smell and clattering thunder signaled a downpour suitable for racing toy boats along the curb? We kids on my block did. In the uncertain world of the war years, without material excesses, we enjoyed the easy pleasures of summer. Such as these.

Nature's gift of the ability to record, store, and retrieve the essence of the senses is a hallmark of nostalgia. Without it, we are locked in the present and approach the future lacking full awareness. Its power of instant association is a reconnect sensation serving as one's personal time machine. Distinctive visions from the past live again, fleetingly or for a while. They bring back a life we knew, pleasant or unpleasant.

Each of the foregoing senses of nostalgia of my wartime childhood I experienced in my sentimental journey writing these books. Even though they no longer exist, I can still inhale the unique scents of the small drug stores that provided both necessities and lifestyle: Saunders', Futrelle's, and Jarman's—a delightful unforgettable mixed aroma of cosmetics, medicines, and sweets. I see the black-and-white-checked tile floors, usually sparkling, and hear the clear soda water stream fizzing from the counter nozzle to fill a long v-shaped glass of ice cream with its froth, the real drink of choice for World War II. You just can't replicate those bygone smells, or those thin, wiry steel tables and chairs where kids waited after a movie for their mothers.

The war grasped our lives, but not completely. We made the best with what we had, and it usually started and played out in our neighborhoods. School days always consummated daily reunions of friends, but often chores.

1

Boiling, sultry summer vacation days failed to interfere and somehow invigorated. We awoke early to get going. Because of Wilmington's moderate winters, outdoor play was year-around. My house on the southeastern corner of Colonial Drive at the intersection with Guilford Avenue is still occupied, but with extensions, and the pecan climbing tree flourishes.

My Forest Hills neighborhood was visible and friendly, not only regarding wartime unison but because people seemed more inclined to be hospitable then. Our residents contained many leaders in the war effort and civic life. We were outdoors more and saw each other more, passed the time of day, visited, and went to the other's aid. The mailman knew what was going on, stopped to talk with people, and shared news.[1]

Without air conditioning, shade trees and front porches could be more relaxing than one's second-story bedroom. With two exceptions, the mid-December 1943 "blizzard," which "paralyzed" the area under four inches, and the August 1944 near-hurricane which tore up the beaches, the weather deterred neither play nor the war effort.

* * *

The McEacherns. George McEachern lived on Guilford Avenue directly behind me with parents Walter and Tabitha. Although several years younger than my gang, we included him because he had more toys and equipment, a big downstairs play room, and an outdoor grill. "It always drew a crowd," Mrs. McEachern recalled. She and husband Walter were widely known for their charcoaled hot dogs, a cinch to appeal to warriors or ballplayers needing a noontime break. And (maybe most of all), her Hutaff family owned the area's Coca-Cola bottling company. In days of short or zero supply in the stores, their house was "always stacked with Cokes."[2] I cannot forget the sweet pungent aroma of their huge front-yard magnolia tree we boys climbed because it lives today.

Backyard-next door neighbor George McEachern in play military uniform driving toy airplane on wheels. Background across Guilford Avenue: the house of Emory and Gertrude Southerland.

Author's collection

Diverting from war, we boys played *at sports*, primarily football and basketball. Finding a field for baseball was difficult. We also played cowboys-and-Indians and cops-and-robbers, free and unstructured but competitive. The vacant wooded lot the McEacherns owned next door and their concrete driveway with basketball goal made decent playgrounds. Friendly, George was a reservoir of war assets, and willing to play the enemy.

George surpassed me with metal toy soldiers and military gear, treasured and hoarded commodities, naturally deeming me envious. One day I snuck home with a bagful of his precious lead soldiers, put them on parade, and dreamed away the afternoon. Enamored with my new collection, I completely lost track of their origin, re-bagged and took them over there that evening, boasting of my luck. Mr. McEachern announced they looked awfully familiar. Suddenly I left them and raced home embarrassed with bruised pride, having stolen the only thing in my life. They said nothing to my parents.*

Mr. McEachern, whose war effort service was the Coast Guard Auxiliary, farmed with George Hutaff in Castle Hayne. A most colorful character of my childhood, often he pinned my ears back with elongated chatter, pacing the azalea line between our properties, pipe firmly in tobacco-stained teeth, while I dribbled my basketball or recovered pecans beneath our tree. He flooded this boy with information.

The Kalfins. The McEacherns and only one other family, the Herman Kalfins, lived on Guilford's block-long south side. Between them also was an abandoned clay tennis court, on which my future brother-in-law, Lieutenant George H. Garniss, in 1944 taught me baseball fundamentals. Mr. Kalfin owned one of Front Street's finest women's shops. His daughter Sondra along with Bobbie Lounsbury, Charlotte Jones, and Jeanne Gresham were neighborhood girl playmates. The games they participated in usually were "hide-and-go-seek" or "ain't-no-bears-out-tonight" types, until we disappeared or they dropped out on purpose. They, too, had other interests.

Although the suburbs were relatively crime-free, on November 1, 1944, thieves stole jewelry valued at $2,018 by forcing the Kalfins' door. One month later two Negro men suspects were dismissed for lack of probable cause. The family recovered nothing, and the neighborhood understandably was ill at ease for a time.[3]

The Southerlands. Emory and Gertrude Southerland, and their pretty teenage cheerleader daughter Patty, lived across from the McEacherns. He managed the Penney's store, and she reigned as the neighborhood's classic fastidious housekeeper. He, as the classic weekend fisherman and hunter, kept boat, trailer, and gear back by the garage, and enjoyed entertaining friends by cooking their catches on his fireplace and downing a drink or two in "Emory's Night Club on the Sound." Her demands: outside, and woe unto any who entered the house after such excursions.[4]

One night her sofa caught on fire from a cigarette and caused a "big alarm. She was beside herself," a neighbor recalled.[5] "I admired everything

---

* I admitted it finally in 2000, my redemption. George does not remember this incident. We lined up the soldiers and shot Tinker Toy sticks at them to see who could knock down the most.

about him. He had his own little dog house out in the yard." Mrs. Southerland, a prim and proper lady, liked to invite my mother and a few refined friends for tea. Patty, well she was about the cutest high school girl I ever saw. On weekends I hung around my backyard to glimpse her going out on dates. Today I can still see why I had a crush on her.

The Solomons. At the western end of Guilford on Forest Hills Drive, Harry M. and Louise Fick Solomon raised three daughters, Marie, Jean, and Catherine. Marie and Jean finished NHHS during the middle of the war. Catherine was a couple of years older than I. Harry owned the established family business, S&B Solomon Wholesale Dry Goods Company, and served faithfully during the war and years after as head of the city housing authority.

The Copelands.[6] Next door to the Solomons on Forest Hills Drive were the Copelands, who sported one of the neighborhood's most entertaining playthings. Grover, an Atlantic Coast Line Railroad executive, and Clara had one child, Bobby, my friend. They built a miniature railroad in their backyard with cars you could sit in and brakes that actually stopped them, metal tracks, plus a trestle. Boys from all over gathered, occasionally supervised by ACL employee Negro DeWitt "Dee" Metters. "If he had been a white man he would have been president of the line, he was so smart," Clara said. You pushed the cars uphill and rode downhill. A little station house was added "for the boys to put their secrets in."

The Copeland house was like many built in Forest Hills and Oleander during the 1930s and until after the war started. The garage in back had an upstairs apartment which functioned as more than a bedroom. Owners rented these garage apartments to war workers or servicemen. Nearby, Dr. Charles P. Graham added one so his wife, Jean McKoy Graham, would not be alone while he served on navy duty.

The Stanleys. In Forest Hills, only Bonner Thomason's house kept horses. The Charles Harringtons, living at "the point" where Colonial and Forest Hills Drives converged, stabled their horse there. But around the corner from Colonial on Market Street, on his seven acres, Dr. J. W. Stanley raised a cow, mule, hothouse, and 60 pecan trees.[*] On a dare or when feeling frisky, we boys teased the mule, shook nuts off the trees, and swiped watermelons—always shooed away and sometimes apprehended. The dentist Stanley "sold enough [pecans] to pay his taxes," remembered daughter Blanche Stanley, and also raised and sold non-acid tomatoes and tomato plants. He had "quite a side business." Her mother, Frances Stanley, rented rooms and made every closet into a bathroom. The home was called "Pecan Lodge."[7]

---

[*] A number of trees still stand, but the house long ago was razed when the YMCA relocated from 3rd and Market.

The Greshams.[8] Sam and Mary Emma Gresham lived in the first house inside Colonial from Market. Only Obby Allsbrook and Bobby McCumber from my boyhood still live in their homes. Mr. Gresham ran his own gasoline hauling firm and spent many hours in tank trucks heading out of the port storage area. Porch sitters, they monitored the Stanleys' pecan business, the large corner Herbert McClammy house and their transient renters, and vehicle traffic on the concrete street. One car in particular made a lasting impression. The Barefoot boys (Graham, Poli, and Murray) drove their Model A Ford on bare metal rims through the neighborhood. "You could sure hear it coming." Horses and riders were normal.

The Hansons and Mitchells.[9] The Louis Hanson and George Mitchell houses across the street from me backed up to the Stanley property. Dick Hanson hunted on the Stanley acreage with 22s and 440 shotguns. "It's a wonder we didn't shoot somebody." High school boys played ball on the Hansons' side yard. "That's where we all would meet." The group included Graham and Poli Barefoot, Charlie Mitchell, Jere Freeman, Jr., Charlie Harrington, Jr., and Louis Hackler. We younger boys sat and learned, and once in a while received an important assignment. Dick and brother Louis, Jr., raised chickens and pigeons in a coop beside the garage. Mrs. Hanson's mother, Katherine Vollers, visited them often in a big black limousine with capped driver, duly impressing us.

My across-the-street neighbor Lt. (j.g.) George L. Mitchell, Jr., a veteran of several Pacific invasions on LST-124.
Emma Mitchell Wilcox

The Humphreys. Next door lived one of my wartime buddies, Billy Humphrey, a close friend to this day. My father's real estate firm built the house for Liston and Eloise Humphrey in 1942. Our mothers visited frequently whether at the side yard or in the kitchen, but true to Southern etiquette of the day, rarely called each other "Viola" or "Eloise," only last names. Close associates in our church and civic life, our fathers called each other by first names. Mother and Mr. Humphrey, Hemenway school mates, thus were more familiar. Daddy and Mrs. Humphrey addressed each other formally. (I never figured out this arrangement.) Billy and I called all parents "Mr." or "Mrs." and responded to adults with "sir" and "ma'am." Kids had no problems.

Billy and I each had dogs, Wimpy and Jip. They liked growling and going at the other, requiring separation. Every boy owned a dog. They followed us everywhere, often swept up in our battle play-outs.

Until she had her second and final child, Elise, born on V-J Day, August 14, 1945, Mrs. Humphrey acted as my surrogate mother. Driving Billy someplace, she might include me. If I needed supper, she might bring me some.[*] Both my parents were often out of the house active in civilian defense, fraternal, civic, and church organizations. My mother's war effort activities included responsibilities as a Red Cross Nurse's Aide and with the American Legion Post 10 Auxiliary.[†] Mother usually drove our car, and Daddy got rides or caught the bus.

I emerged as a prototype latchkey kid, spending hours at home alone, including at night doing homework, listening to the radio, and playing with my war collections. When my sister Elizabeth began working at the shipyard in mid-1943, she often fixed our supper and monitored my assignments.

In those years of strict segregation, only whites lived in my extended neighborhood. Negroes worked there as yard hands, chauffeurs, cooks, nurses for young children, and servants, or peddled fresh vegetables through the neighborhood. Otherwise they were unseen. The closest Negro settlements were in Foxtown, a nearby area around Princess Place Drive and 29th, and the north end of Mercer Avenue. It seemed like they were in the next county. We boys never ventured there except with our father at the wheel.

A Negro couple came our way several times a week pulling two red wagons with wooden slats (like on an ancient pickup truck) loaded with pole beans, corn, cantaloupes, squash, turnips and garden greens—if they hadn't sold out. Her voice still rings: *"Niiicce freeessh green peeeasss, butterbeannnssss and ooohkra!"* They made their living this way. Mother was a loyal customer. Like the voice, the taste of juicy, slimy okra (ate heads and all) Mother cooked still lingers.

Negroes never came to a white's front door, but to the side or back. At our back door on Guilford we often gave the couple canning jars of ice water while they rested under our tree or sidewalk steps. Mother did not use a glass we drank from, but kept their jars washed.[‡]

The Brookwood Neighbors

The Brookwood folks were neighborhood kin, even after some switched from Forest Hills to the new Chestnut Street School in 1942. Market Street

---

[*] Until her death at 91 in September 2000, she remained the dearest, sweetest of persons, quick-witted as ever, with a radiant smile remembered from long ago—a special friend of my family.

[†] The four scrapbooks she kept on people in the service helped my research. When my sister and I closed her housekeeping, we donated two of them to Post 10, who later donated them to Randall Library at UNC Wilmington.

[‡] Vernon Gigax knew this late couple whose names were Will and Kate Robinson. For years people saw them all over town selling produce and collecting junk.

running east-west was an invisible yet definite dividing line between north-south neighborhoods. You might know people on the northern side, but the line held you back. Market was an extremely busy road into downtown, and had the county's steadiest traffic.

There one night I saw my first dead man, killed instantly when struck by a dairy truck on the south side of Market opposite Kenwood Avenue and the Broad Circle Food Store. Billy Humphrey and I were biking in the dusk of January 20, 1945, and heard the commotion, arriving right before the ambulance. The sight of produce truck operator Sam Lewis Cauley, 45, lying on the pavement terrified me. The dairy truck, driven by Otto Leeuwenburg, traveling east at 25 mph, had crashed into Cauley's parked vehicle.

The highway patrol arrested Leeuwenburg, who escaped injury when his truck overturned. A coroner's jury concluded the death was "through the 'careless and negligent operation' of a milk truck....[But] no [damning] evidence was forthcoming...,"[10] and he was not indicted.*

We boys tried impressing Brookwood girls, especially Lucy Ann Carney, Cecelia Black, Mary Low, Nancy Sneed, Mary Ann Snakenburg, and Carolyn Simpson. Brookwood kids lived in older, smaller houses with narrow lots and driveways. Shorter east-west streets were called the "dirt road connectors." Lucy Ann remembered when David Darden moved away after his father went to jail. His friend Billy West fought a boy who said something bad about David. Billy had many friends. "One of the greatest joys of my life was Billy's class at Forest Hills," said his mother, Rae West, an unofficial neighborhood den mother—the kind every kid summons when blocks from home needing a bathroom or snack.[11]

When Cecelia contracted scarlet fever, the Blacks moved her sisters Betty and Barbara and brother Jackie over to her grandfather's and stayed home to nurse her, aided by Dr. Auley Crouch's house calls. Mary Belle Ormond's railroad family lived on Metts Avenue behind the Walker Taylor house.† "It was nice and quiet....I knew everybody in town practically." The air force pilot son of her neighbors, the A. R. Hardwicks, once buzzed their house indicating he was headed home.[12]

Johnny Butt was a Brookwood pal until his father's company transferred him. Fanatics over the late afternoon serials, we proceeded with our game of dirt-pile "little soldiers" and cars while listening to a radio blaring

---

* His son and my schoolmate Bill Leeuwenburg recalled the grand jury determined his father not at fault. They found the man had been drinking and was seated on the ground behind the truck without truck lights. "My father was upset a long time after that." [Interview with Leeuwenburg, July 24, 2000]

† Mac Wilson remembered growing up "she was the epitome of what a lady should be." [Interview with McCulloch B. Wilson, Jr., March 1, 2000]

from the house. Kids constructed forts next door. Once in Johnny's kitchen sink I thought I might die from gulping ice water. He heard of a man who dropped dead after doing it and thought I should know. I gagged, spit out the remainder, and breathed hard.

Harold Laing lived in the family-run Powers rooming house with a neon sign at the corner of Keaton and Market where he was raised as an only child. A number of tourist homes and rooming houses populated that section on the south side of Market, including one owned by the John W. Kings next door.[13] Harold was fearless and unblushing (i.e., slightly reckless), a boy you wanted on your side even if you didn't like him. Burnt Mill Creek, an intimate play site loaded with squirrels, was "always a place of interest," with snakes and tortoises and other belly crawlers along the banks, some squashed in the streets.[14] Lucy Ann feared the creek, not only because of varmints, but because the reckless Delgado neighborhood boys congregated there.

To county school superintendent H. M. Roland and wife Perida, the neighborhood was "very amiable, can't remember anyone who didn't get along." But Borden Avenue spawned some "destructive" boys. Her circle of friends tilted toward educators. Unlike the Joneses and Humphreys, these ladies set rules for addressing each other formally by Mrs.-last-name, even with the most intimate of friends.[15]

The Other End of Colonial Drive

In those days boys bullied each other with threats and fists. Whether a scuffle or full-fledged fight, learning how to start it or end it was essential in growing up male. Matters were usually straightened out on the street, or at most by parent-to-parent conversations and severe discipline, never by filing charges or pleading social agency intervention. We had our share of sissies. Some were "mama's boys"; others, trouble looked for them. Eventually the word got around: some went home to Mother, the rest stood up for themselves. With age I gained adequate moxie to prove myself, but my mother was prone to shelter me nevertheless.

Obby Allsbrook, whose father, O. O. "Red" Allsbrook, ran the White's Ice Cream and Dairy Company, was a favorite target. "He was picked on a lot," said his mother, Elizabeth. "I told Obby if anybody hits you again, you just hit them back. 'Mother, I'm just not that type of boy.'"[16] Meanies also hassled boys on either side of him, Angus Olmstead, Jr., and Q. B. Snipes, Jr.

I experienced the evolving power of discussion, persuasion, and confrontation avoidance, a lifetime practice successfully employed. Q. B.'s father worked with mine at the Carolina Building & Loan and his mother was a school teacher. One of our idols was champion boxer Barney Ross. After he became a Marine hero, we alternated days acting his part, whether on Guadalcanal or in Madison Square Garden.

The Broad Circle was a first-class neighborhood corner grocery. "The owner was always there," provided personal service, and they delivered.[17] My mother, a regular shopper, received her due rewards with scarce items, and owner Mr. Olmstead saved Camels for Daddy. Thurston "Gene" Edwards worked there for six years as a student, contributing to the family income. Chores included the unsavory task of cleaning the meat block every Saturday. He remembered the sound of Mr. Olmstead popping caps off the six to eight Coke bottles he swigged daily. Edwards also worked next door at Brinson's Odorless Dry Cleaners. "I didn't have time to get into trouble."[18]

Edwards waited on customers, took orders, fetched and boxed the items, prepared the bill, and delivered by bicycle. Approximately 80 percent of the store's business was on charge accounts due monthly. "Some people who didn't pay regularly were those who would normally be expected to pay." Most Forest Hills residents we knew shopped at Broad Circle for convenience and familiarity. Folks gathered as an informal assembly post swapping news about boys overseas, or the New Hanover Wildcats football season.

Trading with friends and neighbors was normal business practice. Physicians and other practitioners bartered or exchanged professional services in lieu of fees. So, the Harringtons might naturally trade at the Broad Circle, owned by Angus' father. Instead they frequented the Davis Grocery Company one and one-half miles away on 17th Street.

Whistles played a supporting neighborhood role. There was the trademark shift whistle at nearby Spofford Mills in Delgado which neighbors had

The popular Davis Grocery Co. store at 17th and Dock Sts., owned by Norman Davis' father.

Norman Davis

tuned out. Civilian defense officials tooted theirs during blackouts and drills. We boys blew them during cops-and-robber games. And James G. Thornton hired a patrol policeman with a whistle to blow in case of emergency. "We were scared of the people in Dry Pond" coming over, his daughter Lucretia said.[19] The banker Mr. Thornton, an active supporter of the war effort leading war bond drives, continued even after his son Jimmy was killed in action.

The Colonial Village Kids

Two tragedies hit the new (1941) Colonial Village subdivision, part of my extended neighborhood. In February 1944, a gas leak killed Leroy Blake, who was awaiting navy duty. *Star-News* carriers Billy Venters and Ronnie Phelps, delivering the morning paper, smelled fumes at 168 Colonial Circle, knocked on the door and got no response. Someone later smelled lingering gas and called police. Leroy had been overcome. Three family members asleep in their beds saturated with sweat were revived with artificial respiration.[20] In 1945 a blaze destroyed a favorite hangout, the Colonial Village Ice Cream Parlor at Mercer Avenue and the Old Wrightsville Beach highway (Old Shell Road).

Classmates Joe Johnson, Betty Buck, Willie Stanford, and Phelps, born to be ringleaders, honed their skills early. Their houses attracted the Colonial Village gang. Joe's family endeavored to make ends meet like so many others in wartime Wilmington. Joseph H. Johnson, Sr., worked for the Railway Express Agency and "was gone on the train all the time." His mother, Elizabeth Woodcock Johnson, "did a lot of cooking and baking with Grandma, and gave some to the USO [United Service Organizations]."[21] Joe and his father plowed with their old mule named Maude. "I remember winning all the garden contests at school, and had all the biggest potatoes and onions."[22]

Joe knew the neighborhood like an Indian scout: every ripple of the creek, freight train schedules, and how to annoy and then avoid the charging black bull on the Taylor farm. He taught me something about sprinting. After a couple of near misses beating the bull to the nearest fence, I figured my luck had expired—exhilarating, another "notch in my gun" proving fearlessness (but little did they know the truth).

Have you ever tried smoking "rabbit tobacco"? Surely it isn't domestic just to Wilmington. A light gray weed in the fields, once dried and rolled into cigarette papers (not newspapers!) you puffed it like a cigarette. At best you only turned green. They both tasted so awful I can't remember which was worse, rabbit tobacco or "Indian cigars." But I can still sense the bitter roasted tongue from numerous tries. Some of the "tougher" boys preferred the real thing, but no grocery clerk would ever sell to 11-year-olds. True daredevils therefore would acquire "borrowed" smokes. If Tracy, Bogart, and every GI you met could, why not them?

The Johnson property backed up to both sides of Burnt Mill Creek. Some kids fished there (but not me) periodically hooking a half-pan size scaly scooter, usually tossing it back but sometimes carting the trophy home to a mother all too willing to dump it. The brown water was deep enough in spots for swimming. Trying to see underneath meant bloodshot eyes, something you couldn't hide from Mother if you disobeyed by going into the water anyway. Trees with massive vines for swinging and leaping covered the north side. Aaahyeeeaaah! —this was "Tarzan and Boy country."

The creek provided a haven where social and racial groups mingled on equal terms, rich boys with the sons of mill spinners and shipyard welders. I wondered why Negro kids otherwise were kept apart from and beneath us. We had no rules, but when the group decided to shed trunks, you either went along or went somewhere else. The creek served many useful purposes, including solitude when, with nothing else to do, skimming rocks across silent pools, or watching the swirling algae could pass a bit of a boring afternoon.

Colonial Village life centered around my schoolmates' families. Mercer was paved where they lived but not on the northern end where Negroes and lower-income whites lived. Folks kept Victory gardens and animals. "When they got tired of their animals they would bring them to us, including a deer," Bertha Buck remembered.[23] "Everyone on Colonial Circle came to our house because we always had a pony, goats, and other animals," added daughter Betty. Next door neighbors to the Bucks were military renters from out of town. "We kind of adopted the families. They couldn't understand why we didn't have double names."[24] Oscar D. Buck, "tall and slender and looked like Abraham Lincoln," worked at the shipyard.[25]

Willie Stanford's father, Jonathon Stanford, paid $4,000 for their house in 1941. The neighborhood teemed with wild summer blackberries. Willie willingly dug caves and mounds for war games behind E. B. Bugg's house. Athletic and a "big old tomboy," along with neighbor Janet McVey, "it was always play the boy games or just us two girls playing hopscotch." The Stanfords often walked to and from their grocery store at 13th and Castle without being bothered. Sometimes Mr. Stanford slept there to open up at daybreak for shipyard workers.[26]

These kids daringly roamed on their bikes, fitting in equally well anywhere. In those days parents didn't drive children to play. At school they could tell the Forest Hills bikes from theirs because the rich kids had Iver Johnsons with pants guards. Regulars included "villager" Jerry Outlaw and Forest Hills kids including Mary Van Walbach, Billy Dosher, Pender Durham, Bobby Cameron, and Betty Bugg, whose maid produced tasty vegetable soup sandwiches. Joe Johnson's territory expanded eastward to the Lingo City gas station where the railroad tracks crossed Oleander Drive. He adorned his room with all sorts of war paraphernalia like cardboard airplanes; war maps covered mine.

Ronnie Phelps, also a typical adventuresome boy and constantly on the go, wore out school shoes playing basketball on asphalt courts, plugging holes with cardboard and wearing them to school anyway. His dirt-road house had no address. Brother Kenneth accumulated marbles before leaving for navy duty. When he returned after the war he found Ronnie devoured them as slingshot ammunition. (The driest, hardest, flattest surfaces for shooting marbles were behind the school—the best.)

Collectively or individually, our gang could be naughty, nuisances, and slightly destructive. Red Ryder BB guns were a choice toy weapon if you could get one. Target practice included moving objects (cars, people if necessary), tin cans, bottles, branches, and reflectors from the stop-look-listen railroad crossing signs.[*] The reflectors proved hard to remove.

The Mercer-Wrightsville Avenue area created its own subculture. At the corner was a warehouse-type building with a jukebox. "Kids enjoyed going in there."[27] For boisterous weekend entertainment, few could top the "Bloody Bucket" tavern behind the Esso station, a combination beer joint, soda shop, and night club. Patrons settled loud boasts and disputes with fistfights, broken glass, knives, or worse. Regular Ralph Woods lived on Mercer near the tracks. "A part-time painter and full-time drunk, he would get religious some of the time. Then he would cut you in a heartbeat. The story was he threw his wife into Burnt Mill Creek, wouldn't let her out."[28]

The dairy farms of Wilbur Taylor and John Leeuwenburg adjoined the area. "Old man Taylor...sold all the firecrackers in town" across the Cape Fear River.[29] His farm contained an infamous Covil Avenue pond loaded with leeches, water moccasins, and trash. "Not the cleanest place around," according to Ronnie. "It provided an excellent place to swim, was cool, we went in our birthday suits, and joined with blacks from Mercer Avenue."[30] Ronnie and Donald and Jack Andrews never could convince girls to jump in.

The Oleander Kids

Oleander kids were tougher than you might think, considering their upscale neighborhood. They played tackle football year-around, and when brave enough, on the Cape Fear County Club golf course. The object was to scramble out of the way of approaching golfers, even if a game dragged until dark. I might join older boys H. L. Keith, Emsley Laney, Bryant Hare, Bill Garrabrant, and Howard Penton. They might bring in ringers from Delgado or Mercer; that meant we were serious. We wore cleats and partial pads and

---

[*] About 1945 while I walked home, my good friend Graham Burkheimer shot at me with a BB gun. A pellet hit the right eye, nearly putting it out and starting lifelong slight vision problems. The guns were fun but dangerous.

uniforms. Tired, dirty, and thirsty, with scratches, bruises, and torn clothing, it was a long bike ride home at twilight.

Enterprising George "Finny" Rountree, a natural organizer, and friends shined shoes for the military renters at the brand-new Oleander Court Apartments. On Halloween, he and cohorts went through the streets "doing things I would now regard as malicious." An amusing prank was to lean a garbage can on end with top off against the front door, ring the bell and run. The can emptied inside. Bonfires lit up Park Avenue. "We were certainly the scourge of the neighborhood."[31] These were the rich kids, a sociologist's wonderment.

Oleander homeowners rented to Camp Davis and Camp Lejeune senior officers with children. Catherine Russell "had a lot of army brat friends" as well as Laura Roe, Jim Burns, and Alena Matthes. "Living in Oleander we were kind of cut off from other neighborhoods." Catherine's father built a dance floor over part of their house called the "Top Hop." There high school students and soldiers played 78rpm records and danced on weekends till they dropped. Laura's father bought a pony and surry for Laura and the neighborhood kids, using "hay power instead of gasoline power" for the war effort.[32]

In late 1944, Brigadier General Lewis Griffith Merritt, known to Joe Knox's family, visited their Magnolia Place residence. General Merritt commanded the Marine Corps Air Station at Cherry Point, North Carolina, following combat in the Marshalls. "I can remember him standing on the front porch throwing footballs to the boys." Magnificent in uniform and ribbons, he overwhelmed the kids with his down-to-earth but military manner.[33] Gene Robinson's house became the principal basketball arena where you played either a simulated full-court or legitimate half-court game. The goals had no nets. Nothing was east of Hawthorne Road but woods. Trolley tracks, idle since 1940, ran down Park.

In my extended neighborhood, Oleander possessed the best looking girls near our ages: Evelyn Bergen, Bootie and Marjorie Penton, Virginia Harriss, and Honey and Sugar Page. While we dedicated boys ventured out defeating the Axis, Oleander boys hung out around front porches, pairing up on five-minute dates, learning spin-the-bottle—quite advanced for that period. Betty Bugg ran with that group. The first boy who ever asked her out invited her to a boxing evening at Thalian Hall, a popular wartime event. Betty's mother said no. "A boxing match was no place for a lady."[34]

The things we did at that age—later as parents if we caught our own children doing them, we would go ballistic. What generation gap?

Forest Hills Extended Neighborhood

Members of the Armed Forces (Partial)

A -Army; AAF - Army Air Forces; CG - Coast Guard;
MC - Marine Corps; MM - Merchant Marine; N - Navy

Name	Branch	Address
Alexius, Pvt Harold D.	A	104 Live Oak Pkwy.
Berkheimer, Pvt Peter	A	210 Colonial Dr.
Block, Sgt Joseph	A	141 Forest Hills Dr.
Broadfoot, Bryan	MM	133 Forest Hills Dr.
Broadfoot, Maj William G., Jr.	AAF	133 Forest Hills Dr.
Broadfoot, Lt Winston	N	133 Forest Hills Dr.
Brown, Maj William A., Jr.	A	2305 Market St.
Garey, George	CG	205 Colonial Dr.
Garey, 1stLt Robert R.	AAF	205 Colonial Dr.
Garrabrant, Capt John R.	A	28B Mimosa Pl.
Gerdes, Ens Herman John, Jr.	N	114 Keaton Ave.
Graham, LtCdr Charles P.	N	123 Forest Hills Dr.
Hackler, Maj James F., Jr	AAF	129 Forest Hills Dr.
Hanson, LtCdr Louis A.	CG	15 Colonial Dr.
Hanson, Pvt Louis A., Jr.	A	15 Colonial Dr.
Harriss, Lt David S.	N	2211 Oleander Dr.
Hundley, WarOff Harry L.	MC	133 Forest Hills Dr.
Kester, S/Sgt A. Truett	AAF	106 Borden Ave.
Loughlin, 1stLt John W.	AAF	143 Forest Hills Dr.
Lounsbury, Lt(jg) James B.	N	2517 Guilford Ave.
Low, 1stLt Avery C., Jr.	A	123 Keaton Ave.
Low, Ens Kirk H.	N	123 Keaton Ave.
McCumber, Col J. B.	A	Colonial Dr.
McGirt, Sgt Harry G.	AAF	2429 Market St.
McKay, Lt Fred, Jr.	AAF	Oleander
Mitchell, Lt(jg) George L., Jr.	N	17 Colonial Dr.
Mitchell, Seaman Charles	N	17 Colonial Dr.
Morse, Capt Cornelius, Jr.	A	14 Colonial Dr.
Murphy, Yeoman 1/cl Marvin B., Jr.	N	209 Keaton Ave.
Phelps, Seaman 1/cl Kenneth	N	Wrightsville/Mercer Ave.
Preston, 2ndLt Lester W., Jr.	A	145 Forest Hills Dr.
Robertson, 2ndLt LeRoy C., Jr.	A	Guilford Ave.
Sneeden, Jack	—	2706 Market St.
Soverel, Capt Ralph W., Jr.	AAF	239 Brookwood Ave.
Taylor, Walker III	MM	130 Forest Hills Dr.
Thornton, Capt James G., Jr.	A	208 Forest Hills Dr.
Thornton, Lt William H.	N	208 Forest Hills Dr.

Volk, Lt Ralph C., Jr.	AAF	102 Columbia Ave.
Walbach, Col James DeB.	A	145 Forest Hills Dr.
Walker, Sgt George H., Jr.	A	142 Colonial Village
White, C. Ellis, Jr.	—	121 Forest Hills Dr.
Williams, Charles D.	AAF	210 Brookwood Ave.
Williams, Harry T.	A	210 Brookwood Ave.
Williams, James Lee	AAF	210 Brookwood Ave.
Williams, Ralph C.	A	210 Brookwood Ave.
Wrean, Col Joe T.	A	2506 Guilford Ave.

Chapter 2
The Bottoms, Brooklyn, and Dry Pond

In addition to Foxtown and Mercer Avenue, numbers of Negroes re-sided in Love Grove between the Atlantic Coast Line Railroad passenger tracks and Smith Creek, and in "The Bottoms." * *Both races populated The Bottoms, a broad neighborhood stretching from South 5th to 15th and Market to Dawson. Dr. Hubert Eaton, a physician and distinguished Negro citizen, lived there.† Most streets on the south side of town and The Bottoms were unpaved. I can only guess that levels of income and influence on City Hall might have been why.*

South 11th Street in The Bottoms where Cornelia "Nealie" Haggins' family lived was a dirt road. After rains she walked in slush and mud on unpaved roads to see friends, and to the Negro Williston Industrial (High) School. In warm weather the fire department sometimes turned on corner fire hydrants so the children could cool off, but also making more mud.

The German prisoner of war camp across from Williston confined her neighborhood even more. Children spent most of the time playing ball and hopscotch, sitting on porches, listening to phonograph records, and going to parties at friends' houses on weekends. She lived with single mother Inez Quick Haggins. "Mama was sort of strict with us. We only went out if she knew the parents well." Nealie graduated in 1945, and sisters Auldrie and Mary in 1946. After the war she married Wilmington veteran Elmer Campbell.[1]

George Norman, a graduate of Williston and North Carolina College for Negroes,‡ moved to 805 South 15th in July 1942 the day he married

---

* To Negroes, it was with an "s." To whites, "The Bottom."

† Dr. Eaton took in Althea Gibson and helped develop her game on his backyard court. The Williston graduate, who died in 2003, won the Wimbledon championships in 1957–58. Too bad I can't retrace my steps as a historian. As a student, I wrote sports for the *Wilmington Star-News*. In 1953 my feature on the growth of local tennis stated Wilmington tennis is improving, but it's doubtful a local would ever play in Wimbledon. Like other whites I was unaware of events in the Negro community. Little did I know.

‡ North Carolina Central University.

Edna Richard. They lived there until his death in 2000. His father, James Norman, was an Atlantic Coast Line Railroad fireman for 46 years when Negroes performed railroad jobs only as firemen—perhaps the dirtiest job—waiters, porters, and laborers. "Didn't get no white collar jobs." At the U.S. Employment Service, George helped Negroes into defense industries. Three brothers survived army service, Isaac, Thurman, and James, who was captured in the Battle of the Bulge.[2]

Inez Quick Haggins, single mother of two Williston Industrial School students and resident of The Bottoms.
Cornelia Haggins Campbell

* * *

The Carolina Place Area

We Forest Hills kids interacted with friends from other neighborhoods primarily through church, the YMCA, and other organized activities. One area I occasionally biked to was Carolina Place around 17th and Market.

Boys slept over at each other's houses, but not many cared to with Walter Yopp in the family funeral home on Market. Bobby Cameron did. One night he and Walter were alone listening to "Gangbusters" and tuned to a report of an escaped convict headed for Wilmington. Walter heard a noise, got excited, retrieved his father's shotgun, and blasted a big hole in the back door. Bobby's parents came to the rescue.[3] Bobby rode his pony Flicka to Forest Hills or Oleander, and his fox terrier would "bite anything that came around. Don't know how many pairs of pants we had to repair." He and friends roller-skated in the driveway of the Jessie Kenan Wise mansion at 1703 Market, climbing over its walls to get away.[4]

Roddy Cameron (unrelated to Bobby), fascinated with military equipment, led his group at soldiering through Chestnut and Princess Streets and down by Burnt Mill Creek. When a British minesweeper veteran of Dunkirk called here, it was "a big deal to hear them tell their war stories." Roddy recalled B-17 *Flying Fortress* crewman Ed Crane, shot down over Germany and a prisoner of war, substituting for our Sunday school teacher.[5]

The position of respected Judge John J. Burney, the father of John, Jr., and Louis, did not deter them from being themselves or leaders. When home the judge drove boy scouts in his car, spitting tobacco juice out the window. "Riders always kept the rear window up just in case," reported Norman

Davis.[6] John employed the special talent unsparingly playing in football games. Louis ("Loo-ee") ran with a feisty crowd including Charlie "Barrel" Niven, later my New Hanover High School classmate and an outstanding athlete, Jimmy Council, Lawrence Powell, Thurston Watkins, Bobby Lucas, and Howard "Fish" Troutman, who had three brothers in the service.[*]

Davis' father owned Davis Grocery at 17th and Dock, one of the finest and best-stocked markets. People came from miles around.[†] Best friends Norman and John Burney hung out at Lane's Drug Store at 17th and Market, even though John jerked sodas at Jarman's on the opposite corner, owned by Delmer Seitter's father. At which drug store to congregate was a coin flip for the NHHS wartime generation. Nearby the school, they offered identical services and smells.

Lee Lewis lived at 16th and Ann. With Mavis Sykes and Diane and Marilyn Costello, "we would sit on the sidewalk and play poker. I wasn't really the best of students. I thought going to school was to have a good time."[7] Lee later married Norman. Her sister Miriam married Wilmingtonian Harlan McKeithan, who served with the army in Trinidad. Sister Betty married Wilmingtonian Robert Waters, a navy PT boat commander in the Pacific. Norman's sister Caroline married army pilot Richard Turner. Something about a uniform.

Bill Kingoff lived at 301 North 15th. He palled with Glasgow Hicks, Dalziell Sprunt, and Bobby Romeo. Older teenagers claimed neighborhood seniority. "When the high school boys got out of school [in afternoons], they cleaned up the streets of my crowd. John Burney had a way of 'tying up a person.' My crowd did not date much."[8] Close since childhood, graduation and military service finally broke up Woolcott Avenue's Mitchell Saleeby, Junior Highsmith, Vic Piner, and Raymond "Football" Smith.

The Burneys resided at 1705 Orange across from Herbert and Eugenia Coughenour. Jimmy Coughenour's 1945 combat death added to their tragic story, having already lost two toddler girls. Daughter Frances survived. A number of her NHHS 1938 classmates and neighbors served, including Medal of Honor recipient Charles P. Murray, Jr., Sam Bissette, and Billy Brown, killed in action in 1944, who lived a few blocks away. "He had great big brown eyes, was nice looking, very friendly,"[9] Frances recalled.

*　*　*

---

[*] After the war I buddied with those boys and played on the 18th Street Commodores baseball team that used the 13th and Ann field. When future pro football Hall-of-Famer Sonny Jurgensen beat me out for third base, my role became utility.

[†] Davis Grocery disappeared long ago. While so many WWII-era local structures are gone, the familiar blue-top Pure Oil Pep filling station owned by Warren Sanders and the fire station across from the Davis store are now businesses.

The North Side

Many Negroes also lived north of Market in the racially mixed areas of Grace and Red Cross Streets. James Otis Sampson, Jr., grew up on North 10th with Benny Wright. Both still live there. Whites Albert and Ida Wilson lived next door to the Sampsons at 10th and Grace and ran the corner store. "We never had any problems with whites. People were always nice to me and my father." His father, James Otis Sampson, worked with my father at the Carolina Building & Loan Association for 32 years. Young James helped after school and on weekends. Cousin Margaret Sampson, whose father shoveled coal on ACL engines, lived in The Bottoms, a stone's throw from Williston Elementary.

James had few friends. "Times were hard. I was raised strict, in the old school. You did what your parents said to do. First Baptist Church at 5th and Campbell, evolved from the white First Baptist, was their main social outlet. Reverend J. J. Howes served as pastor, with Ada Pearsall in charge of kids' activities. You were in church just about all day Sunday, and the church was full."[10]

Until his 2000 death, Bill Childs owned the house where he was born at 918 Grace. His part-time preacher father cooked for the ACL. Nick Ponos, whose white family operated the New York Cleaners on Grace, grew up next door. Bill enjoyed lifelong membership in one of the oldest and most respected churches, St. Stephens AME. Dr. L. W. Upperman, civic leader and physician at the Negro Community Hospital, lived on

Williston Industrial (High) School class of 1944 friends, *left to right, front row*: Lee Shelton, Marie Smith, Barbara Mason, Gloria Mason. *Rear*, Henry Lee McCrimmon, and Andrew "Gee" McGee ('45), who later played with the Lionel Hampton Orchestra.

Cornelia Haggins Campbell

North 7th. So did Derick Davis with his mother, Nettie, a Peabody School (one of the two Negro grammar schools) teacher and stepfathers Walter Green and later Robert Scott, both morticians. Green worked at Sadgwar's Funeral Home. He and his friends generated their own entertainment: trips to

Seabreeze Beach by bus or pickups, porch sitting, courting, and movies in
the downtown theaters' "crow's nests." "My mother was a very strict woman,
and I didn't see all I should have seen." Williston friends went to war, including pal Johnny Mallette, like Derick a 1940 graduate of North Carolina
A&T. Mallette saw action in France as an army major.[11]

The Brooklyn area of North 4th was on the edge of town, covering from
2nd to 5th, and Red Cross north to the Hilton area with its "world's largest
Christmas tree." High school classmate Bernard Rabunsky and friends "didn't
have much money to buy things, so we improvised. My brother invented a
baseball game that we played with two dice. I still have a scorecard or two."[12]
They entertained themselves with marbles, played ball in the street, used a
rubber bladder for a basketball, and made toy guns and slingshots with
rubber inner tubes and tree branches. Saturdays meant the Bijou Theater,
and summer a beach trip with kids loaded on his father's transfer truck.[13]

The Rabunskys had plumbing but not the house across the street. A
number of Jewish families called racially integrated Brooklyn home, Bergers,
Shains, Rubins, Molkowitzes. "We were not afraid to leave the door open,"
reminded Janet Rabunsky Evenson.[14]

Owner of a one-truck transfer company, Samuel David Rabunsky, father of my high
school classmate Bernard, on North 4th St. in Brooklyn.

Bernard Rabunsky

Negroes and whites shopped in North 4th's cheap stores. James Whitted remembered, "Albert Axler was one of the nicest Jews in the area. Started out selling clothes carried on his back. Sam Berger also came through selling furniture, 'a dollar down and dollar when I catch you.'"[15] Axler owned a meat market, Berger a department store. In late 1943, Axler ran afoul of the Office of Price Administration "as an habitual violator of the OPA regulations as he had been investigated a number of times during the past few months." His lenient 12-month suspended sentence was because "he doesn't speak or understand English very well, but Axler promised to obtain help to assist him."[16]

Rural Castle Hayne and Wrightsboro in northern New Hanover County were integrated in pockets, but "Blacks were segregated against themselves, city *vs.* county." Whitted and the predominantly Negro Rock Hill area had no electricity until the mid-40s, and no inside plumbing.[17] Polish and Dutch first generation bulb farmers settled in Castle Hayne and attended Saint Stanislaus Catholic Church. They harvested flowers without machinery, employing mostly Negroes. "Everything around the Castle Hayne loop road was flowers and more flowers," said Lottie Marshburn. They shipped fresh blossoms daily by train to Washington, D.C., and other points.

Lottie's father shipped vegetables to New York and drove a train at the shipyard. Other flower-grower families included Tinga, Brock, Ludeka, Janicki, Swart, Van Ness, Vander Shalie, Gmytruck, and Lewandowski.[18] The Swart family operated a dairy farm. The area also provided our region with much of its truck crops.

* * *

Dry Pond

Dry Pond between South Front and 5th is one of Wilmington's best-known neighborhoods. From the decades-old houses and fringes of The Bottoms, many men left for the military, mostly as enlisted, and along with nearby downtown realized large numbers of casualties.

After living in an apartment over his father's grocery store on South Front, navy pilot Joe Reaves' family moved to Castle into a one-story brick bungalow for most of the war, then to South 3rd. His father, Joseph W. Reaves, was in business with uncle J. R. Watters until 1945. His mother, Mittie, knitted for the war effort and sisters Rosa Lee and Eleanor worked as USO volunteers. The NHHS '38 gang remain friends, including Reaves, Charles Murray, Dan Cameron, Ray Funderburk, and Sam Bissette. Joe served in the first ROTC program in the state with classmate David Brinkley.*

---

* Reserve Officers Training Corps. Although growing up north of Market, the late Brinkley is often associated with Dry Pond. Activated along with other members of the local Company I, 120th Infantry, in 1940, he was discharged before the war. The Dry Pond group congregated at Hall's Drug Store, now a café.

The Newbold family at 1 Church Street and their six children were hospitable hosts. Sometimes my mother deposited me there while chasing her activities. Caroline was the oldest, followed by Jesse, Ann, Hayes, Jerry, and Raynor. Sundays meant First Presbyterian Church. To Caroline, "get-togethers were important."[19] To Jim Stokley, an NHHS ('39) classmate of Jesse and my sister Elizabeth, the "big social thing was Sunday night 'league' at church, and then to the Newbolds' house."[20]

Mrs. Newbold worked at Wrightsville Beach's Oceanic Hotel cafeteria and met Dutch marines waiting for a bus into Wilmington. Training at Camp Lejeune in 1945, they asked if she knew any nice girls. "'I have three at home,'" she replied, and took them home for dinner. They returned a few times.[21]

Lake Forest School opened on the South side in 1944. Behind it loomed a heavily wooded, almost junglelike area where Marines trained. Student Delane Eason and friends climbed trees to watch. One day a colonel ordered them away, pointing to warning signs. To actually observe the Marines—how swell that must have been.

By late-1941, the Sunset Park area, founded in the 1920s as a "suburb" along the Carolina Beach Road near Greenfield Lake, sensed the oncoming surge. Shipyard worker demands accelerated housing construction. Except for being all-white, it took on an All-American complexion as a solid blue-collar community. Old-line families and money would not live there, but it thrived at the center of the boomtown.

Children went to brand-new Sunset Park School which opened in late 1942 as another federally financed rush job. Jim Fountain bought *Charlotte Observer* newspapers from a local dealer daily and resold them at the ship-yard main gate. "They just wanted to buy from a kid who was trying to make some money."[22] Mike Michaelis delivered the *Star-News* on his bicycle through his junior year, earning enough to buy three boats which he rented at the lake. Michaelis paid for his own clothes, dates, and in his senior year a 1931 Chevrolet. Constant companions included William and J. C. Rogers, and Bill and Jimmy Applewhite—known to fish the lake from sunup to sun-down. They enjoyed a secret swimming hole in the middle. "Kids smoked too much, especially rabbit tobacco. We rolled it up in old burlap bags."[23]

* * *

The Sounders

Across the county on the sounds and creeks near the ocean, Haskell Rhett "thought he owned Bradley Creek in the summertime. It was pretty deserted," unknown to builders and residents who since have flocked. "It was a long way psychologically from home to Front Street." How far? Once in 1942 he and buddy Weddell Harris were unable to get home to the Rhetts after a movie downtown. They spent the night on the road before catching the first morning bus. As they entered the door, his mother thought they were coming downstairs for breakfast.

Rhett's social life also suffered. "I remember one or two [dates] but I don't think I ever scored. I was very limited living down there without a car."[24] Haskell loved to hunt and fish and went dove hunting on the Airlie estate next door. The caretaker didn't like it but owner Mrs. Harry Walters said okay.[25] Rhett still lives there.

If you resided at Bradley or Hewletts Creek, Wrightsville or Carolina Beach, or Greenville, Middle, or Masonboro Sound, you were remote. The second-smallest North Carolina county in geographical size seemed expansive then. "The sounders were a different breed in those days," someone reflected. "Anyone who lived on the sound couldn't participate in outside activities at school because they had to ride the bus home. They seemed a bit tougher than the city kids."[26]

At the war's end, the Masonboro Sound area finally received electricity when the Tide Water Power Company installed facilities to 70 Masonboro Loop Road customers and a line five and one-half miles long.

Those kids were tough, all right.

Chapter 3

"Tired of Buying War Bonds"

"When you feel tired of buying war bonds, multiply that by 15 and try to realize the way men carrying the rifles feel," combat fighter pilot Captain Roland Wooten exhorted in 1944.[1] *The talk helped. The county then broke its war bond drive records by investing $8.279 million.*

"Keep on buying," the beat continued into 1945, with victory nearing.* Officials fervently tried from 1944 on to sustain public interest in the war effort. Thanks to those "who dug down deeper than ever before...the war bond is America's best investment today....Don't let up...."[2] Downtown "Retailers for Victory" spearheaded a $150,000 bond drive to buy an aircraft carrier to be named "Shangri-La," the mystery ship from which the 1942 Doolittle raid on Japan was launched. "Bomb Tokyo with your extra change."

Achieving measurable success proved often tenuous. About the same time in January 1944 we learned of the Bataan "Death March" atrocities, the newspaper noted,

> Labor leaders were calling strikes, halting war production, handicapping the war effort, wasting millions of man-hours of output...to get more pay for workers living in complete safety and comfort at home....And by contrast consider the present lag in war bond sales....We, right here in Wilmington, have left every defense unit undermanned from the start....We'd rather keep right on with our social and business engagements than do a trick...on the home front....The blood shed by our men in the Philippines calls for retribution.[3]

When holders attempted to cash in bonds in October 1944, chairman James G. Thornton decried, "'Persons who buy bonds with the thought in mind to immediately cash them are not helping the war effort but impeding it. It would be better not to buy at all.'"[4]

---

* Three previous bond drives: the Fourth, $5.7 million; Third, $7 million; and Second, $4.9 million. For the Sixth in January 1945, the mark was broken at $8.287 million, but for the Seventh and final drive, the total was $5.6 million.

Only employees taking a payroll deduction could vote for "Miss or Mrs. North Carolina Shipbuilding" in November 1942. Heralding the opening of the movie version of *This Is the Army*, a September 1943 fund raiser for Army Emergency Relief, local army units and the boy scouts paraded through downtown. The tank "Miss Texas" led the way, followed by vehicles mounted with machine guns and antiaircraft weapons.

Star-News route carrier boys sold almost $1,500 in war stamps. Carriers Hardy Wessell and Olin H. White received new bicycles for selling the most stamps.* In January 1943 Washington Catlett School earned the U.S. Treasury Minute Man flag recognizing its 90 percent participation in the bond-stamp drives. Lake Forest School pupils "contributed" two jeeps by selling $2,191.70 worth during

Army air cadet Hardy Wessell in basic training, Miami Beach, Florida, 1944.

Hardy Wessell

March 1943. Approximately 1,300 children attended a cartoon-comedy show at the Bailey on February 12, 1944 "as the reward for obtaining pledges from citizens to convert stamp albums into war bonds."[5]

* * *

Manpower and Production

Governor J. Melville ("work or fight") Broughton appointed Mayor Bruce B. Cameron in 1943 to head the county's "campaign to get rid of the 'idlers and loafers' hindering war production." Police chief C. H. Casteen had already promised to enforce the laws and rid the city of vagrants. "Any man who willfully refuses to work and carry his share doesn't deserve any mercy."

First Baptist's Reverend Sankey Lee Blanton prophesied, "If we lose this war, we'll lose it on the home front....The man who slacks his hand at work, the man who wastes his country's substance, is guilty of doing something closely akin to treason."[6] By November 1943, being unemployed was a

---

* Wessell served in the air force training command. Yeoman 3rd Class White was KIA in 1945.

misdemeanor, and everyone between 18 and 55 had to be employed for at least 35 hours per week.

The Federal Government offered incentives in recruiting Wilmington workers for jobs in Washington, D.C., and Hawaii. "Colored laborers wanted, indoor work. Free sleeping quarters or free transportation furnished."[7] Classified ads pleaded for female laundry workers, restaurant waitresses, and live-in domestic help. The shipyard and other firms sought men either 4-F or more than 40 years old, then as the war dragged, upped it to 50–65 for light work. More job training was conducted through the National Youth Administration complex on Carolina Beach Road until it became the first prisoner of war camp in February 1944.

The New Hanover High School Victory Corps program prepared students for military life or industry. Vocational director George H. West referred to it as "pre-induction [draft] training." By early 1943, girls were sought for, and by March some 2,000 trained workers had been furnished to local industries since July 1940. "It means that 2,000 older men, fathers, mothers, brothers and sisters have left their places...[to build] Liberty ships here, to go to Camp Davis shops...."[8]

As America neared maximum war production, new August 1943 Washington regulations dropped many local industries from designation as essential to the war effort, freeing up employees from being "frozen" to the job and making them draft-eligible. With major undertakings nearing completion in October 1944, the Federal Works Agency estimated that county construction had cost $7.4 million. Federal financial assistance provided about 60 percent.*

* * *

"Tommies" in Town

In July and November-December 1943, a unit of British Royal Artillery, the First Composite Antiaircraft Battery of 17 officers and 329 men, visited Camp Davis and Wilmington on their national study and training tour.[9] In a July 17 parade down Front Street, the battery "won high praise for the impressiveness of its exhibition...." Led by Major T. C. Metcalf, the British wore tropical khaki shorts and shirts, high woollen hose, and high shoes, with "overseas caps cocked at a jaunty right angle...[and] demonstrated sharp precision, strided [sic] with high-swinging arms, and stamped to a sounding halt." Wilmingtonians invited them into their homes and eligible-age girls went crazy with the diversion.

---

* The 1945 city directory listed 28,256 adults in the city and 16 suburbs, a total of 51,620. In April 1946, after the immediate postwar shuffling of departing workers and military and returning veterans, the "semi-official" count was 46,882 in the city, a 40 percent increase over 1940's census. See *A Sentimental Journey* for more numbers.

British soldiers of the First Composite Antiaircraft Battery, Royal Artillery, visit the shipyard, 1943.

North Carolina Shipbuilding Company

Seventy-five Wilmingtonians attended a July formal dance at Davis honoring the British. "Thrilled by their first sight of the British Tommies...the young ladies all expressed a keen desire to meet the visiting soldiers. No less anxious to become acquainted were the Tommies themselves, who for years have heard colorful accounts of the American type of 'swing' and 'boogie-woogie.' The Tommies picked two favorites...North Carolina as the state they like best to come back to and Wilmington as the city where they feel most welcome."

On December 3 the group bade farewell with another parade. From City Hall, British ambassador Lord Halifax praised the two nations' cooperation. "The tall jaunt diplomat, dressed impeccably in dark clothes that would do credit to the best Bond Street tailor, made an impressive picture as he moved slowly among the lines of ruddy Tommies in khaki...." Ann Hewlett Hutteman remembered her mother, Margaret Hewlett, wrote the mothers of her British visitors, and received replies. "It meant a lot to their mothers. The men had not seen fresh eggs in years."[*]

* * *

---

[*] In November 1945, the city hosted a contingent of 700 Netherlands marines training at Camp Lejeune, a postwar feel-good visitation also fondly recalled.

Churches and Other Organizations

Established and ad hoc groups planned, organized, and executed much of the war effort. By late 1942, the Salvation Army shipped more than 300 packages of stationery, handkerchiefs, and toiletries to county servicemen. By March 1944, the Red Cross chapter issued 4,367 first-aid certifications, aided 3,018 servicemen or families, prepared thousands of surgical dressings, and knitted garments.

As the area's religious life flourished, houses of worship provided substantial contributions in spiritual enrichment, rest and relaxation, and social contacts. Foremost was the warm welcome given armed forces personnel on weekends at services, meals, and overnight stays. "All you had to do was to go to church in Wilmington to get an invitation to dinner," Marine Vince Norako said. He and Camp Lejeune buddies, "an ecumenical bunch," included Mormons who visited that church at Borden and Market.[10] Groups provided units stationed nearby with toiletries, phonograph players and records, and of course, Bibles.

Church basements filled up every Saturday, like the one at First Baptist, where liquor was prohibited. Ruth Middleton's father helped Reverend Sankey Lee Blanton set up. The church paid professional singer and Camp Davis soldier David Melchoir to sing. In November 1943, while walking home from her Temple Baptist Church, Muriel Williamson brought home two British soldiers unannounced. "Mother always had something to eat."[11]

Fire consumed St. Luke's Zion AME at 7th and Church, a favorite among Negro soldiers, on January 2, 1944.[*] "Many servicemen, both white and Negro, were pressed into service, as were many civilians, who got up from their beds to help combat the blaze...."[12] Negro servicemen also frequented St. Stephen's AME and Chestnut Street Presbyterian, whose seven-year pastor, Joseph D. Taylor, became an army chaplain. After a brief illness, Taylor died in New Guinea in March 1944. Doctor L. W. Upperman and Reverend J. Harry Whitmore of my Church of the Covenant Presbyterian led a memorial service of "commemorative expressions."

Servicemen enjoyed the convenience of downtown places of worship, including St. James Episcopal, First Presbyterian, St. Mary Catholic, Fifth Avenue Methodist, First Baptist, Temple of Israel, and B'Nai Israel. Emma Mitchell recalled that her First Presbyterian was so popular it needed the services of Kentucky minister Samuel Vander Meer to help pastor Dr. William Crowe, Jr.

In October 1943 Crowe observed that "'Wilmington has faced its difficulties and made more progress in overcoming them than many other cities similarly situated.' His chief concern is with the spiritual and cultural aspects of community life," one being "the irregularity of formerly constant

---

[*] St. Luke's rebuilt and still stands.

attendants upon church services." He estimated 80 percent of Wilmingtonians had no church connection, compared to 25 percent in 1941. "We face a spiritual crisis....With everybody overworked we are rapidly becoming slaves to the job," citing serious neglect of spiritual training for children.[13]

Crowe and other ministers from main-line churches, including Blanton, C. D. Barclift of Fifth Avenue Methodist, and Walter B. Freed of St. Paul's Lutheran, frequently spoke out supporting the war effort, morale, and righteous uplifting. Barclift, a strong inspirational leader and 1943 Exchange Club president, worked tirelessly, preached religious virtues, and performed air raid warden duties.

Each Sunday morning hundreds of shipyard employees paused for religious services led by the Wilmington Ministerial Association.[*] By 1943, my church was packed every Sunday at the 11:00 a.m. and 7:00 p.m. services.[†] St. Mary under pastor Right Reverend Monsignor Cornelius E. Murphy held four Sunday Masses and a Sunday afternoon devotion.

For Jewish residents, religious and cultural life around the two downtown synagogues was augmented by each weekend's open doors. The Temple, under congregation President Herbert Bluethenthal and Rabbi Mordecai M. Thurman, established a lounge for military personnel and held special Passover Eve and other Sunday morning services for those unable to attend Friday services. Camp Davis and Fort Fisher Chaplain Sidney I. Goldstein also helped. Members of B'Nai Israel "showed true southern hospitality, taking soldiers into their homes for meals and comforting many a homesick soldier. Some...became sons-in-law to Wilmington families. It is hard to imagine...the small...synagogue was packed when the congregation hosted a Passover Seder for 250 men."[14] Families played the role of "foster parents."

B'Nai Israel rabbis were Harry Bronstein and Samuel Friedman. Families with relatives in Europe included Bill Kingoff's. One came to Wilmington from Austria a week before Poland was invaded and volunteered for the U.S. Army. The two congregations split on many issues. "There was a schism," Dan Retchin of B'Nai Israel remembered, "two opposite poles to a degree." They did form the Covenant Club.[15] In April 1943, 800 area Jewish servicemen participated in Passover and the Festival of Freedom at sundown on the 19th.

(Like other Wilmington Jews, Bill Schwartz was aware of Hitler's solution to the "Jewish question" through relatives trying to get out. Until he

---

[*] To my knowledge, the Ministerial Association was perhaps the only racially integrated organization in town.

[†] Principal staff included minister Dr. Whitmore, Lucilla White, director of religious education, and Arthur John, music director. With more than 600 members, on June 1, 1944, Covenant merged with St. Andrews at Covenant's 15th and Market location, forming a congregation of about 1,600 with Whitmore as temporary minister.

entered navy midshipmen's school in New York he had avoided antisemitism. After signing up for the "home hospitality" program where people invited men into their homes, he finally realized why he was excluded: his name.[16])

* * *

Families Left Behind

To Peggy Warren, the R. B. Warren family maintained security and morale in "a time of high suspense, heart-felt emotions and feelings of self-sacrifice for a great cause. Our family contributed to the war effort, and our parents taught us to be proud Americans and to be thankful for this wonderful, free country. The war changed our lives. It gave [brother] Pat the opportunity to save money he earned overseas and to go to college on the GI Bill. It gave my parents greater financial security with my father starting his own construction business."[17]

When Pat left for the navy, "it was a sad day for all of us.[18] I remember my mother and I followed his bus as long as we could, waving out the window and with tears in our eyes. We wondered if we would ever see him again. My mother put a star in our front bedroom window....I guess my thoughts were that this was something we would get through and that everything would soon be OK again...there would be 'blue birds over the White Cliffs of Dover....'"

Jean McKoy Graham, whose husband, Charles Graham, served as a navy medical officer on the battleship USS *Indiana* (BB-58), remembered the plight of military wives.[19] "You didn't have any friends as long as he was gone, not even relatives, but when he came home they flooded around. They didn't have any use for service wives then," and were attracted to returning uniforms.

Jean McKoy Graham with her children Adair and Jean in front of the Front Street post office, 1945.

Jean McKoy Graham

"He said he wasn't going to war with one child [Charles, Jr.]. He wanted me to have another." So daughter Jean Victor Graham was born October 13, 1942. "I wasn't different from other war wives. I didn't have the time or gasoline to get anywhere," and no maid. In their Chevrolet coupe she carpooled to kindergarten at St. James Church, run by Louisa Howard and Margaret Bellamy Alexius, whose husband, Harold Alexius, was in the army.

Charles entered the navy in 1942 and served in South Carolina, Maryland, and California. "I had a baby about that time, and I took castor oil, quinine, and pituritin to have the baby come early so I could go with him." Then another baby came. "In two weeks I was on the train with them [Charles and the children]" to California.

Changing trains five times, at each stop she got off to sterilize baby bottles. In San Antonio, Texas, a conductor arranged for them to board a troop train to Los Angeles, but it had food only for troops on the two-day trip. Charles obtained coffee at some stops. Finally they ate with soldiers before arriving in November.

Shortly Charles received orders to join the *Indiana*. "He got leave and brought me home to Wilmington [in late 1943] right before he left for overseas." Their third child, son Adair, was born here December 13, 1943. "I sent him a telegram saying he had a 10-pound son, and he sent me one back saying 'that's great. I've got sea duty.'" She moved into their Forest Hills garage apartment awaiting completion of their house. A number of owners built these apartments to accommodate wartime renters.

Jean's parents and Charles' mother helped with the children. She received no government benefits. "I don't think the doctors charged me anything because he [Charles] was still in practice here." Her pediatrician was Dr. J. Buren Sidbury. Charles, Jr., and little Jean contracted infantile paralysis. The nationally known Kenney Treatment cured them: rubber sheets and blankets, with hot applications two hours on and two hours off. As wife and mother, Jean almost had to do it all.

* * *

Every Little Bit Helped

The *Star-News* printed periodic columns of happenings at nearby posts, some written by servicemen. Bluethenthal Field's "Wings Over Wilmington, With Air Base Boys" announced its "attempt to present the life of the soldier, his problems in Wilmington, and news events which might be of interest to townspeople (1942)."[20] Before entering the army in 1944, high school student Jim Lee was an assistant at the shipyard and Camp Davis. "Yankees came down to work. They talked oddly. I'm sure they thought we did."[21]

In May 1944, WMFD launched a weekly radio series called "Crisis in War Town" describing national and community war service. The shipyard hosted 80 convalescent soldiers in 1945 on visits to Wrightsville Beach, the 2nd and Orange USO, and other sites. Twelve thousand young people joined the Junior Red Cross filling Christmas stockings and boxes for refugee children, sewing, making favors, and working in salvage drives. Mrs. Alfred

Sternberger was chairman. Bluethenthal staged the largest military recognition program on August 1, 1945. Harry L. Gardner and base commander Colonel C. T. Edwinson coordinated activities. The public program included a flyover by aircraft from Cherry Point Marine Corps Air Station and Bluethenthal and static displays.

The Brigade Boys Club housed 4,125 servicemen from September 1942 to March 1943. Local boys shined shoes and pressed clothes, and furnished them with cots, blankets, overnight necessities, and weekend movies. "White's DeLuxe Ice Cream Has Gone To War," a 1943 newspaper ad read. "Our soldiers, sailors and Marines are enjoying White's nourishing DeLuxe ice cream....It is our patriotic privilege and duty to help you understand the reason why we can no longer give you this rich ice cream...."[22]

In 1943 the YMCA accommodated 14,000 servicemen in the social room, and regular membership increased to 1,007. Maffitt Village converted an entire dormitory into a hostel for merchant marine crews. The post office stopped some afternoon automobile mail routes outside the city limits to conserve tires and gasoline. Coal and ice shortages developed. Increased customers and lack of sufficient equipment and labor generated "badly overtaxed" laundry facilities by 1943. "Operators are begging the public for 'more cooperation and understanding.'"[23]

Scrap-metal drives sputtered. "All owners of idle metal are not doing their full part. There is a great quantity of old machinery, boilers, mechanical appliances of one sort of another....Certainly it could never be put to such good use as being converted into tanks and shells and ships....The government is paying for all scrap turned in...."[24] A May 1945 drive staged by president W. Elliott O'Neal's Junior Chamber of Commerce produced 95,000 pounds of waste paper, largest in the state per capita. That corner of the war effort continued.

Although maintaining exhilaration in the war effort fluctuated, morale remained high. "We were anxious to get involved and do our part," said Leon Stein, who served as a combat naval officer. "This was the thing to do. The war effort was an education...made a better man out of me."[25]

B-17 bombardier-navigator Heyward Bellamy couldn't "remember anybody who wasn't a nationalist at that time. It was a sure thing you were going into the service. No one talked about losing the war. It was a question of when we would win it. I remember riding the train and little old ladies would try to get me to take their seat. You were just something special because you were in uniform." When he came home he found locals very supportive, "always had a good feeling they were behind you."[26]

*   *   *

Adults continuously sought to instill patriotism in children through the war effort. One example was membership in the Lone Ranger Safety Club. "I Promise to Cooperate With My Air Raid Warden," a Merita Bread advertisement admonished.[27] "Half a million boys and girls have developed safety habits by following the club's rules to guard them from accidents at home and on the street. They have pledged their loyal enthusiasm to America's Victory effort in many ways...."

The never-to-be-forgotten culture of the times (1943) is easily reflected here:

"'The customer is always right'....[Now] the opposite is true, if signs in the local stores are any indication."

No pants pressed while you wait —"Since business is too much to handle people may wait...if they can sit patiently for a day or two.

"Please help us speed up the line—please have change ready. Don't worry our clerks—they're harder to get than customers; help the new employee.

"No beef today—'Saves trouble; people wanting beef don't come in then and bother the clerks.' Imagine contriving devices for keeping the customers away!'

"Bus driver: 'Why complain? It's a small enough sacrifice if it will help win the war.'"[28]

I remember countless such exhortations—the foregoing definitely sensible—and I guess they worked.

How true this had become. If it will help win the war, then buy more bonds. Save more fats. Turn in more scrap. Suffer a bit of inconvenience. Again.

"Showboat" Sunk at Least Six Times[29]

"'Sunk' at least 6 times in Japanese propaganda, the mighty battleship *North Carolina*, known affectionately to her crew as the 'Showboat,' is still a worry to the Japanese high command," reported an item in January 1945. She had sailed more than 250,000 miles and participated in 15 campaigns in three years of combat. She beat off more scores of air attacks and shot down 17 planes, suffering one major casualty, a torpedo hit in the Solomons on September 15, 1942.

The former USS *North Carolina* (BB-55) has been a living state memorial to World War II berthed at Wilmington since 1961. Although not associated with the area during the war, her presence as a leading tourist attraction makes her the hub of WWII activities and living history in Southeastern North Carolina.

Jesse Helms and the Nylon Hose

"What a U.S. naval officer in England doesn't know is that any American woman would give her eyeteeth for a pair of nylon hose. Still, in an effort to suit the fancy of an English maiden," North Carolinian Lieutenant (Junior Grade) Ed Rankin sent $20 to Wilmington navy recruiter Jesse Helms "'to buy as many pairs of nylons as possible.'"[30] Petty Officer First Class Helms arrived in May 1942 for two years of duty in the navy's post office recruiting station. In September 1943 he became the petty officer in charge, and later served the state as a five-term United States Senator.

The Atomic Bomb[31]

Navy Petty Officer First Class Isaac Hobbs heard resoluteness and sensed veracity from his brother Frederick at the family reunion in late July 1945, in their home in Wilmington's Winter Park. Frederick, an army warrant officer immersed in a highly classified weapon program, knew. Expect something of great importance soon regarding the war against Japan.

A few days earlier the army secretly successfully test-fired history's first atomic bomb at Alamogordo, New Mexico. Days later, on August 6 and 9, U.S. B-29 *Superfortresses* "Enola Gay" and "Bock's Car" respectively dropped the uranium bomb "Little Boy" and plutonium bomb "Fat Man" on the large military and industrial cities of Hiroshima and Nagasaki. On August 15, Japan surrendered unconditionally, and World War II ended.

At least two Wilmington people worked directly for the Manhattan Project, which developed the atom bomb. Mary Helen Moore, a Women's Army Corps technician fifth grade, clerked at Los Alamos, New Mexico, the project headquarters. Her mother, Bessie I. Willetts, lived here. Frederick Hobbs worked at Oak Ridge, Tennessee, the project site producing uranium U-235. An administrative manager, he performed courier duties and liaison with Washington, D.C., and Los Alamos.

The story of the Hobbs family's contributions to the war effort hardly ends there. Without going overseas or firing a shot, the five brothers compiled remarkable achievements on the home front in science and technology, weapons development, procurement, administration, and transportation. The sons of electrical engineer Julius C. and Maude Player Hobbs, each graduated from Winter Park School and New Hanover High School.

The oldest, William J., a lawyer with the Reconstruction Finance Corporation, traveled extensively buying tires, down for flight jackets, and other military items. Isaac, a North Carolina State chemical engineering graduate, helped develop phosphorus and ammonium nitrate for ordnance use, trouble-shot aircraft radar systems, and worked on the application and installation of "IFF" aircraft identification systems. "We had to make sure the stuff was up to snuff," he recalled to me.

Marcus, with three Duke degrees including a doctorate in physical chemistry, left the Duke faculty on loan to the Office of Scientific Research and Development, where he helped develop the frangible bullet used for gunnery training and propellants for rockets. "We were trying to develop an early-stage missile with solid propellants. The war wouldn't last forever. We better get out of it as soon as we can. I don't regard myself as anything other than a worker in the vineyards."

The youngest, Carr, was an Atlantic Coast Line Railroad official supervising trains carrying troops and materials through Goldsboro.

Before joining Oak Ridge, Frederick also served with the OSRD, the government's principal agency for science and technology, which spent nearly half a billion dollars and accelerated a revolution in modern warfare.

Chapter 4

"Robbers Row" and the Downtown Economy

Everything commercial was situated downtown next to the Cape Fear River. Retail stores, banks, insurance companies, movie theaters, lawyers, most decent restaurants, bars, hotels, whore houses, many old-line churches—except beach establishments and a multitude of filling stations and corner groceries dotting the county. To visit the area's principal attraction ranged from treat to pain (if trying to park). Wilmington had a couple of so-called "supermarkets," but no shopping centers. Sears and Penneys catalogs supplied mail orders. Downtown had almost anything within reason, even when teeming with soldiers and war workers. For sure, it was an outing.

Its hub bounded by Front, Dock, 3rd, and Walnut Streets, downtown thrived during the prosperous war years well into 1945. Retail stores and movie theaters populated Front, the "main drag." To Bob Cantwell III, the two-block stretch of the Princess financial center between Front and 3rd—also the site of numerous real estate, insurance office, and law offices—became "inevitably known as 'robbers row.' At least it had the advantage of ready identification, and you could find or avoid the inhabitants thereof, as was your desire."[1] He was neither far off nor alone.

The Wilmington area boomed because of the war. But in the beginning, who might have visualized what opportunities for economic enrichment would present themselves—as long as we won. In an unusual advertisement, prominent businessman Hugh MacRae wrote four days into the war:

Visioning victory—what does this mean to Wilmington, N.C.? It means, if we awaken to the opportunity, and we will, that Wilmington will become a city of not less than 200,000 inhabitants, it will regain its position as the largest city in North Carolina. Wilmington...has the greatest purchasing power of any city except one in the state....New Hanover County, before the coming of Camp Davis [et al.]...had the largest per capita purchasing power of any county in the South except three. It now undoubtedly stands first in the Southern States.[2]

Postcard looking north along Front St. at Market St., late war. Most buildings seen are still in use, including Tom's Drugstore (left corner).

Aaron May

* * *

The Boom is Underway

As February 1943 began, the brief wartime business record looked solid and the forecast rosy, aided by war industries. The newspaper gleaned: Wilmington looked "ahead to consolidating and expanding the greatest gains ever made in the city's financial history as its industries and businesses produce on a 24-hours-a-day schedule for the war effort....The city was the scene of unprecedented business activity and [observers] could see no reason why last year's records could not be duplicated or surpassed again." Growth and optimism were being fueled by the shipyard, Camp Davis, and Camp Lejeune "involving payrolls, and purchases of foodstuffs and commodities through Wilmington channels."[3]

Operation and expansion of old, established industries and small businesses also contributed. Area yearly bank clearings exceeded more than $362 million. As shipyard employment grew from 6,000 to 18,500 during 1942, January payrolls totaled $40 million. Among financial charts, only postal receipts declined, because the government allowed military personnel to mail their letters free.

Construction neared peaking, barely any of it private. "The largest program of public works construction in a decade continued in full swing here," including the city's Federal Works Agency-financed $2.5 million waterworks program with a new filter plant, renovation of the mains and sewers system, and larger city water source. Water now came from the Cape Fear River above Dam Number 1 at King's Bluff in Bladen County via a 22-mile concrete, lock-joint pipeline. At year's end the new filter plant at Hilton Park was almost completed.* Both city and county finances "were at their best operating levels in years." And Wilmington in June 1942 ended its first year of council-manager government.

From 1941 to 1943, area manufacturing plants increased production by 45 percent, retail firm activity 22 percent, and total employees 18 percent. Some business activity such as automobile sales, affected by rationing and material shortages, had decreased.[4] Businesses adjusted to wartime restrictions. In early 1943, downtown stores altered shopping hours to 9:00 a.m. to 7:00 p.m. to "operate within the national conservation of fuel and dim-out limitations."[5]

Wilmington, on the threshold of a new day economically, "probably exceeding the hopes of its most active citizens a few years ago," faced "many serious problems which must be solved as a result of its tremendous growth in such a short period," Greater Wilmington Chamber of Commerce official F. O. Gockler predicted. Not all was well. "If the opportunity is not...handled properly and expanded, we stand to lose a gain which under normal conditions would require a half century of work and effort. One opportunity we are now tossing aside every day is the advantage to sell Wilmington to the many persons now coming into our community....Some of the stories...will most certainly cause many people never to return and other people who hear the stories not want to come."[6]

Yes, undoubtedly some influential locals wanted the town to remain small and unknown, ergo *their town.* Would it bother them that wartime visitors might not return? Progressive area leaders faced this mindset over again for the next three decades, finding it instrumental in retarding both natural and stimulated growth.[†]

Businesses continued to open or grow in 1943.[‡] An August page advertisement announced the opening of the Reno Billiard Parlor. "All equipment

---

* This project was one of the most important upgrades to local infrastructure. Planned prior to the war, and expedited thereafter, without it needs of the exploding population would have been even more seriously strained.

† The Chamber also added, "For in every direction after the war, will be change in transportation...industry...products...methods of manufacture...food...populace." The Chamber, "conscious of the new world of great opportunity which lies ahead," dedicated itself to the city. [Chamber advertisement in *Wilmington Sunday Star-News,* February 7, 1943]

‡ Telephone usage measured business growth. Originating long distance calls increased from 13,500 in 1940 to 65,500 monthly in the late 1942. By early 1946, Wilmington recorded 10,823 telephones, an increase from 7,373 in 1944. Long distance calls in 1945 fell to 36,900. [*Wilmington Sunday Star-News,* February 17, 1946]

brand new—9 Brunswick Tables, cigars, cigarettes, tobaccos, wine, all kinds of soft drinks—comfortably cool—Meet Your Friends...."[7] The Tide Water Power Company bus line set a record by carrying 12 million passengers in their 60 buses during the 12-month period ending in May. Bank clearings indicated the city was maintaining its "all-time record financial paces."[8]

"Mr. and Mrs. Wilmingtonian went on their biggest Christmas buying spree this year," merchants experiencing their "greatest volume" ever.[9] Next Christmas, "abroad in large numbers," shoppers received advice:

> In order to prevent blockades they are to be encouraged not to stop to converse with friends in the middle of the sidewalks....Drivers therefore are to be reminded that pedestrians have right of way at street crossings....Boy Scouts...will be out in numbers to restrain impatient persons afoot at the curb line until the green light gives them the go signal.[10]

* * *

Establishments of the Economic Boom

Saleeby Produce Company. Mitchell Saleeby, Sr., owned the wholesaler at 115 Dock. Customers bought right off the truck. "My father wasn't college educated. He just knew how to run a business," Mitchell, Jr., recalled. Brother William often traveled to Florida and Maryland for produce, preserving it on ice. They hauled local produce to New York. A number of Negroes worked there. "The best one was Robert Wilkins. A very strong man, he could take a [100-pound] bag of potatoes and move it easily."[11]

Spiritine Chemical Company. Neighbor Louis Hanson owned the company with offices on South Front. Until he entered Coast Guard active duty he operated the Leland plant which made cleaning solvents, bug sprays, distilled pine, creosote, and nose drops, and sold to the Atlantic Coast Line Railroad and bases and stores. Spiritine is still in business.[12]

S&B Solomon Wholesale Dry Goods Company. Harry Solomon owned the firm at Front and Market that sold bolts of material and notions to independent stores "up country—had to give them credit until their crops came in." Solomon's was the area's principal dealer, as was J. W. Brooks for wholesale grocers, and South Front's W. H. McEachern & Sons for produce dealers. Solomon's closed in 1975, but McEachern's remains a family business.[13]

Bellamy's Grocery and Market. D. Frank Bellamy owned a general store three blocks from the hospital. "He sold everything," son Heyward said, including dry goods bought from Solomon's. Heyward delivered 100-pound rice sacks on a bicycle. "I got to be a physically sound fellow working at that store." Some customers asked him to get them molasses when sugar was rationed so they could make moonshine.[14]

Berger's Department Store. Advertisement: In Brooklyn on North 4th Street, "Just Across the Bridge, Plenty of Free Parking Space....One of Wilmington's outstanding retail business expansions.... The public seems to greatly appreciate our service under wartime conditions, and the indication of our aim to stay in business and grow!"[15]

Robert C. Cantwell Insurance Agency. When he was 19, Bob Cantwell III took over a portion of his father's insurance and real estate business. While Bob was in the army his wife ran the firm. "Betty was able to retain most of the business we had. Some of my friends who didn't go to war tried to snip away at my clients."[16]

Will Rehder Florist. Henry Rehder ran the family retail store on North Front. Brother Stanley, a horticulturist, operated the 40,000-square feet glass greenhouses before serving as an army officer in Europe. On special days the family stayed up all night making corsages for next-day delivery. Soldiers wired flowers by Western Union on holidays to girlfriends and mothers. Other popular florists included Dorothy Owen, Lena B. Westbrook, the Blossom Shop, and Lucy B. Moore Florist, run by F. D. Edwards, and Roudabush's. Only Rehder's remains open.[17]

Wilmington docks along the port area of Water and Dock Sts., ca. 1943.

George J. Green

Wilmington Hotel. E. B. Bugg owned the Wilmington Hotel at Front and Walnut since 1929. The city's second hotel behind the Cape Fear, it advertised services as "Fire, Rat & Vermin Proof," and "We Please the Cranks," an attraction to servicemen seeking short-term interludes.[18]

Brownie's Beauty Shop. Gladys "Brownie" Brown owned a popular shop in her 809 Chestnut home.* Previously she worked in Ollie Whitman's Sunshine Beauty Shop nearby. Brownie never advertised, relied on old regular customers, and had no trouble obtaining supplies.[19] Husband Alex Taylor Brown served in the merchant marine, sons Alex "A. T." and Wilbur in the army, and Robert "Gene," in the air force.

L. Schwartz Furniture Company. Bill Schwartz's family store ("Your Credit is Good") was located in the rougher Brooklyn section of town. They "sold everything they could get." Stores were allotted stock on a waiting list according to past business, receiving it in driblets without style or color choices. Customers bought it before it arrived by train. "No such thing as debt during the war; people paid off everything in cash."

The lucrative business created problems on what to do with earnings. Many merchants converted assets into cash, quickly ridding items languishing on the shelves. Paydays required merchants to have full cash drawers, on Fridays withdrawing large sums from banks, but many stores made workers buy something.[20]

John H. Shaw's Sons Funeral Homes. Advertisement: "47 Years of Continuous Service—Home office, 520 Red Cross Street, Wilmington, N.C. Branch Offices in Jacksonville, Whiteville, Lumberton, N.C. 'Join the Shaw Burial Association: $100 for a Few Pennies a Month'—'Funeral Service, Quiet, Private, Dignified.'"[21] Both Shaw's and L. Schwartz's still operate.

Block's Cantfade Shirt Company. Block's (Southland Manufacturing Company), Wilmington's third employer in size, was the largest family-owned shirt factory in the country, with plants throughout North Carolina. All three sons worked for William "Daddy Block," the father-in-law of Hannah (Mrs. Charles M.) Block, who established the firm. Located at 3rd and Greenfield, the follow-on company recently sold.[22] Blocks made one million military shirts and delivered all but one of them to the army and navy. Manufacturing military shirts caused the company to adopt the army-type collar, "said to be superior to the company's pre-war style." Pacific-veteran Joe Block later joined the company.[23]

Crystal Restaurant. Probably the most popular downtown café, it was next door to Freeman's Shoe Store on Front and two doors from the Bailey Theater. Meals went for 30–40 cents. Cousins Mike and Theodore Zezefellis ran it. Steve "Pop" Fokakis worked there before opening the Hot Shoppe on South 17th. High school brothers and bus boys Nick and George Fokakis,

---

* A weekly customer, Mother often left me in Brownie's care while she performed volunteer duties. Brownie became sort of a "kidsitter" and allowed me to play all over and with Perry Whitman. In 1999, at 92 she escorted me where I had not entered for 50 years. The pungent smells of shampoo and hair color are embedded, and although she has not "fixed" hair for years, her outdated equipment was just where she put it down after her last customer. I went to her funeral in September 2000, another link to my mother gone.

recalled long lines of people waiting to get inside, sometimes wrapped around to 2nd and Market. Nick remembered the soldiers "tipped the girls but they wouldn't tip me. The Crystal was the place."[24]

Real Estate and Construction. Contrary to assumptions, people bought and sold houses, and real estate business thrived. Daddy was associated with three companies, Carolina Building & Loan Association (his principal position), Moore-Fonvielle Realty Company (January 1943 principals were W. A. Fonvielle, president; W. D. Jones, secretary-treasurer; Salesmen Louis O. Fonvielle, Paul A. Bergen, and John V. Fergus), and Moore's Insurance Agency. They were co-located in different offices of the building on the northeast corner of 2nd and Princess (amidst "Robbers Row"). The Carolina daily sold money, war bonds, and Christmas Club savings accounts.

In 1941 local building volume and value hit a peak, the highest in 12 years. Wilmington had 10,182 dwelling units by 1942. In January 1943 Sunset Park homes were listed for "immediate possession" at $3,500 and $6,000, and at 1415 Dock, $5,000.[25] Figures for 1942 revealed a $700,000 drop in private or commercial construction due to federal restrictions and vital materials conservation for the war effort.

There are two ways to
BUY A HOME TODAY

1 Building immediately is difficult . . . but home foundations can be made with War bonds bought now! In this way bonds serve a two-fold purpose . . . to hasten victory and to provide a home for your returning serviceman.

2 If, however, you should find a home on the market to serve your needs, we can still help you! We will arrange with you to finance your home with a direct-reduction loan and your payments will be like paying rent.

ASSETS OVER 3½ MILLION DOLLARS

The / Three Million Dollar

CAROLINA

BUILDING and LOAN ASS'N

MEMBER FEDERAL HOME LOAN ASS'N

ROGER MOORE, Pres.   W. D. JONES, Asst. Sec.-Treas.

W. A. FONVIELLE, Sec.-Treas.

M. G. JAMES, V-Pres.   J. O. CARR, Atty.

Home buying continued through my father's Carolina Building and Loan, a bulwark location at 2nd and Princess.

Wilmington Evening Post, May 23, 1945

Real estate transfer activity (2,518) in New Hanover County's business and industry life peaked during January 1944.[26] By then, county military construction since Pearl Harbor totaled $5,674,502. Camp Davis accounted for $12,417,003. To date engineers had constructed 21 miles of county roads and 27 miles at Davis.[27] One of the city's largest civilian construction jobs, the Atlantic Coast Line headquarters, opened on January 24, 1945.[*] The new Building D at Front and Red Cross "will afford much needed relief from the present congestion in the general offices...."[28]

The "Smart Restaurant." Advertisement: St. John's Tavern at 114 Orange. "Here's Food for Thought—There's no rationing of the quality of our tempting dishes!...A bit of Old Wilmington restored to its former beauty where the NEW Wilmington and old friends may find delightful meals, courteously served."[29] St. John's, in a colonial-era building, attracted military officers and sophisticated civilian sets. Along with the Governor Dudley Restaurant, they were the only ones of their caliber.

The Black and Corbett Trucking Firms. D. J. Black "stayed in business as long as he could operate trucks, then parked his trucks, and got a job at the shipyard in the transportation department," remembered wife Catherine Black. He operated Black's Motor Express with eight Chevrolet closed-freight trucks. The scarcity of parts, tires, and gas forced him out of business, and he sold his hauling rights.[30]

R. E. Corbett owned and operated Corbett Transfer, a general freight hauler with contracts with Swift, Armour, and Nabisco, and daily runs to Camps Davis and Lejeune. On Highway 17 heading for Wilmington he loaded up his canvas-covered open truck with servicemen thumbing rides.[†]

* * *

1945

Building permits, most for private construction, bottomed out and began climbing in 1945, and by year's end would surpass 1944. Retail sales decreased nearly 12 percent by summer 1945. One merchant selling lower quality clothing said merchandise was unavailable. A women's clothing shop reported after a New York buying trip, "In Wilmington we have to take what we can get, and consider ourselves lucky."[31] As if Front Street needed another jeweler,[‡] "throngs of local public" visited its newest venture, David's Jewelers, "Wilmington's newest and finest," in June.[32]

---

[*] The D building is one of three remaining structures from the days when the ACL dominated the north end of downtown. Currently housing the Wilmington Police Department, the unsuitable building's future is unclear once the department relocates. The other two structures form the Coast Line Convention Center, Wilmington Railroad Museum, and businesses.

[†] Although their fathers' trucking firms never merged, R. E. Corbett, Jr., and Cecelia Black did. They were married in September 1954.

[‡] Of the hordes of jewelry stores, only Kingoff's and Finkelstein's are still in business, each at its original site.

Summer 1945 opened with mixed economic news. Cash bank deposits and postal savings increased over 1944, but "no estimate of Wilmington's cash wealth can be made."* Wilmington stood in a "favored position for business expansion in the postwar era....The one great need is for united determination to escape a letdown."[33] By July, bank deposits nosedived attributed to the "decrease in activities such as those at Camp Davis...[and] wartime travel difficulties...." Vacations were few.[34]

Observers looked for silver linings at Christmas. "The 'prophets of gloom' who predicted the commercial death of Wilmington after the departure of soldiers...were apparently wrong....Wilmington has enjoyed a proportionately better year than at any time in its past history...." The city lost an estimated 30 percent of its population since last Christmas, but business volume dropped only about 15 percent. Postal revenue, "always a good business barometer," declined about 16 percent. Holiday travel increased "as a heavy civilian load coupled with normal travel of servicemen taxed transportation facilities to the peak."[35]

Stores stocked the largest choices of goods since 1941, but some items remained unavailable. The brightest news: the Hilton Park Christmas tree—touted as the world's largest living Christmas tree—was lighted for the first time since 1940, and Santa arrived on a special ACL train.

---

* In 1944, Wilmington's 53 manufacturing plants—all here before the war—paid more than $52 million in wages. The average number of persons employed (less the shipyard) was 4,071. [*Wilmington Morning Star*, April 4, 1945]

Chapter 5
"Serving with Uncle Sam"

The first Star-News *column reporting news of military personnel appeared on September 9, 1942, called "In The Service." It ran throughout the war several times a week titled "Serving with Uncle Sam" and "Our Men in Service." It added "and Women" in 1943. Items noted duty assignments, home leave, decorations and honors, and combat action seen—a clearinghouse or bulletin board for good news only. Information came from the government, family, and friends. Pages elsewhere reported casualties and prisoners of war.*

A number of local families qualified for multiple stars on the flags hung in front windows denoting members in the armed forces. Bessie G. Williams sent four sons to the army: air force Captain Charles D., in France; First Lieutenant James Lee, B-25 bombardier-navigator on Corsica and veteran of 56 missions; Technician/5 Ralph C., in England; and Harry T. All had worked for the Atlantic Coast Line. Out of five sons, by 1943 Mr. and Mrs. W. P. Troutman had given three to the navy: William, David, and Marvin.

The six sons of Mr. and Mrs. C. C. Webb, Sr., were in government service by August 1942. All grew up in Wilmington and finished New Hanover High School: Homer, merchant marine; Glenn, army master sergeant; George and Alton, navy; and Clayton McDonald, air force. Austin McDonald served in the FBI. Homer survived the sinking of SS *Esso Houston* in May. The McDonald men were from her previous marriage.

The J. F. Hobbs family on Castle Street presented four sons: army Private First Class Orbert, in the Southwest Pacific; Seaman First Class Ottis, aboard a Liberty ship; Seaman First Class Richard, in California; and Staff Sergeant Robert, in Europe with the 82nd Airborne Division (March 1945). The Webb/McDonald and Hobbs boys survived.

Occasionally our boys came home from the front. Donald Whelpley, 23, of Carolina Beach, who served one and one-half years with the Flying Tigers in China and Burma, visited in September 1942. Required to register with the draft, he preferred to enlist in the navy. Technician/5 Alonzo L. Jones, Jr., 29, among the county's first draftees, returned after 43 months in the Southwest Pacific. One of the original men discharged on the point system, he remarked, "'Everything's still a blank.'" He saw his 15-month old son Allen for the first time. In May 1943 he had been home on emergency leave when his mother died, and his father died shortly after he rejoined his outfit.[1]

Three Gibbs family men served. NHHS graduate Second Lieutenant Richard G., a P-51 *Mustang* pilot with the 55th Fighter Group, downed two German aircraft while escorting B-17 *Flying Fortresess* in March 1945. His brother Donald was a Marine, and their father a Coast Guard lieutenant on North Atlantic duty.

Twin brothers Seaman First Class James Taron Lockamy and Seaman Second Class Robert Allen Lockamy in July 1945 visited their parents for the first time in 20 months. James saw action at Surigao Strait, Saipan, Leyte, Luzon, Iwo Jima, and Okinawa. Robert entered during his New Hanover High School senior year and performed Atlantic convoy duty. Marine Private First Class Clyde Leonard, Jr., veteran of Guadalcanal and two and one-half years of Southwest Pacific with the First Marine Division, said "the average serviceman returning from overseas appreciates more the plan for rehabilitation of returning soldiers rather than the question, so generally asked, 'How many Japs did you kill?'"[2]

*   *   *

"Your Patriotic Duty"

It didn't take long for local draft boards to get tough with "delinquents." In December 1941, Clerk Glenn J. McClelland warned all: "It is your patriotic as well as your legal duty to keep in close contact with your local board now."[3] Keeping track of registrants was a never-ending problem. In March 1943, the delinquents list contained 72 names. Draft violations were serious offenses. Raymond Worth Alexander, 40, received 18 months in the Atlanta penitentiary for failure to maintain contact. At the war's end, 36 delinquents faced FBI investigation.*

The number of local men drafted in 1942 reached 1,021. Because of "stepped-up draft machinery...1943 is expected to bring a heavier draft call." The two local Selective Service boards, City Board No. 1, averaged sending 75 per month, and County Board No. 2, 150 men over the previous three months.[4] From 1940 through December 1943, 3,018 men were inducted.

---

* After January 1, 1943, all men entering the armed forces came through Selective Service, which at induction would parcel out men to the services, sometimes granting preferences. Enlistment exceptions were 17-year-olds with parents' permission. The Marine Corps had a special arrangement with draft officials.

Volunteer local drafts boards endured charges of favoritism or discrimination, but on the whole appeared fair and objective.

When the 1943–44 high school year convened, the draft's impact on 18-year-old students was evident, exacerbated by those dropping out for defense work. Soon the military manpower pool also shrunk drastically, partly because of deferments. "'We've reached the bottom of the barrel.'"[5] A traveling board soliciting volunteers for the Naval Aviation Cadet program spent two days here in May. Seven men signed up. By January 1946, the two local boards merged and operated "in a reverse manner" processing men back into civilian life.[6]

In 1942 shipyard worker John King walked into the army office at 9 a.m. to enlist. A few hours later, his twin brother, William, unaware, applied for enlistment. Recruiting sergeant Frank Humphries noticed the information similarities and asked if William knew John. A few days later they headed together for Shaw Air Force Base, South Carolina. Tanky Meier told his Atlantic Coast Line boss he was joining the air force with friends Herb Houston and Victor Mintz (both were killed in action). But the boss threatened to fire him with no postwar job promise, saying: be drafted and come back with one leg and it's yours. Tanky waited until January 1943 to save family embarrassment over being fired.

Denied by the navy, Don Blake received two weeks at home before departing for army training. He joined the 556th Anti-Aircraft Artillery Battalion of the Ninth Army in Germany before it crossed the Rhine, soon meeting the Russians on the Elbe River. He helped run a redeployment camp at Antwerp, Belgium, for men returning Stateside. Discharged in 1946, he later served in the Korean and Vietnam Wars.

Sailor Leonard Quick, former Williston Industrial School student.
Cornelia Haggins Campbell

By March 1944, since Pearl Harbor, 205 former NHHS men and women were in the service: 72 in the navy, 65 air force, 48 army, 15 Marines, five Coast Guard, and one in the nurses' cadet corps. Some would avoid service. Jim Robertson had written his friend Billy Broadfoot in India in 1944 that he "was sweating out being drafted." Billy wrote his own parents, "I give you a quote. 'I am trying, however, that the navy, with whom we have contracts, will be able to get me a deferment.' The whole tone of the letter was a little of fear. He's not made of the stuff his old man is."[7]

Negroes became eligible for enlistment in 1942. "Not only because this is the first time in the history of the navy that the colored man has been eligible for such enlistment, but because it is a step the navy has been considering for many years. Many Wilmington Negroes have asked for information." In June three became the first to enlist in North Carolina. "Formerly, Negroes were enlisted as mess attendants, a post which requires very little actual combat duty,"[8] recruiter Jesse Helms remarked. The navy in July sent a Negro chief petty officer "to discuss enlistment...with members of his race."[9]

Fathers also volunteered. Real estate and insurance man and World War I navy veteran R. C. Cantwell, Jr., asked for a recall. Son Bob Cantwell remembered, "He was 50 years old and still slightly crippled, but he was sure that there were jobs he could do." A doctor noticed missing teeth, which might reject him. Mr. Cantwell remarked that "he had anticipated that the government would supply him with a weapon and not require him to bite any enemy troops. They took him up on his offer and he and Mother were off to a new war at the Portsmouth (Va.) Navy Yard." Bob then ran the business. "I didn't think it looked nice for me to have a father in the service and not go to help him....I didn't mind bleeding a little bit, but didn't want to

Army Lt. R. C. "Bob" Cantwell III and wife, Betty Garrabrant Cantwell, *right*, with father, Navy Lt. R. C. Cantwell, Jr., and mother, 1943.

Bob Cantwell III

bleed much." Commissioned in September 1943, "I went to France to fight the Germans, but there weren't many left there."[10]

* * *

James Sampson, Jr.,[11] became an army cook with the all-Negro, white-officered 24th Infantry Regiment. "It seemed so natural I don't know how I did it. When you're young you look for challenges." On Saipan in early 1945, a general inspected his kitchen and praised him. "I was just trembling." He worked his way to staff sergeant. The 24th landed on Okinawa after the invasion. He saw no combat but "I was around people who were dead and dying. You don't think things were bothering you because you were young. It was later on you realized what you had been through. I saw drugs when I was overseas." About race relations on Okinawa: "You were jumping into the foxholes together, you were doing everything together." He experienced segregation while heading home.

Bill McIlwain[12] and football teammate Whitey Auld and several other friends enlisted together after graduating in 1944. "Whitey said, 'I'll take the army,' I said, 'I'll take the Marines, another guy took the navy.'" The newspaper heralded, "The nation's armed services will be strengthened considerably today when it takes into its fold Bill McIlwain, baseball and football star of the NHHS, sports writer, sports authority, high school leader, *ad infinitum*, and who, until last night was sports editor of the *Star*." Bill's World War I veteran father taught him how to shoot, but he failed to qualify for marksman. "At age 18, that [failure] was about the worst thing that could happen to me." A foot disability caused Bill's March 1945 discharge. A football injury did the same for Whitey. "Even if you had something wrong with you, you knew you could get in the service."

Shipyard worker Bill Childs[13] received his draft notice in January 1943 but a psychologist rejected him. He missed being part of the 80 Negroes inducted, then the largest such Wilmington contingent.* "I was not unhappy because it would give me the opportunity to do something else." He moved to Chester, Pennsylvania, to work at Sun Shipyard.

Because of a leg injury, the draft rejected Clayton Smith while he worked at the shipyard. "All this time [December 1943] I felt I wasn't doing what I should have been doing." His aunt "made appropriate noises at the draft board in Raleigh," and he was inducted in September 1944. "Anybody going in at that time was strictly replacements." As an army seaman he helped sail Doris Duke's yacht in Florida.[14]

"Many Williston [Industrial School] graduates and former students are now connected with the armed forces," the *Cape Fear Journal* reported in November 1942. "It is interesting to note that many of these young men

---

* The peak number of Negroes assembled here for induction was 411 in March 1944.

have made steady advancements since they entered. Many letters have been received...stating how the skill and knowledge received at Williston had helped them to advance."[15] On the next Navy Day, Williston honored its sons.

Wilmingtonian Fred N. Day III played on the 9th Infantry Division football team in Germany after the war. Air force Corporal Algernon Meigs, son of Mrs. M. G. Meigs, was among soldiers received by Pope Pius XIII in Rome. Yeoman John L. Casteen won a $1,000 war bond on the CBS Phil Baker radio program as its 1,000th contestant.

* * *

Wilmington, the Small World

Our boys were always running into friends around the globe. For a small county of 43,000 before the war, it must have seemed half served in uniform. When landing at Le Havre, France, in January 1945, Mac Wilson encountered Lieutenant Whit Benton, "the last person I ever expected to see. We grew up right around the corner from each other." Attached to the 273rd Infantry Regiment, 69th Division, Mac "had grown up with it." He made the army a career.[16]

Jack Hart asked H. G. Carney, head of the city draft board, to change his 3A classification to 1A so he could volunteer. Carney hesitated to break the rules, but went ahead. Jack enlisted in October 1942 and served three years with only 15 minutes on home leave. Already with nine months in the Tunisia and Sicily campaigns and in his 11th month in Burma, Jack met brother-in-law Technician Sergeant Horace Hicks, a veteran of Algeria and 14 months in India-Burma, by accident in 1945.

Army transportation officer Bob Cantwell III, offloading troops in Algiers, Algeria, saw the Wilmington-built Liberty ship "SS *Walker Taylor*, Wilmington, N.C." In Marseilles, France, in late 1944 he bumped into school-mate Herbert Jones, a merchant ship purser. ("He very kindly supplied me with 48 bottles of Coca-Cola....") Later in Dijon, France, he exchanged mess visits with Wilmington army Captain Joe B. Fox.[17]

In 1940 Joe Reaves had flown here with Warren Pennington and later began lessons at Bluethenthal Field.[18] Two hours short of his license, in October 1942 he entered the navy's V-5 cadet program at North Carolina. Instructor John Anderson of Wilmington asked for Joe, giving him "a leg up in a world of many washouts." Joe requested dive bombers but instead flew OS2U float planes and R5D four-engine transports in Pacific forward areas carrying cargo and litter patients.

Dick Jones was scheduled to graduate in 1945 but quit at 17 to join the merchant marine.[19] "All the boys were either in the service or going. So I thought I ought to go too." Wilmingtonian merchant marine officer Harry

Payne assigned Dick to sail on a Liberty ship converted into a hospital ship. On a 1945 trip he returned wounded Americans. Among them was Wilmingtonian Malcom Rhue whose footlocker "was a pawn shop in there. Everything imaginable, captured stuff." The first thing they did in a German town was clean out the bank. "He had some wild stories. He would have been one of the dead-end kids."

Herman Hartis, drafted in September 1942, served 38 months.[20] A member of the 840th (construction) Engineers Battalion attached to the air force, after arriving in France, he became part of Patton's Third Army building airfields and roads. His company had several local men including Jerry Rogers, James Vereen, and Charles Davis. There "wasn't much talk about back-home stuff. We found little things to make us laugh. Me and a boy from Pennsylvania went over the hill [AWOL], wanted to be the first in our battalion to get into Paris."

Bill Walton, Jr., was ready to be drafted.[21] "I did not feel the urge" to volunteer, "just wasn't my nature to run down to the recruiting office when it started." He drew 5th Air Force duty with a mobile radar unit duty in New Guinea and the Philippines. Home "seemed like it was another world away." He saw occupation duty on Kyushu, Japan. "We didn't have any compassion for them, and they had less for us. We had some misgivings about them once we entered the occupation, but found them congenial." He had run into Wilmingtonians Leon Stein, Dick Dunlea, Jr., and David Ormand.

Martin Willard joined the navy a few weeks after Pearl Harbor. His first duty was in a merchant ship armed guard detachment. "I knew some boys who got three or four ships sunk from under them," but not him. "For all that time at sea, I was never injured—I was lucky. If you were on a merchant ship you either were sunk or you made it through." He sailed on four. While a USS LST-1012 crewman off Southern France in August 1944, he found future brother-in-law Miles Higgins. On V-J Day at Okinawa, his brother Emerson Willard came aboard bringing him a pair of loafers purchased in Hawaii for Martin's 29th birthday. The Willard family sent five relatives and close friends to the Mediterranean at the same time in 1943: Higgins, Johnny Smith, and cousins Edgar Williams, Cecil Sanford, and Terry Sanford (future North Carolina governor and U.S. Senator).[22]

Jeanette Hanson married Marine Corporal Nils Harry Hanson four days before he went overseas in December 1942. Since then she saw him at the Bailey Theater in a newsreel closeup taken in an Iwo Jima landing craft, and later, awaiting WAVES service in New York, in another newsreel.

Probably no one encountered more Wilmingtonians than John Burney. Called "Tar Heel" and "Redneck," John was a rifleman and platoon sergeant in the 254th Infantry Regiment, 63rd Infantry Division in Europe, attached temporarily to the French army. Deployed straight from the United States and landing in Marseilles, he fought up to the Vosges Mountains. In Dijon he crossed paths with Tom Gregg. Classmates Bill Farmer and Tom Campbell served in the 63rd. A. L. King rode 43 miles to visit John in France, but missed him. John was wounded in Germany three times. The last one on April 17, 1945, left him with shrapnel throughout his body except the left arm. On the hospital ship home in July he saw friend Killer Huffman.[23]

John's father, Judge John J. Burney, a World War I veteran in France, told him how to fight. "What did the judge tell you today to do to the Germans?" his buddies asked. The first Christmas away in 1943 on guard duty, he cried. On Thanksgiving in 1944 near Benwhir, Alsace, he stepped into a covey of quail (the family always hunted quail around Thanksgiving).

Without a girlfriend (lacked the money), instead John wrote girls from school. On furlough, he rode on his duffel bag on crowded trains. Once at Florence, South Carolina, Wilmingtonian Colonel McCormick picked him up and delivered him home.

Family reunions occurred thousands of miles from home. Major William F. Corbett met his army nurse sister (NHHS graduates), First Lieutenant Mary Nettles Corbett, in New Guinea in 1944 and the Philippines in 1945. Their father, W. Z. Corbett, lived here. Brothers James F. and Paul Melton met for the first time in five years at the Anzio, Italy, battlefield in September 1944. James went overseas in January 1943, serving in North Africa, Sicily, and Italy, and Paul went to Italy in December. In Naples Paul encountered their Wilmington first cousin, Corporal M. M. Brooks, Jr. Another Melton brother, William P. Melton, Jr., was in Sardinia. Paul received the Bronze Star and Combat Infantryman's Badge.

* * *

"Raggedy-assed Heroes" and Other Exploits

Wilmington native and officer Robert Ruark commanded the naval detachment on the SS *Eli Whitney*.* "'The armed guard was shoved aboard merchant ships to annoy the merchant seamen....We were very probably the most raggedy-assed heroes ever put to sea....My boys were getting $60 a month, the Chinese mess boy who served me was making $550 a month, with bonus areas and extra bonuses for bombing, so my morale problem was tough for a cadre of 30 guys and me.'"[24]

Three sisters joined what became the Women's Army Corps: Virginia Ward and Mabel Lee of Wilmington, and Bessie Lawson. Navy WAVES Storekeeper Second Class Gladys Sheets saw Hawaii duty. She and her husband, merchant marine Chief Yeoman Francois Sheets, were former Wilmingtonians.

---

* In his posthumous 1965 autobiography *The Honey Badger*, the author Ruark described his WWII experiences. During the war he wrote articles for *Colliers*, *Saturday Evening Post*, and *Liberty*, and served with Admiral Chester Nimitz.

Army nurse corps First Lieutenant Elizabeth Barry in 1944–45 was stationed on a hospital ship. By March 1945, 23 graduates of James Walker Memorial Hospital nursing school served in the army or navy, six awaited call, and two more worked for the government. My great aunt Lillian George, who maintained the local Nurses Registry, said, "'The nurses here and elsewhere have not fallen down in response to military needs....We are making every effort we can to supply the civilian demands. We have a very acute shortage....'"[25]

Civil engineer Henry Von Oesen entered army duty three weeks before Pearl Harbor. He advanced as an infantry company commander and battalion operations officer, served in the Philippines and in the Japan occupation. While teaching rifle tactics he was laughed at because of his Southern accent. When he came home from service, his parents thought he had lost it all.[26]

Army Lieutenant George Bethell wrote from North Africa in late 1942.[27] "The officer's club here is opening tonight and we're having a dance with the nurses....All this is seemingly out of place but we're so far behind the front that life is very peaceful....I haven't seen any of those mysterious Eastern women of the [Hedy] Lamar type, but I'm looking."

James Walker Memorial Hospital nurse Ruby Bissette in 1945 received news about husband army Staff Sergeant Sam Bissette. Blue Network commentator Ted Malone, who met him in Paris, telephoned her later from New York. Motion picture projectionist Mark Venters served at the New York naval hospital using projectors like those at Wilmington's Bailey Theater where he previously worked. Refusing a medical discharge, his closest brush with combat was his favorite movie: "Mother, when the picture 'Destination Tokyo' [1944] comes there, don't fail to see it."[28]

After receiving his wings in 1941, George S. Boylan, a member of my church, began antisubmarine air patrols out of Newfoundland.*

Seaman Mark D. Venters, Jr., with showgirl, St. Alban's Naval Hospital, Long Island, N.Y., 1945.

Mark D. Venters, Jr.

---

* At least 94 boys from St. Andrews-Covenant Presbyterian Church served in uniform. Army Major Francis Rivers Lawther and air force Captain Ralph W. Soverel, Jr., died in

With the 8th Air Force, he commanded the 329th Bomb Squadron and 93rd Bomb Group as a lieutenant colonel. He led B-24s for 18 months on 25 missions over Germany before returning to the United States in late 1944. Actor Jimmy Stewart flew with him. George received the Distinguished Flying Cross and Air Medal with three Oak Leaf Clusters and retired as a lieutenant general.

In 1942 while studying at Davidson, Emerson Willard received an Annapolis appointment. Soon "I decided that was not the place for me....They would not let us resign." So he and others decided to flunk out. Authorities knew what they were up to, and furnished a bus to drive them to Washington to enlist. He entered navy flight training in 1942 and flew PBM and PBY patrol planes from Saipan in 1945.[29] Because he had taught Spanish at Hampden-Sydney College, the navy slotted Joe Whitted, a Willard first cousin, as an intelligence officer in Panama. Joe and Martin Willard rode through the Canal together several times.

* * *

Soldiers, Businessmen, Community Leaders[30]

The first duty assignment for Wilmingtonian Bruce B. Cameron, Jr., a 1938 Virginia Military Institute graduate, was at Camp Davis in February 1941 when headquarters was in the Wilmington post office. He volunteered for duty, living at home at 1810 Market Street and commuting until the end of December. As a civil engineer, Bruce helped plan construction for Davis and Fort Fisher while an aide to post commander Brigadier General James B. Crawford. Bruce later accompanied Crawford to Fort Bliss, Texas, before returning to Davis in 1942 for AAA training.

At Camp Hulan, Texas, in the spring of 1943 and now a captain, Bruce joined the 382nd AAA Battalion, a 40mm-gun unit. While undergoing desert training in California, in January 1944 he married Mary Dail of Santa Rosa.

Bruce shipped out to New Guinea, taking 50 days on a Dutch ship without escort. "[General Douglas] MacArthur fought a damned smart war" and the 382nd, with Bruce as executive officer, went with him. In July 1944 he learned of the death of his father, Wilmington Mayor Bruce Cameron, at age 53 from a brain blood clot during a trip to Philadelphia. Friend Robert Williams informed him by telegram. The army sent him home after eight months without his advance knowledge. Older than brother Dan, he figured that was why it was he instead of Dan. By November, Bruce had assumed responsibilities for his father's business interests and Dan remained in Europe.

aircraft accidents. Multiple family members served: four Sprunts, Gaylors, Holmeses, and Kings, and three Merritts, Nisbets, and Troutmans. All 94 are remembered on a plaque inside the chapel.

Dan Cameron graduated from VMI in 1942 with a reserve commission "in the horse cavalry." Immediately placed on active duty, he requested AAA and was assigned to the 430th AAA Battalion at Camp Davis, "a real swamp" requiring duckboards and truckloads of Topsail Beach sand to maneuver. After landing over Normandy's Omaha Beach on June 8, ("strewn with all kinds of equipment, dead bodies stacked up like cordwood"), his unit protected field artillery. "We were always exposed, but did not take too many casualties." He watched the breakout around St. Lo, the smoke, noise, planes crashing, the bombardments. A Red Cross telegram told him about his father. He "worked himself to death." In the Battle of the Bulge, the 430th set up behind the infantry in antitank positions. "We wouldn't have been able to stop a [German] Tiger tank."

Like many other local men, Dan encountered fellow Wilmingtonians, including friends VMI roommate Gene Fonvielle, soldier-artist Henry MacMillan, Jurgie Diehl, and Bill Mears. Henry for much of the war in Europe was given a car and driver and went place to place painting watercolors of combat. His commander needed details of the Normandy hedgerows for intelligence purposes. Dan remembered spotting him near St. Lo. "I saw some nut out there in a field and found out it was Henry." He and his mother had been in business with the Camerons at MacMillan & Cameron Company. The army allowed Henry to bring home the paintings. The Cape Fear Museum exhibits them too infrequently.

When the war ended, Dan was on R&R (rest and relaxation) in the South of France and Switzerland. "We should have

Virginia Military Institute ('42) classmates Capt. Daniel D. "Dan" Cameron, *left*, and Lt. Chris Eugene "Gene" Fonvielle at Ludwigsburg, Germany, 1945.

Daniel D. Cameron

Henry MacMillan at Bad Neuheim, Germany, 1944.

Daniel D. Cameron

stayed longer; nobody missed us." While training for transfer to the Pacific, he guarded Nazis, including Hitler's barber. Dan received the Bronze Star with five battle stars.

Bruce and Dan became highly successful businessmen and developers, respected and powerful civic and political leaders, and generous community benefactors including the University of North Carolina at Wilmington and the arts. Much of the area's resoluteness, foresight, and achievements in arising from the 1960s doldrums is attributable to them. Their father set high standards.*

* * *

At the War's End

En route to a May 1945 linkup with the Russians at the Elbe River, Technician/5 William Turner rode a tank destroyer spearhead guarding six U.S. generals. "After 10 or 15 minutes of spontaneous fraternizing, back-slapping and handshaking between Russian and American officers and enlisted men, the two groups adjourned to the city's best hotel."[31]

Lieutenant (Junior Grade) Ralph Buckner Barden, son of Mr. and Mrs. James T. Barden, Sr., of Winter Park, a TBM *Avenger* carrier torpedo-bomber pilot, proceeded toward a Tokyo electronics plant target on August 15. Directed to jettison bombs and return to the USS *Lexington* (CV-16), he stated, "'The order to 'return to base' was difficult to realize. It was the first strike from which I had ever been recalled...[and] the greatest strike I had ever flown.'" Barden flew nine and one-half strikes in 10 months, the "half strike" being the final one.[32]

So it was. The final strike. The war ended. Among the first Yanks to arrive in Japan was radio operator Staff Sergeant David L. Ormond, at Atsugi airport outside Tokyo. Five Wilmington boys on the destroyer USS *McDermott* (DD-677) sailed into Japan in October. The ship had seen heavy action. They were Clarence E. Newsome, Jr., Morris J. Tatum, Morris F. Powell, Ralph H. Buck, and Earl Hilburn.

Obviously Wilmington's sons and daughters had given their all in combat and on the home front to help bring an Allied victory. But the carryover of war lingered. Almost a year later, while studying dentistry at Emory University, Barden received the Navy Cross for an earlier attack.

Decorations and Honors

My decorated Forest Hills neighbors included:

First Lieutenant John W. Loughlin—Distinguished Flying Cross and Air Medal with one Oak Leaf Cluster; flying transports in India-China (1945).

---

* In 2002 Wilmington's new Louise Wells Cameron Art Museum opened, a family gift spearheaded by Bruce. I had the pleasure of lecturing there on the MacMillan paintings. A *Wilmington Star-News* survey ranked Dan as the community's leading businessman.

First Lieutenant Robert Ranor Garey—Air Medal with OLC; P-51 pilot, for action against the Japanese.

Army Colonel Joe T. Wrean—Legion of Merit; antiaircraft commander at Port Moresby, New Guinea, April–November 1943.

Others included:

Captain George H. Chadwick, Jr., 23—DFC and Air Medal with two OLCs; B-17 pilot in Italy with 15th Air Force, his 50th mission against the synthetic oil refinery at Brux, Czechoslovakia (his first was the Ploesti, Rumania, oil fields).

Capt. George H. Chadwick, Jr., 23, B-17 *Flying Fortress* pilot in Italy, completes 50th combat mission against the synthetic oil refinery at Brux, Czechoslovakia. His first was against the Ploesti, Rumania, oil fields. He received the Distinguished Flying Cross and Air Medal with two Oak Leaf Clusters. My mother sent this Wilmington newspaper clipping to his wife, Jo Chadwick, in 1969.*

Jo Chadwick

Air force Staff Sergeant Herbert L. McKibbin—Bronze Star; service as ground crew chief in a P-51 squadron.

Lieutenant (Junior Grade) Robert Edward Waters—Silver Star and Presidential Unit Citation; Southwest Pacific, tactical commander of three patrol-torpedo boats in aggressive attack on Japanese vessels.

Captain George E. "Roddy" Kidder—DFC; pilot in China-Burma-India Theater (1945).

Paratrooper Private J. A. Willis, former shipyard worker—Silver Star; action near Bastogne, Belgium, January 3, 1945.

Tech Sergeant William E. Butler—DFC with two OLCs and Air Medal with one OLC; B-17 crewman in more than 200 combat flights against the Solomons, Rabaul, and New Guinea (1942–43).

Commander Richard S. Andrews, Pacific submarine skipper—Bronze Star; for sinking 3,000 tons of Japanese shipping; awarded by Admiral Chester Nimitz.

Lieutenant Edward C. Hines, Jr.—Legion of Merit; destroyer USS *Cole* (DD-155), invasion of North Africa (1942).

* * *

---

* "Dear Friends, Enclosed in the very nice picture I found in my scrapbook about the boys in the services....I'm sure it will bring back memories. Thank you both for being so nice to me. Kindest regards, Viola M. Jones." [Mother to George and Jo Chadwick, August 12, 1969, enclosing clipping (probably 1945) about George's decorations]

And the Boys Came Marching Home

The three military members of my father's "business family" at 2nd and Princess began arriving in late 1945. Lieutenant (Junior Grade) Lloyd W. Moore rejoined Moore-Fonvielle Realty Company and Moore's Insurance Agency in October, after commanding an LCT (landing craft, tank) in the Aleutians and Gilberts. Navy Lieutenant W. Alex Fonvielle, Jr., came home in November 1945 after more than three and one-half years. He received the Bronze Star for commanding patrol-torpedo boats at Guadalcanal, Vella Gulf, Choiseul, Empress Augusta Bay, and Bougainville. The other son of my father's partner W. A. Fonvielle, army Lieutenant Chris Eugene Fonvielle, 7th Armored Division, returned in January 1946 with the Bronze Star after 20 months in Europe.

Doctor Major Samuel E. Warshauer reopened his office after five years in Australia and New Guinea. Navy flight surgeon Lieutenant Worth Sprunt visited his parents, Mr. and Mrs. Walter P. Sprunt, after 25 months with carrier aircraft units in Pacific combat (March 1945). Five boys returned with the 86th Infantry Division from Europe: First Sergeants Simpson Fuller Sistrunk and Glen Shipley, Staff Sergeant Clyde W. Lassiter, Tech/4 Talmadge Batson, and Private First Class W. D. Smith. Sistrunk, "after 'talking Fort Bragg officials blue in the face' was allowed to come home...for a one-night visit with his parents, wife and baby," and then return for discharge (June 1945).[33] And, the first local man granted a GI Bill loan was Mark C. Scott for a house at 1814 Perry through Peoples Building & Loan.

After three years service, neighbor Lieutenant Commander Charles P. Graham returned in November. His USS *Indiana* (BB-50) saw extensive combat against Truk, Saipan, Iwo Jima, and the Philippines, and was the first ship to enter Japan's home waters. He resumed practice with Dr. James F. Robertson. Others arriving in late 1945 included neighbors Sergeant Harry McGirt; nurse First Lieutenant Mary E. Martin, and navy Lieutenant John Taylor Schiller, a Pacific veteran of the destroyer USS *Gwen* (DD-772), battleship USS *North Carolina* (BB-55), and the carrier USS *Midway* (CV-41).

For some it took longer. My backyard neighbor, navy doctor James B. Lounsbury, finally resumed his obstetrics and gynecology practice in March 1946. His assignments included Mediterranean convoys and minesweeping near Japan. Across-the-street neighbor, Colonel J. B. McCumber, who commanded the

Wilmington army air forces flight surgeon Capt. William J. Wheeler, M.D., son of Mrs. Jeanette Wheeler.

George N. Norman

504th AAA Gun Battalion on Leyte and Okinawa, in April 1946 was among the last of the old 252nd Coast Artillery National Guard veterans who entered in September 1940 to resume his career.

"To Whom It May Concern"[34]

NHHS Principal Thomas T. ("T-Square") Hamilton, Jr., assisted boys entering the service by penning "To whom it may concern" letters vouching for certain positive characteristics. For Nick Fokakis(1943), he wrote: "Is a young man of excellent character and pleasing personality. Mr. Fokakis maintained a satisfactory scholarship record and his class citizenship was excellent. We found him to be cooperative, courteous, and dependable." Regardless, infantryman Fokakis slogged through combat in New Guinea and the Philippines.

Wilmington-Area Residents at Pearl Harbor

Besides the three Wilmingtonians killed in action on December 7, 1941,* at least 23 other Wilmington-area persons were stationed at or living around Pearl Harbor. Navy: Lieutenant (Junior Grade) Clarence Earle Dickinson, Jr. (USS *Enterprise* [CV-6]); Seaman Second Class Lawrence Homer Henderson of Hampstead (USS *California* [BB-44]); Taylor Marion Jeffords, (NHHS '39, baker, USS *West Virginia* [BB-48]); Joseph G. Nesbitt (seaplane tender USS *Avocet* [AVP-4]); Conrad Lott (Leland, *West Virginia*); Roscoe A. Cole, Jr. (harbor defense unit); M. C. Dobson (naval air station); Nelson Robinson (destroyer); William H. Barry (ship); Lieutenant Benjamin E. Adams, Jr. (submarine; wife Catherine Cantwell Adams of Wilmington lived on Waikiki); U. S. Mintz (NHHS '39, USS *Oklahoma* [BB-37]); and Seaman First Class William Pressley Troutman.

Army air forces: Tech Sergeant J. W. Thompson, Jr., Marsden S. Ward, Jr. (both Hickam Field). Army: Private William S. Smith, Harry Redrick (Schofield Barracks). Other civilians: Justus Sistrunk (Hickam Field); Mrs. Emil (Rosa Burch) Peterson; Drexel High (shipyard); Mrs. Glenn Frazier (husband on USS *Arizona* [BB-39]); and Blanche Stewart (nurse), who airmailed her mother, "'We are working day and night. Everything has been orderly, and we are not expecting another attack.'"[35]

Navy master diver Garland "Jack" Suggs salvaged sunken and damaged ships in 1942, escaping death several times. Once a ship's hull shifted, almost burying him alive. "'I dug like a demon and managed to crawl out from under the falling hull without snaring my air line.'" For that "he gets qualms only after he returns to the surface and recalls some of his narrow squeaks."[36]

---

* Signalman First Class Harvey Howard Horrell, *Arizona*; Boatswains Mate Herbert Franklin Melton, *Oklahoma*; Radioman Second Class Clyde Carson Moore, USS *Shaw* (DD-373).

Wilmington Jews in Uniform[37]

Members of both the Temple of Israel and B'Nai Israel Synagogue, serving by January 1944:

Maj Samuel E. Warshauer
Capt Mortimer Herzberg, Jr.
Lt(jg) Bernard S Solomon
Lt(jg) John Taylor Schider
Lt(jg) Erwin Jaffe
Lt Noah J. Plisco
Lt Frank Retchin
Lt Arthur Bluethenthal
Lt Carol S. Goodman
Lt Louis S. Solomon
Lt Bernard J. Warshauer
Ens Leon Stein
Ens William Schwartz
Ens Joseph M. Schwartz
2dLt Robert A. Goldberg, Jr.
Staff Sgt Moe A. Kotler

Tech Sgt Arnold Neuwirth
Tech Sgt Marx Neuwirth
Sgt Joseph M. Block
Sgt Adolph O. Solomon
Cpl Solomon B. Sternberger
Cpl Nathan Schwartz
Cpl George Dannenbaum
Cpl James Herzberg—(KIA)
Cpl Daniel D. Retchin
Cpl Sidney Rubin
Cpl Bernard Davis
Cpl Leon R. Moskowitz
Cpl Frederick H. Scherr
Pfc Samuel S. Rubin
Pfc Irving Kaminsky
Pfc Irving Schwartz

Chapter 6

"If War Took a Summer Vacation"

Rationale prevailed, and enough manpower was available at the Information and Filter Center temporarily. By July 1943, "the regular summer let-down has come....As the summer advances the staff falls off....That would not be so bad if war took a summer vacation and the danger of attack faded....Any business, domestic or social sacrifices involved is more than offset by the value of this service."[1]

New Hanover County blew hot and cold in its number of volunteer aircraft spotters and plotters. In February 1943 the filter center, the area's Signal Corps aircraft status office, sought 600 volunteers immediately, men especially for night duty. Shifts doubled to 24 hours. But with the threat of a German air attack substantially subsiding, the task loomed difficult. By March, the newspaper suggested "there would seem to be no course open but to draft workers for the center."[2]

By April, "It is perhaps too much to expect that another appeal for volunteers...will receive more attention than the many previous pleas....Without this service an enemy attack could lay Wilmington waste and spread destruction throughout Southeastern North Carolina before defending planes could get off the ground."[3]

In the summer of 1942, spotter posts opened weekly. One, a heavy 10-foot wood structure on John Nuckton's Castle Hayne field, afforded "spotters a safe place from which to watch for enemy raiders...equipped with electric lights and a dial telephone system." Staffed by more than 50 volunteers, the post "is one of the best manned in the county....No one knows where or when the enemy may strike."[4]

As the City Council in July approved funding a post on the Cape Fear Hotel roof, downtown's prominent building, it charged the Federal Government with refusing to help bear costs.[5] "This is one of the many requests that has been made of us. I'm afraid that we are near the breaking point unless the government helps us," said Mayor Pro-tem Edgar L. Yow.

Establishing that "model" installation post was intended to eliminate several nearby. "You can order a soldier to stand guard in the rain; that's his duty," a filter center sergeant said. "But you can't expect Volunteer Joe Smith, a civilian, to stand a three-hour shift in the rain." The Council eventually appropriated construction of the filter center control room and other equipment, telephones, salaries, a blood bank, a siren system, and medical equipment. The glassed-in spotter hut began 24-hour operations in July.

"Wilmington is deeply indebted to the men and women, who setting aside every personal and household demand upon their time, climbed the steps to the control room and remained on duty," an observer noted in June 1944. "They were weary, lagging, boring hours, especially on the night tricks," but admonished, "...It is still possible that an enemy agent might commit some act of sabotage...."[6]

* * *

Living with One's Own Defense

"Although every effort was made to keep the [U-boat] sinkings secret in order that the Germans might not know how successful they had been," a state history recorded, "it was not possible to conceal from the coastal inhabitants the explosions at sea, the oil and debris on the beach, the flames against the eastern sky, or the men 'horribly wounded and burned' who were taken to local hospitals...."[7]

During the height of ship sinkings in 1942, Governor J. Melville Broughton wrote Navy Secretary Frank Knox, "'...The defenses against submarine depredations certainly in the North Carolina coastal areas are wholly inadequate and frequently inept and that there is a shocking lack of coordination between army, navy, coast guard, and air forces....'"[8] But by spring 1944, Admiral Ernest J. King, the navy's senior officer, reported German submarines were unlikely "to terrorize Atlantic shipping lanes again" as two years ago.[9] Area sightings and other evidence of sinkings had dramatically tailed off.

The Germans laid mines off several major Atlantic seaports. Early in the war authorities closed Wilmington for a week, unreported publicly, but found no mines in North Carolina waters. Still, the threat and rumors continued well into 1944 when the submarine menace all but disappeared, a shift unreported but assumed as restrictions expired or became lax, and normalcy along the beaches gradually resumed without obstruction.*

---

* The newspaper in 1945 erred that Germans mined our port in 1942 and 1943, emanating from the previous day's paper stating it was Wilmington, Delaware, and other key ports. The June 17 item continued. "...[The mining] comes as a complete surprise to everybody not engaged in the minelaying and other phases of the defense program....Wilmingtonians for the most part contented themselves in patience and on the whole indulged in little obtrusive inquisitiveness." [*Wilmington Sunday Star-News*, June 17, 1945]

Private boats of the Cape Fear Division, Coast Guard Auxiliary, prepare for drills from their Inland Waterway base at the Harbor Island drawbridge, Wrightsville Beach.
Wilmington Sunday Star-News, May 9, 1943

Telephones functioned as both salvation and scourge. Critiquing a June 1943 alert, the *Morning Star* blamed "thoughtless residents" for the "chagrin and disappointment [for] the incessant use of telephones....During alerts and blackouts...the phone is needed exclusively for transmission of orders, assembling of wardens and other defense units....Friends and strangers calling to know what was happening harassed the police chief...."[10]

In January 1942 Louis J. Poisson succeeded *Star-News* publisher R. B. Page, pre-war Defense Council chairman, for the duration. Governor Broughton then appointed Page as the area State Defense Council representative. County sheriff C. David Jones began duties for the duration as New Hanover County Civilian Defense Corps commander, subsuming many of the Council's functions. F. P. O'Crowley (city) and Elbie L. White (county) served as chief air raid wardens.

Lucinda O. Denton and her family spent each July 4th at Carolina Beach's Gwendolyn Cottage. To keep cool inside drawn shades, "they placed a block of ice in a tub and ran a fan in front of it. A kerosene lamp gave them enough light to pass the time playing cards."[11] One night Bill Leeuwenburg and friend played soldier on Wrightsville Beach, shining flashlights into homes. Real soldiers, threatening to tie them up and execute them, "scared us totally to death." Walter and Tabitha McEachern kept the only kind of light allowed, a blue one, by their telephone at Wrightsville.

To Peggy Moore, summering at Wrightsville, if the shipyard lights—visible from the beach—went out, "we were in real trouble." One night they did. Her Marine officer neighbor left on his lights even though illegal. Every night the beach patrol told him to extinguish them. The night the shipyard lights went out (the U-boat shelling of the Ethyl-Dow plant on July 25, 1943), the Marine turned his on.[12]

Peggy Moore, *left*, and friends entertain Camp Davis officers at Wrightsville Beach, ca. 1942.

Peggy Moore Perdew

Threats of espionage continued. At Fort Fisher where Earl Page's family lived, his grandfather used binoculars to enjoy viewing porpoises. "An alert MP confiscated his binoculars and detained him while the army tried to figure out what sort of espionage he might be up to. Fortunately, it didn't take long to deduce that this 75-year old didn't pose a grave threat to national security."[13]

Officials arrested Stanley Dennis, Jr., "a 15-year-old 6-foot youth" from New York, in January 1945, thinking he was a German saboteur. Instead he was a patriotic youth attempting to enlist in the navy. He hitchhiked here and contacted Judge H. Winfield Smith stating he was Smith's "long lost relative," and asked to be adopted. Smith called the County Bureau of Identification. The boy's description fit one distributed by the FBI that a Nazi saboteur might be in Wilmington. Dennis' father took him home.[14]

Frances J. Wagner's family lived temporarily in a Carolina Beach waterfront cottage.[15] "All house windows facing the ocean were required to be covered with opaque black shades. No automobile headlights were permitted....One was lucky to have a passenger who could stick his head out the window or ride a fender for a better view to guide the driver." On the boardwalk, all oceanside businesses had to board up their windows or doors. "No street lights or such were allowed on the front side....Since it was said that persons on shore had heard Germans on the ocean talking, they in turn probably could locate the beach from the noise on the boardwalk!"

"Air Raid Quiz Test"[16]

The *Star-News* frequently ran defense-related items including an "alert quiz" from the Office of Civilian Defense. By early 1944 the items had all but disappeared. A 1943 question asked, "If you are driving your car when an air raid siren sounds, do you (a) continue driving with lights on, (b) turn lights out and stay in car, (c) pull car to curb, turn off ignition, seek shelter, (d) take a side road." If you answered, "am I driving at night or in the daytime?" you fail. Answer: C.

The Italian *Villaperosa*

Under presidential authority, the Coast Guard in early 1942 seized the enemy Italian merchantman *Villaperosa* moored in the Cape Fear River near Wilmington. The 6,255-ton freighter was in the United States when war was declared. For sabotaging the ship's engines, Captain Adriana Marlano Bersia received three years in the Atlanta penitentiary, and 18 crewmen got 18 months. In the North Atlantic in April 1944, a torpedo sank the ship, renamed *Colin* under a Panamanian flag.

Chapter 7
Going Overseas Single

Billy Broadfoot "wanted to go overseas single because if I didn't, I knew I would get shot down. Married men didn't make it. I was dating Mary [Bason] in New York, and about to get cornered. I felt sorry for them. They had families and someone to love. They pulled their punches." The ratio between married and single pilot casualties "was ridiculous."[1]

An August 1944 letter home underscored Billy Broadfoot's sentiments regarding Marian Dixon, a "Pat," and other eligible girlfriends. "The best way to stay healthy in this racket is to keep your mind unfettered. Little boys that run around worrying, or even pondering, don't run far." (By that time he had received the Distinguished Flying Cross, Silver Star, and Air Medal.)[2]

Billy and Mary dated in 1943 when he was stationed on Long Island and she worked for Dell Publishing Company. In March 1945 he returned from 125 combat missions as a P-38 pilot in India and Burma. While huddling from the rain in Chapel Hill, North Carolina, they became engaged. On April 1 they wed at her home in "a wedding uniting two families prominent in North Carolina."[3]

The "problem was keeping the women off" when wearing the uniform, Billy recalled, smiling, one being that Wilmington girl named "Pat" for whom he carried a flame. "I wonder if you all would do me a favor and send Pat some flowers," he wrote his parents in 1943 from India. "They should be sent (telegraphed) so that they arrive on February 5th."[4] The relationship fluctuated. "You asked about Pat? She writes...sometimes only spasmodically. Considering her ineptness as a correspondent, she writes very often indeed...."[5]

In January 1944, "In Pat's last letter she seemed really pleased about her 'Indian' orchid. Thank you, Mother, for thinking of it....I guess it takes women to know what pleases women."[6] Four months later, failure. "I haven't heard from Pat for quite some time. I suppose she's found herself a fat 4-F."[7] With Mary waiting, why care?

Sixteen months later, his honeymoon letter home from Sea Island, Georgia, summed it up: "Whew! Whew!—Billy & Mary."[8] Mary had caught him. A week later: "As I told Mother over the phone, never has there been a more obvious bride than Mary....I tried nonchalantly to sign 'Major & Mrs.' on the registers. Mary would stand by, moon-eyed, and admire her rings....The boy I sent up for her bags said 'Mrs. Broadfoot'...and Mary, by her own admission, jumped and said 'who me?'....[We] were sitting in a chair the night of the President's death. She gave me one of those wide-eyed looks and said, 'Oh, Billy, everything's so different now. Roosevelt dead and—and—me married.' So it goes."[9]

* * *

A "GI" for Christmas[10]—Fighting in Germany in 1944, Private Clyde B. Case, Jr., wanted to give "a very particular present to his sweetheart for Christmas." Enclosing a $20 money order, he asked the *Morning Star* to advertise in the classifieds for a male cocker spaniel as a gift for "Winkie" Rivenbark. (The army censor removed part of his letter stating how long he had been overseas.) The newspaper found a black cocker spaniel and delivered it on Christmas Eve. "Miss Rivenbark's astonishment was unbounded. 'Gee whiz....This makes me the happiest girl in Wilmington this Christmas.'" She named him "GI."

An orange Model T[11]—What attracted Dotty Harriss to Ransey Weathersbee, Jr., in high school was his orange Model T Ford and deftness with cars: He "could take apart a car and put it together for our date that night." They married at St. James Episcopal Church while he was in dental school in Atlanta, Georgia. It was so "hot, the men were in tails, formal wedding, no air conditioning, tiny reception in our yard at 901 Market." They left Wilmington for Atlanta in a 1937 Chevy to Lake Waccamaw for their honeymoon. Her mother saved enough gas coupons, and Betty Henderson helped drive them. Dotty worked for the War Production Board and Coca-Cola headquarters. Ransey graduated in June 1945.

"Remember Me"?[12]—"Remember me [sic] sure hope you do well how are you doing now just fine I hope well tell [every] one up there I said sweet hello for me," Private T. L. Roach hurriedly wrote from Fort Bragg to Thelma Merritt, Post Ordnance Machine Shop, Camp Davis. "Remember you asked me if I was ever busted you wanted one of my stripes well I [sic] sending them to you [enclosed]....I would write more but I have a broken finger...and it hurts to write...."

(Was this the start of something big, or the end? What would you have done if you were Thelma? Wonder how many scribbled "remember me" letters just died with the recipient? Read on.)

"Forgotten?"[13]—"Dearest Cornelia, I thought that you had forgotten about me," lonely soldier Charles James wrote to Williston Industrial school girl Cornelia Haggins.

> But later I found out that my thoughts had been in vain. It was indeed a pleasure, a pleasure to hear from you....Everything is all right in New Guinea but it's not like home. No young girls as fine as you are....You said that there is no cupid that would appeal to you right now. Am I right?....Three fourths of the young men are in the armed forces. I hope you won't change your mind until after the war. Yes I really want one of your pictures. [Cornelia says she never sent it.]

* * *

Some Wartime Weddings

While most military marriages involved a male service member and civilian, occasionally the bride was on active duty. In the Wrightsville Beach town hall's first wedding, Women's Army Corps Staff Sergeant Eula B. Page married Lieutenant William P. Byrne of Camp Davis in April 1945. "Three times secretary to a general" and the first WAC assigned to Davis, she had returned from 14 months in England, Italy, and Tunisia.[14]

Neighbor Blanche Stanley, daughter of Dr. and Mrs. J. W. Stanley, a James Walker Memorial Hospital nursing graduate, and Marine Russell Sneeden, son of Wilmingtonians Mr. and Mrs. Steve Sneeden, in October 1943.[15] ● Navy Lieutenant (Junior Grade) Wayne Alexander Fonvielle, Jr., of Wilmington, and Margaret McLean Faw, of North Wilkesboro, North Carolina, in March 1944 in New York City, reception in the Waldorf-Astoria Hotel. She graduated from Greensboro College and the University of North Carolina law school, he from UNC.[16] ● Wilmingtonians Army Sergeant Fuller Sistrunk and Dorothy Coleman in St. Mary Catholic Church, in March 1944, after an eight-year courtship.[17] ● In January 1943 newly commissioned air force Second Lieutenant James Franklin Hackler and Josephine Love Bridger, of Bladenboro, North Carolina, at West Point, New York. ● Nurse Ensign Charlotte Armond Meier, daughter of the F. L. Meiers, in Maryland to Roger Morris of New York, in June 1944.

And overseas: In Belfast, Ireland, in April 1944, Wilmingtonian naval officer John David Colwell and Luvenia Wickens, of Belfast. ● Frank Elliott White of Wilmington, and Mavis Elizabeth Lattimore, in Australia in May 1944. ● Air force Private First Class John T. Capps and Leslie May Clark, Braintree England, there in 1944. ● Wilmingtonian Cynthia Anderson, in London in June 1944, to army Captain William J. Maroney, a former local businessman.

* * *

Classmates and Sweethearts[18]

Aline Hufham and Billy Spencer married on October 16, 1943, in Carlsbad, New Mexico, where he was in air force flight training. New Hanover High School '39 classmates and sweethearts, they never enjoyed a honeymoon. His parents, Stephen and Elizabeth Spencer, and sister Silva, and her parents drove Aline to the wedding. They obtained gasoline because the driver, his army brother Marion Spencer, received an extra ration.

The newlyweds went home together for three days at Christmas 1943 in a station wagon loaded with seven people, experiencing breakdowns and blown tires. (Not uncommon, servicemen with leave often spent much more time traveling than at their destination.)

As they headed westward, his father "was standing there crying, maybe thinking he was seeing him for the last time." Another tire blew approaching Kingman, Arizona, his new duty station. "We were really worried. We stood in the middle of the room and prayed. I've believed in miracles ever since." Billy made it. She rented a Kingman hotel room with other wives and worked those two months in the telegraph office. She followed him to Utah, Wyoming, Nebraska, and Kansas. He departed in June 1944 ultimately for Europe, and she returned home by train.

Following two years at the University of North Carolina, Billy became a B-17 *Flying Fortress* and B-24 *Liberator* bombardier. In September 1944, on his 13th B-24 mission over occupied Europe, his plane was shot down over Koblenz, Germany. The left-waist gun malfunctioned and a fighter hit them there. Two crewmen ejected. "Surviving crew members said he remained at his post until it was too late."[19]

Aline received a telegram on September 11 stating Billy was missing in action. "It was real upsetting, but for a long time I felt he was in a prison camp or with the underground and they would get him out. When the war ended, surely we'll hear something. I had gone to the movie with an aunt and cousin at the Bailey and heard the war in Europe was over. But we still didn't learn anything about him then. After a while you just assumed."

Five years later while teaching school in Raleigh, North Carolina, she learned the government declared him killed in action. Authorities found dogtags belonging to him and other crewmen. His remains and two crewmen are buried together in the St. Louis, Missouri, National Cemetery.

Aline's parents were Gurney J., who worked for Larkins Credit Clothiers, and Flossie Hufham. Sister Glenn was eight years younger, and brother Jack four years younger than Billy. "He was the perfect guy for Aline," Jack said. "I left for navy boot camp the same day Billy left for Europe," eventually serving on a destroyer escort in combat. When Billy was announced as MIA, the Hufhams wrote Jack about the anxiety of living in anticipation of the doorbell ringing.

Before being shot down, Billy sent his sister the money to buy Aline red roses and the remaining Prelude silver set she wanted—and a letter for delivery on their first anniversary. Silva took them to Aline that day, wondering if it would upset her. "But I was very glad she did."

Aline, now married to classmate Herman Hartis, lives in Wilmington. The 1939 *Hanoverian* said about Aline: "Her quiet nature seems to be tuned to each season's harmony." She showed me the telegram of September 11, 1944.

*   *   *

Mary Daniel, Addie Lee, and Barbara[20]

In 1944 Mary Daniel Carr went to work at Camp Davis with her sister Ann Carr. Ann had dated friend Addie Lee Gaylord's brother Robert, now in the army. "She wasn't wearing an engagement ring; so until you were wearing one you were free to date." Robert came home on leave before going overseas. That night Ann had a date with Marine Lieutenant Jack Ormdall, and Robert surprised her. Mary then took Ormdall as her weekend date so Ann and Robert could be together.

On Monday morning their mother, Mrs. J. D. Carr, seeing a packed suitcase, sensed an elopement. Yes, Ann and Robert responded. The mother told Robert he had better ask Mr. Carr for her hand. Robert said, "Mrs. Carr, I would rather face the Germans than face Mr. Carr." The next day they were married at home. "We had 10 weddings in our living room," Mary Daniel remembered. Robert left later that morning for Fort Campbell, Kentucky, and in six weeks he shipped out.

Addie Lee Gaylord became engaged to three men, and with each Mrs. Carr hosted an engagement party. One man, Camp Davis soldier Jack Babicky, fought in Italy and came home in 1945. She had corresponded with his family. "I couldn't leave Wilmington to go to California with him. I'm a very mother-conscious person. He wanted to see his mother. I told him to go home to his mother." She never married, partly because Mrs. Gaylord didn't approve.

In 1944 Mary Daniel took a government job in San Francisco, California. Ann, bored ("She couldn't date"), joined her. A Wilmington friend from the Plantation Club ("That's where all the servicemen went") went along. "There was no problem getting a job. United Nations was starting up, lots of parties." Mary and Ann became hat check girls. "They were particularly fond of us because we were Southerners." Governor Earl Warren attended the same parties. Mary remembered seeing President Harry Truman and parades for General Jonathan Wainwright and Admiral William Halsey. "I was an old timer compared to the rest of them," Addie recalled.

Their mutual friend Barbara Allen had been engaged to Wilmington soldier Rodger Russell, killed in action in 1944. Barbara "was so upset about it, was reading Rodger's letters to everyone," said Mary. In mid-1945 Barbara visited them "to get over Rodger." Ann prepared to return to Wilmington, but Mary "was having a good time." Barbara loved to dance and play cards. When she arrived in San Francisco by train, a sailor carried her luggage to Mary's apartment. Mary "thought this was going to work out very well," but the sailor soon left.

From left, Barbara Allen; her brother Lt. (j.g.) Gleason Allen; a friend; Mary Daniel Carr, in San Francisco, California, 1945.

Mary Daniel Carr Fox

"I wasn't sure how she would get by in San Francisco," Mary remembered. "I was a virgin. We were the most sheltered people. The boys didn't expect anything."* Mary worked for the War Department and part time as a hat check girl. Barbara also checked hats. "We saw Henry Rehder and other Wilmington people," Pete Page and Barbara's brother, Lieutenant (Junior Grade) Gleason Allen.

Men who knew they were there phoned. Gladys Sneeden McIver visited husband Lamar McIver before he shipped out. "It was like old home week. There were so many things to see, it was like a fairyland." Their jobs expired once the war ended.

* * *

* Mary Daniel was one of my wartime Sunday school teachers at Church of the Covenant.

Barbara and Rodger

Wilmington native Rodger P. Russell, Jr.,[21] served as a sergeant in Company A, 17th Engineer Battalion (Armored), Second Armored Division.*

Rodger and Wilmingtonian Barbara "Babs" Allen, "madly in love," became engaged in August 1942. "Once again the holiday season finds us far apart sweetheart," he wrote. "All though I can't be with you at this happy time of the year, my love and thoughts are with you ever...."[22] A few weeks later, "Happy New Year Babs—May this be our year and bring us together again....The little girl in the picture reminded me of you. I don't guess it's that blond hair and blue eyes. How I love them."[23]

In late 1943 he wrote his parents about life in Sicily. "I am getting lazy now. I don't have to wash my own clothes anymore. The bivouac is full of people taking in washing.... Our squad has a special old lady we give our work to....She sends us spaghetti on Sundays. I have a tailor too. I couldn't get any pants to fit me so I got the smallest size they had and let my tailor fix me up.

Sgt. Rodger P. Russell, Jr., 17th Engineer Battalion (Armored), 2nd Armored Division, engaged to Barbara Allen, was KIA.
Isabel Russell Gore

He speaks English. He used to run a tailor shop in the States....They think that everybody in America is rich and have lots of money....What I can't understand is why they come back here...."[24]

His August 1944 letter "from a foxhole 'somewhere in France'" revealed, "'Kids are the same the world over—they all want candy and chewing gum.'" By then a veteran of three fierce campaigns, he had been overseas two years. "'These old Jerries are plenty tough but we are just a little tougher. I have been able to attend several church services since we have been here, and they surely help, especially at times like these.'" Rodger, then in the hospital with malaria, was doing well.[25]

Rodger's sister, Isabell Russell, married Marsden Gore in June 1943. She remembered her brother vividly: only son, a happy childhood, slender, about 5'-11", and very protective. On December 7, 1941, he was working at

---

* The division landed in Morocco in November 1942 and fought in Tunisia and Sicily in 1943. Landing in Normandy, France, on June 9, 1944, the division entered Germany on September 18. Rodger joined before its deployment to North Africa.

the Atlantic Coast Line Railroad. "When he was drafted he gave Barbara the diamond, didn't want to marry her for her to be obligated. He would marry her when he came home." Barbara visited him during training.

A December 1944 Wilmington newspaper revealed the tragic news. "Rodger Russell, Wilmington Soldier, Killed at War Front—Sergeant Rodger P. Russell Jr, son of Mr. and Mrs. Rodger P. Russell, 1404 Grace St., was killed in action in Germany [sic], November 24, according to word received by his family here from the War Department. Sgt. Russell is survived by his parents, and two sisters, Mrs. Wesley Blake and Mrs. Marsden W. Gore, Jr., of Wilmington....Sgt. Russell was engaged to marry Miss Barbara Allen, of 1813 Princess Street."[26] He stepped on a landmine and died from wounds in a hospital in Holland.

The final citation for his service read: "He stands in the unbroken line of patriots who have dared to die that freedom might live, and grow, and increase its blessings. Freedom lives, and through it, he lives—in a way that humbles the undertaking of most men.—Harry S Truman, President of the United States."

Isabell recalled her mother "was very bitter about the war. It changed her life. She idolized him. It just about destroyed her; it was so the rest of her life. It was just grief for the whole family, hard to understand. Father was a very private person. He had to be strong for Mother. They had to put her to bed and call the doctor." To the day she died in 1978, at age 86, she never stopped grieving. Mrs. Russell and Barbara were very close. "Rodger

Engaged sweethearts Rodger P. Russell, Jr., and Barbara Allen, New Hanover High School graduates, at Wrightsville Beach before he left for army combat in North Africa, 1942. He was KIA in Holland in 1944.

Newspaper clipping provided by Gleason Allen

sent his money home to Mother to bank for the wedding. Once he was killed, she withdrew it and gave it to Barb."[27]

Barbara knew Paul Darden, of Wilson, North Carolina, when he was stationed at Camp Davis. They corresponded after Rodger's death. She decided to return to see him. Mary Daniel Carr said, "OK, I'll go home and be an old maid. Wilmington was back to being its sleepy self." So in June 1946 they returned from California together. In less than two weeks, Mary met ex-GI Ed Fox whom she eventually married, and Barbara later married Paul.

In November 1948, four years after he fell, Rodger was re-interred at Wilmington's Oakdale Cemetery by Yopp Funeral Home. His parents and sisters attended, but whether Barbara did is unknown. Barbara Darden died in 1981 and is buried in Wilson. Her daughter Jane Spicer lives here.

* * *

"Story of a Wartime Marriage"[28]

Jane Ellen Baldwin Yates, a Wilmington girl, fondly recalled her love story.

On the desk before me is a small picture, just a snapshot, in an inexpensive frame. The faded date written on the bottom is 6-16-42, and the subject is a couple standing next to a Ford convertible. The setting is Wrightsville Beach, N.C., and the people are a first lieutenant, U.S. Army, and a short slender girl with long dark hair. He is in his summer khaki uniform, sharply creased, and she has on a pink dress with a white belt and white embroidered daisies on the pockets. She is wearing brown and white spectator pumps.

I know all the details because I was that young woman, Jane Ellen Baldwin, on that beach date with Lieutenant Jack Yates of Dallas, Texas, stationed at that time at Camp Davis. We had first met in May 1942. I was working for the Wilmington Savings & Trust Company. Like many local girls, I was going out with men from all over the country....New opportunities to meet men outside of our old acquaintances sprang up all the time.

...Ruth Gholson...asked if I would like to go to Wrightsville Beach...to meet some officers from Texas who were living in Dr. James Robertson's cottage on Raleigh Street....I was told that the fellows wanted to look over the women before they committed themselves to a whole weekend! Later, I learned the men were told the same story about the women wanting to look them over! Ruth explained to me that these four men were all Texas Aggies, a fact that meant absolutely nothing to me at that time....When she asked Jack Yates what sort of girl he would like, he said in an offhand way, "Oh, somebody like you." Well, I know just the one I'll call.

...I don't remember much about that date on May 8, 1942, except that this lieutenant seemed interested when I told him about my volunteer work at the Filter Center. My date...[was] interested in this civilian war effort. We continued to date off and on that summer, with the uncertainties of a wartime relationship. Jack was halfway engaged to a girl back home in Texas and I was dating at least four or five other fellows, even as late as January 1943, a couple of months before we were married.

Early in January, Jack, now a captain, went to Texas on leave, and I got a letter proposing marriage. It came to me at the bank....It seemed so right somehow. We broke the news to my parents and planned a wedding for March 13, 1943, in Trinity Methodist Church. It was not a big formal wedding—we didn't have the time to plan that. Our best man was a fellow Texan who had known Jack in college....He is George Staples, now of Fort Worth, whom we still see a few times a year, but his wife is no longer living. Jack asked two other Aggies to be groomsmen, and I had just the one maid of honor, Harriet Marshburn.

1st Lt. Jack Yates and future wife Jane Ellen Baldwin at Wrightsville Beach, 1942.

Mary Daniel Carr Fox

We had a short honeymoon in New York, and began married life in a room with kitchen privileges, which was the best we could do....Jack had been sure he was headed for overseas, and had requested it. He had been teaching automatic weapons in the OCS, and he really wanted to get into a combat outfit....The day came when he was assigned to an AAA battalion, and...left on a troop train for New York the same day I went to James Walker Memorial Hospital to have our first child, daughter Janet. Jack did learn of her birth before he sailed for Europe.

After he returned to the United States, and was mustered out of the service, we spent time in South Texas where Jack was employed by an oil company.

Jane stays in touch with Wilmington.

* * *

Never Let Him Go

James Arthur "Jimmy" Coughenour, handsome, likeable, and strong, a star football player and ROTC member, was one of the most popular boys in New Hanover's class of 1943. To classmate Gene Edwards, "He was tough, one heck of a running back on the football team. You could look at him and tell he was an Indian."[29] According to sister Frances Coughenour Dinsmore,

Jimmy was 5'10", 154, and had curly, wavy hair. He may have "looked like an Indian" to some, but was in no way. "Perhaps it was because he ran so fast with the ball."

Jimmy, 20, the son of Mr. and Mrs. Herbert Coughenour, entered the army right after graduation with many teammates. By March 1944, the private first class was serving in New Guinea with the 1896th Engineer Aviation Battalion. He saw duty in the Netherlands East Indies from August until he died in January 1945 in the invasion of Luzon, Philippines.

No one remembered Jimmy like his high school sweetheart, Eleanor "Elkie" Burgwin.[30] "It's still hard for me, an impressionable young girl during the war. You don't forget such things. He was the love of my life. We dated from my sophomore year on. He was one year ahead of me."

His parents took her to see him. "We wrote to each other once or twice every day." (She retained all his letters for several decades after the war, even-

New Hanover High School sweethearts ROTC Sgt. Jimmy Coughenour and Eleanor "Elkie" Burgwin, 1943.
Eleanor Burgwin Fick

tually destroying them during a relocation. She needed to forget and proceed with her life—but not so.) After graduation she entered Women's College in Greensboro. "All my friends and my dormitory housemother knew how much we loved each other."

"Beginning in January 1945, I didn't get mail from him for a long time." In mid-February she mentioned to friends she had not heard from him lately. "Looking back I knew that they were solemn and quiet." Her father, attorney Kenneth Burgwin, called the housemother and told her Jimmy had been killed in action. The housemother assembled the dormitory girls and told them. Still, she was unaware.

"One night after supper while my roommate and I were in our room during study hall, there was a knock at the door. There stood my sister. 'What are you doing here?' I said. She said, 'Come with me.'" The two proceeded out of the dorm to their father who was waiting in the car. "He put his arm around me and said, 'Jimmy is dead.' The next thing I knew I was being picked up off the sidewalk."

They got her to a hotel room and a doctor came. The next day she went to the Coughenours. "I just held his picture close to my heart. It still touches." Some of her friends came home from school to be with her. She stayed three weeks before returning to "WC."

Marie Burgwin remembered that after her sister returned to college she "ran off some months later...and married Bob Doss, which broke my father's heart. She was only 18. My father took it very hard. Nine months later she had a baby. This was a terrible time for our family."[31]

Letters from Jimmy's army friends informed her he was on a troop ship headed for action when a Japanese plane crashed into the stern. He died three days later and was buried in the Philippines. "I believe that was to comfort me," alluding his death may have been worse under different circumstances.

When Jimmy's older sister and only sibling, Frances, heard, she and soldier husband Chuck Dinsmore, about to ship out to the Philippines, lived in Texas. "It just tore me up. I tried to hold back my feelings and so did Mother because of Daddy. He just went all to pieces. She held back and was respectful of him. [Jimmy] was his eyeball and Daddy expected him to go to Wake Forest and play football. I just knew they were grieving. You could catch Daddy in the bedroom crying alone. That would start her crying also." Chuck later visited Jimmy's grave.[32]

Sweethearts for several years, Jimmy and Elkie "used to court in the Oakdale Cemetery—they had benches. A lot of couples did. We could just kiss all we wanted to." In her father's sun porch the two also sat and hugged and kissed. From the living room couch her mother could not see them. "Every once in a while she would say something to us and we'd holler back at her."

Elkie kept much more of Jimmy than just photographs, including his army dogtag, the gold ring she gave him before he left home engraved with "JAC" (she

The Coughenour family, *from left*, soldier Jimmy, Eugenia, Herbert, Frances, 1944.
Frances Coughenour Dinsmore

is sure he was wearing it when he died), and the gold football charm he received for playing football at NHHS, with the raised letters "19W42." As if yesterday, she can recite his service record from memory.

What inspires her to keep this relationship alive? "He does. The love I poured on him. He was so trustworthy with my love. He was just my heart and my soul. It doesn't mean I can't love someone else, but it was a different kind. What I have in the palm of my hand, I cannot let it go." Their love "was pure and unadulterated. It was hard to let go. It took me a long time to forgive God, but I've come to terms with Him since."

How have her three husbands reacted? They understood how she felt about Jimmy, and accepted it either openly or passively.

The 1942 *Hanoverian* yearbook noted:

> He believes in playing 2 by 2
> He doesn't know we're living.
> He's the handsome hero of one girl
> and to her full time he's giving.[33]

On the inside back cover in the lower right corner, that "one girl" inscribed: "I think you're swell. I think I'm the luckiest gal in the whole world. Love, Elkie."

In never letting go, perhaps she still finds comfort in that luck of some 60 years ago.

Chapter 8

Surrounded (and Protected) by the Military

Citizens learned right away to live with the frequent antiaircraft firing exercises conducted at Sears Landing on Topsail Island and Fort Fisher. The army dispatched periodic warnings outlining restricted zones, dates, and times, with distances out to 25,000 yards. Newspapers informed the public. Ignorance was no excuse for being caught in the line of fire. Restricted zones included aircraft areas. Planes buzzed water craft to warn them first.[1] Warnings continued until December 1945 when the army combed the areas for live ammunition. Beachcombers still find casings around Fort Fisher.

Camp Davis

Herman Alberti came to Camp Davis in April 1942 after finishing Hampstead High School. He gave up farming and drove a dump truck, building the rifle range in 1942 during his high school junior-senior years. Soon he went to work at the camp post office, served in the army for seven months in 1943, and then transferred to the Camp Lejeune post office. Still residing there, he enriches memories of the boomtown days. The base's perimeters reached two miles both north and south of North Carolina Highway 50 at the stop light, four miles across north to south. During the war the public had access to Highway 50 and Topsail Island.[2]

About the buses that ran between Wilmington and Davis, Martha Vann remembered, "'the big GI bus was an important part of the home front scene.'" Many people who worked there depended on government transportation, "'and many a romance blossomed at bus-side late in the evening after a service club dance. The hostesses would bid goodnight to their heroes after plans had been made for future dates; then they would board the bus and gaily sing their way back into town.'"[3]

Janet Rabunsky served two years as secretary to the hospital administrator, transferring to a Bluethenthal Field job. She took a chartered bus

direct to the hospital and ate in the officers mess. "I put money in the bank
and bought bonds." Earning $1,200 per year, "I thought I was rich."[4]

Lieutenant Justin Raphael trained with the 576th Automatic Weapons
unit at the Fort Fisher advanced base in 1944. With buildings positioned
beneath oak trees that bent westward from prevailing winds, the camp was
dense and pitch black. Men going to latrines at night got lost, requiring first
sergeants to round them up in the morning. "Like living in a forest." Concrete floors from the structures are still there amid oaks that never will
straighten.[5]

Decline and Demise

Now review the chain of events acted out in public leading to Davis'
decline and closing, a dreaded subject deemed inevitable and economically
disastrous.

February 2, 1944. "There was no indication...that Camp Davis will be
among the domestic army camps to be closed during the next few months in
preparation for the overseas expansion program...[and] 'every indication' is
that the nearby installation will remain open."[6]

February 8. The officer candidate school, after commissioning approximately 22,000 in the past two years, will close. "The army has its quota of
officers for the antiaircraft artillery command and has a 'sufficient reserve
to tide it through the war.'"[7]

May 13. "'There is not the remotest possibility'" the AAA [antiaircraft
artillery] school will close.[8] Two weeks later the final (100th) officer candidate school class graduated.

July 28. The War Department announced it will close the AAA facilities
by October 1. The camp will remain on a "standby basis...as fighting strength
approaches the maximum needed."[9]

August 19. "The folks in Onslow County are getting excited about the
prospects of Henry Ford's buying Camp Davis...when the camp is abandoned...."[10]

August 25. Camp Davis likely will remain open after AAA units are
transferred.* "'The exodus of troops...evokes mingled emotions in the command. On the brighter side is the feeling that a great camp has performed a
great mission in feeding trained troops to battle lines to hasten the day of
victory.'"[11]

September 2. "As Camp Davis prepared to silence its heavy guns...[we]
look back upon three years of ceaseless activity which is certain to show

---

* "Many officers and men at Camp Davis had their families living in Wilmington. These families
are now preparing to move elsewhere....What is true of Wilmington is going to be true of several
other towns in this state....It is up to Wilmington...to give serious consideration right now to this
business of planning to meet conditions where the war comes to an end." [*The State: A Weekly
Survey of North Carolina*, August 12, 1944]

Women's Airforce Service Pilots director Jacqueline Cochran and Brigadier General Stearly review Camp Davis women of the target-towing squadron, 1943. Davis was the first duty assignment for WASPs.

Air Force photo, Missiles and More Museum, Topsail Beach

that this camp did more than its share to bring the war to a successful conclusion."[12]

September 7. The final 24-page issue of the base newspaper, the Camp Davis *AA Barrage*, published its last of 74 issues.[13]

December 28. Camp Davis will be sold or salvaged as surplus property "as soon as the evacuation of troops from it has been completed." Evacuation will be completed by December 31.[14]

December 29. The War Department ordered the base to remain open because the air force placed a formal request for its use. Dismantling and an equipment auction sale began.[15] "Terms: 25% at purchase, balance before removal of items. No personal checks."[16]

January 10, 1945. Camp Davis will be given to the air force for a reconditioning and reclassification center for convalescent airmen and personnel rotating to the States.[17]

Would it be back to the nineteenth century for Holly Ridge? In a May 1945 article the revived *AA Barrage* startlingly observed.

> When...[personnel] return to Camp Davis after an absence of a year or more, they can hardly believe their eyes. They are not so much surprised at the beautification of Camp Davis itself, as at the almost miraculous change in the much-maligned community they know as "Boomtown"....Where, they ask, are the mile-long lines at the bus station, the dry cleaning plants, and the lone department store catering almost exclusively to the hundreds of "eager" officer candidates....The roaring spirit of the town that brought prospects for the lure of the yellow dust—army gold—has died.
>
> True, the old carnivals show up each payday, with their essential amusements, including the color-blind rat who always pops into the wrong hole, and the washboard dice game. Why, there is even a new restaurant...as an inducement to GIs craving a taste of home cooking. (It almost outdraws the beer joints.) A sign of the time may be found in a department store which closed out its stock of officers clothing (pinks) in favor of women's and children's clothing.
>
> Yes, one year has made many changes....There's one whole square of cement sidewalk instead of the hip-deep chuckhole....And a new sign, "Town Office," at an alley way indicates civic government is running in high gear. Yes, many changes have come to Holly Ridge, N.C. It may even be inhabited after the war.[18]

July 5. After the post's brief use by the air force, "current rumors again were advanced that Camp Davis would be closed...."[19]

July 7. Wilmington Mayor Ronald Lane headed a delegation to Washington requesting the base remain open. They reported no progress, only that "Camp Davis would be considered purely from a military point of view."[20]

July 17. The War Department announced the base will be discontinued as a convalescent and redistribution center. All unfinished construction work was ordered halted. Its future will be decided after it is offered to other agencies.[21]

July 21. An air force official explained the reason for closing Camp Davis: "a saving to the American taxpayer."[22]

August 8. The Camp Davis Blue Brigade baseball team plays the Wilmington Pirates tonight at Legion Stadium in the final game for a Davis team.[23]

August 18. The Marine Corps will take over Camp Davis on the 19th for use in its Camp Lejeune training program, including for a contingent of Dutch marines (arriving a week later).

January 13, 1946. The Marine Corps will terminate its activities at the $30-million facility as early as possible. The abandonment ended another chapter.[24]

February 17. "Deactivation of Camp Davis...brings to an end one rich source of revenue for Southeastern North Carolina tradespeople....Large sites in the Fort Fisher and Sears Landing areas echoed to the staccato barking and deep grunts of the AA guns,"[25] long gone.

March 16. The navy will assume control of Davis by June 1 "on a highly scientific laboratory and testing ground for newly developed ordnance, including the latest 'buzz-bomb' [Operation Bumble Bee]."[26]

May 24. The newspaper added an interesting footnote to this story. "Wilmington's gratification is that the camp is not to be abandoned...."[27]

July 28, 1948. After 18 months, the navy deactivated the Naval Ordnance Test Facility, Holly Ridge, N.C. "Testing of guided missile components will be carried out at other naval facilities."

* * *

Bluethenthal Field (Army Air Base)

No one has ever known more Wilmington aviation history than the late James C. "Skinny" Pennington and his wife Anna Feenstra Pennington.[28] "[Originally] the airport was just a little grass plot of two runways 750 feet long," Skinny recited. "Depending on what kind of airplanes you were flying it got real short." In 1939 the county began constructing concrete runways.

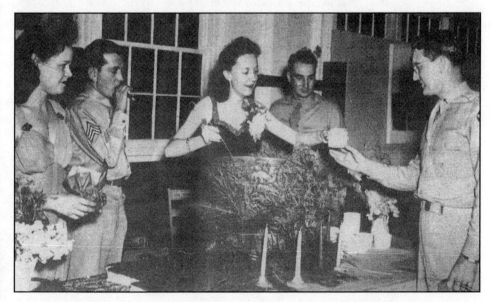

Local hostesses serve at Bluethenthal Field club for enlisted personnel.

Hannah Block

When the army moved in, operations of the civilian airport moved to a grass airstrip on the Carolina Beach Road across from Seabreeze Road, where flying continued for a while. The army had forced the Pennington Flying Service to cease operations until relocating in 1942, and commandeered their Bluethenthal hangar. Anna soloed in 1939 in a J3 *Cub,* with Skinny as her instructor. "I was the third local girl to fly. I never thought about being a pioneer." She worked in administrative and safety positions at the new site. Local civilian flying was restricted to that area, but a pilot could fly elsewhere by filing a flight plan with the downtown Information and Filter Center.

The Penningtons were instrumental in starting the Wilmington Civil Air Patrol in 1941. Unsure of its role, eventually the group assisted in anti-submarine warfare patrols. CAP members drifted off into the army. Homer Barnes and Burt and John Rehder flew ASW for the CAP and Burt and Albert Wooten became civilian instructors for the army. Skinny contracted with Camp Davis for daytime AAA target tracking practice, searchlight tracking, and took aerial photographs of Davis and the shipyard. He shot the photos of the first ship launching, the SS *Zebulon B. Vance,* on December 6, 1941. "I made more money during that time than any other period in my life. They paid me $350 [per trip] for each launching...."

Anna arrived in Wilmington with her parents in 1923 from their native Holland. The Wrightsboro farm of her father, Sipke Feenstra, off the old Wrightsboro-Winter Park road became part of the army's new runway. In late 1942 the family and their buildings were relocated from the burgeoning airport to next door where she lives now. Flowers they grew bloomed prolifically all over the airport.

Quartermaster Office clerk Muriel Williamson recalled when a plane crashed at the field. One of her friends from the chemical warfare office had to go through the pilot's personal effects and found pieces of gum and a half-empty cigarette package. (It had to be First Lieutenant William A. Lowrance from California.) "When a plane crashed on post we would jump in a vehicle and go running after the crash. We knew when a unit was going off to war. They marched by our office. Probably were going to Europe. We knew we'd never see them again. It was sort of sad."[29]

One unusual airfield death became public. A soldier died while donating blood. Private Barney J. Lewis of Brunswick County volunteered at James Walker Memorial Hospital. "It was during the process of securing the blood that the fatal accident occurred." Dr. D. C. Workman, Jr., an intern, and student nurse Lina Walton performed the donation, "but 'through an error,' a tube was then connected to a machine which pumped air into Lewis' vein instead of a suction machine which would have drained the blood." A coroner's jury failed to call Workman or the nurse and ruled it an accident, citing no fault.[30]

Red Cross worker Peggy Moore was on duty that day and accompanied the popular Lewis. "If I had been more mature I would have realized something was wrong. I felt a lot of responsibility. What a way for him to give his life for his country."[31]

By November 21, 1945, the airport assumed a standby basis manned by only 130 army personnel. One year later, the War Assets Administration approved its transfer and 1,308 acres to New Hanover County for the Wilmington-New Hanover airport authority. With this transaction came structures and land for the National Guard.[32] The authority issued its first "private flying school" lease in April 1946, restoring the Penningtons.[33]

* * *

State Praises Local POW Camp[34]

If you missed seeing Wilmington German prisoner of war camps, this May 1944 report on the Carolina Beach Road facility is revealing.

> Commandant Lieutenant R. H. Hazel has 55 men, mostly noncommissioned officers, to handle 277 POWs. The prisoners are sent out as farmers need them, each group going with a leader (usually a German NCO) and interpreter. The farmer employs the detail for a day and gives orders through the leader. On the A. G. Seitter truck farm the men cut the lettuce according to instructions and brought it in hampers to the end of the rows where it was re-packed. An armed corporal stood by, "alert and poised but with little to say. It was his job to see that no prisoners escaped."
>
> Commercial dairyman Otto Leeuwenburg is pleased. The prisoners milk, feed, and wash his 60 cows and keep the barn in tip-top shape. Leeuwenburg uses about eight men on his farm and eight in the barns on a six-day week basis. Some had worked on German dairy farms.*
>
> "This camp is nicely kept with clean, comfortable quarters, a spotless kitchen and dining hall, a small infirmary, and a well-stocked exchange. Here the men spend their earnings, using the small books of canteen checks with which they are paid for their labor." Leeuwenburg paid $576 for labor during that month, and Seitter $1,306.50. Some POWs worked for a higher rate in fertilizer plants. Others cut pulp logs. "If the men will not work when work is available, they get nothing....They get an allowance of at least $3 a month for cigarettes, drinks, and other minor expenses."
>
> The camp is a "model place." Lieutenant Hazel "does not coddle the men neither is he a martinet. He has rules and discipline that must be observed and apparently the men have come to know this....They should

---

* Trucks carrying POWs created a spectacle moving about town. Thelma Barclift waved as the open trucks passed her 5th Street house. Frank Gordon, who lived on North 3rd, recalled not only POWs but almost everything else, it seemed, leaving or entering town came past his house headed north or south on Highways 17, 117, or 421 heading over the city's one river bridge.

be happy at having this opportunity to work for the farmers of North Carolina."

After four months, a U.S. official saw a weakening of fervor for Nazi doctrines. Germans normally take a "very arrogant attitude" when arriving in America. "The army is permitted to force all prisoners below the grade of sergeant to work....The men see no newspapers and talk no politics with guards or visitors, but are permitted to listen to the radio."[35]

Beware, said Hazel, "All are not POWs who look so. Evidently a great many raincoats with 'PW' marked on the backs are being worn around Wilmington....He is being besieged by calls reporting 'escaped Germans.'" Many surplus POW raincoats were sold recently as surplus in a Camp Davis salvage sale. "Even the MPs picked up a Negro who was wearing one of the raincoats." Hazel asked that coat markings be obliterated.[36]

*   *   *

Postscript

With the final announcement that Camp Davis would close, many residents immediately longed for "a return to things-as-they-were."[37] Editorial reaction, previously avoiding the inevitable, countered dolefully as if summarizing the city's fate. In one of the *Star-News'* finest wartime opinions, whether its words consoled or convinced readers, the reality was the natural course of events, and the war's favorable turn, forecast the rapid waning of boomtown days. And the people had better be ready.

> July 30, 1944. "Wilmingtonians are wondering if the city's wartime peak has not been achieved and passed. They are wondering if the coming months will not be marked by a decrease in trade and industry....Some store men have reported that their sales are off as much as 30 percent of late. Restaurants appear to be much less crowded today....Policemen are saying that there are fewer cars on the streets in the early morning. The City of Wilmington has announced that it is expecting a lower income....
>
> Perhaps these are slight indicators that the community is to forego its breathlessness in coming months. They do not, however, constitute cause for alarm or concern about the city's financial and economic health.
>
> How are the citizens accepting the idea of relieved pressure in the future? Some of the talk revels in the thought of a quiet, undisturbed Wilmington...they admit to a desire to return to things-as-they-were. Others worry about what the city will do if the good payrolls are subtracted, if the great war-heightened industrial stimulus is removed and the community is left limp, with too few jobs and too few opportunities....It is the constructive community thinkers who are right.
>
> Wilmington is profiting much by the war production impetus. The city has risen again....[Its] role in the war drama has brought much financial assistance from the government...: witness the vast new waterworks system, the new schools, the new airport, the new fire station, the

housing projects—all additions of permanence. Returning servicemen are going to descend on Wilmington in search of jobs....

Wilmington must not, because the city is tired, drop its ambition for action, new industry, and fuller development....But by and large it will be the imagination, the determination, and the unselfish ambitions of Wilmington citizens...which will order the community to go ahead.

Positive thinking surely, but community leaders balked once the shooting stopped.

Fishing for Targets[38]

Eight-year-old Fort Fisher resident Earl Page excitedly watched target practice. The army installed sandbag emplacements along the beach containing either 50-caliber or 20mm AA guns. "A two-engine plane...would fly parallel to the coast pulling a rather large target sleeve while the guns fired away...meanwhile the general public was fishing from the pier." One day the towline was hit and the 50-foot target sleeve dropped almost on the pier. Luckily, it landed in the water barely missing the fishermen. "Seems like it wasn't long after that the general public was denied access to the pier for a while."

Camp Davis[39]

Mission—Began as army's principal coast artillery (CA) training command, in early 1942 shifted to the army's only antiaircraft artillery (AAA) school and training base; from 1941 to February 1942 was army's barrage balloon training installation

Location—Holly Ridge, on U.S. Highway 17 at N.C. Highway 50, 30 miles north of Wilmington; primarily in Onslow County, some of southern portion in Pender County

Period of Operation—War Department awarded $17 million contract for construction, December 14, 1940; took five months and 10 days to construct; first troops arrived in April 1941; finally closed as naval test facility in July 1948

Size—Holly Ridge post: More than 3,000 buildings on approximately 50,000 acres

Population—Holly Ridge in 1940, 28; troops, 60–65,000 at peak in 1943; civilian, 5,000 employees (2,000 women); total estimates 65,000–110,000 in 1943; 37,000 troops in June 1944

Named for—Major General Richmond P. Davis, USA (World War I)

Physical Plant—18 post exchanges; 2,000-bed hospital; plants for water purification, electric power, central heating, and sewage treatment; 35 miles of paved streets; 90 acres of concrete and asphalt; 22 miles of sidewalks

Satellites

Sears Landing practice firing station, a narrow strip between the Inland Waterway and Topsail Beach, 4-1/2 miles east of Camp Davis, near present Surf City. The army constructed a road through the woods from Davis to the site, and installed a retractable 75-foot steel barge bridge to connect the mainland with Topsail across the waterway.

Fort Fisher Advanced Training Station—Located at the southern tip of New Hanover County where U.S. Highway 421 ends, 50 miles south of Camp Davis on the site of the Civil War fort, 20 miles south of Wilmington.

Camp Davis Air Base—Two target-towing aircraft squadrons and a base squadron stationed here, including contingent of Women's Airforce Service Pilots (WASPs)

Students Trained—22,000 graduates of officer candidate school; range of 57–80,000 enlisted and officer CA/AAA students

Weapons Systems Used in AAA Training and Tests—50-caliber machine guns; 40mm and 90mm guns; M15 quad-mounted guns; rocket-propelled targets; aircraft-towed targets; radar; searchlights

Units Stationed (Partial)—41st, 43rd, 47th, 49th, 50th AAA Brigades; predominantly Negro units were 54th CA Regiment and 99th and 100th CA (later AAA) Regiments

Three Weeks in the Summer of '42[40]

Mary Sutliff, 18, previously engaged, came to Wilmington to visit her sister Winifred Rahlves and husband First Lieutenant Gus (99th AAA Battalion, Camp Davis). A January 1941 Berkeley, California, high school graduate, she had no plans to remain here. Out of money, Mary took a job typing requisitions at the camp until mid-August 1942.

Davis officer Claude Daughtry, Georgia Tech '39 caught the bus with Mary from Davis to Wilmington daily. On June 6, 1942, they formally met en route to her Carolina Temple Cottage residence at Wrightsville Beach. The route went through the Pembroke Jones property on the Inland Waterway over to Market Street. Only Camp Davis people rode. She got up at 5:30 a.m., was on the bus by 6:15, and was due at work at 8:00, five and one-half days per week.

Quickly the bus rides mattered. "The first time I met Claude I knew I was going to marry this man. He was a southern gentleman and a gentle man. He was very attractive. We found our interests were similar." They became engaged three weeks later. Claude "was 24, had been around a while." For Mary, "it [the three weeks] was wonderful, really wonderful. I've never caught up on my sleep. I fell asleep at my desk at work." He sent her "illegal messages" during the work day, proposing to her around July 1st.

He slept on the sofa on weekends at "Belly Acres" where he lived on East Atlanta Street, but otherwise hung out at the Temple. "There was always a party going on." Claude proudly recalled of teetotaler Mary, "She was as pure as the driven snow." They swam at night until soldiers drove them off the beach. "We had a marvelous time. Claude was always trying to get me to go skinny dipping, but I wouldn't." They remembered phosphorous beach sand that left footprints, and "sand wrassling"—going down on the beach on a beach blanket. Mary fixed dinner, and they talked and listened to the radio.

Camp Davis Lieutenant Claude and Mary Daughtry, after their whirlwind three-week courtship in the summer of 1942.

Daughtrys

They spent every night together except when he was camp duty officer. They met for lunch amidst heat, dust, and mosquitoes, and "she never noticed it." "You could stand on muddy sand and have dry sand blow into your ears." We were "trying to fit a lifetime into a few short weeks," he said.

After sitting around all day to connect, she phoned her parents to tell them of the engagement. He heard her father shouting on the other end: "'Is he Catholic?' Father demanded that he write his biography and family history." She was a member of the Christian Church. His father was Catholic, his mother Methodist, and together the lovers became Episcopal. Mary's mother smoothed things over, and asked her to come home.

In mid-August 1942, she and her sister drove Winnie's car to California. "Can't remember how we got gas," but it took 11 days. There she assembled her trousseau. In a few days the mother and daughters drove back across country. Mary was now 19, her mother 52. Mary and Claude were married on September 13 in Decatur, Georgia. His parents attended. He received ten days of leave for the wedding and honeymoon.

Their first child, Dana, arrived on November 27, 1943. The nursery at James Walker Memorial Hospital was rampant with impetigo, so Mary delivered at Bulluck's Hospital on Front Street. Dana was housed in a bureau drawer because no bassinets were available. "Lots of army wives were having babies," she said. Dr. James Lounsbury, my Guilford Avenue backyard neighbor, who had removed Mary's appendix in January, delivered their daughter.

Claude and Mary will forever hold a special place in their hearts for Camp Davis and Wrightsville Beach. For years the Californians have owned a piece of it, and divide their time between Oakland and a beachfront condominium.

Chapter 9

"18, Gung-Ho, and Ready to Roll"

Boys in the New Hanover High School class of 1943 (of about 315 students) realized their fate long before graduation. Several such as Heyward Bellamy left school early for the military. Many members including football players and buddies volunteered for the draft and in July departed in the same bus to Fort Bragg for induction. John Burney, Jr., was "proud to have my 1-A card." His father, Judge John J. Burney, told him, "I'm glad you made an A in something."[1]

The son remembered, "these boys were 18, gung-ho, and ready to roll. I saw local boys cry who were turned down, begged doctors to pass them so they could enter the service." But a few ran up their blood pressure hoping for a 4-F classification by putting ink blotters in their shoes or soap under their armpits. Burney entered the army with classmates George Burrell Byers, C. F. Bell, James Godwin, Clarence Council, Johnnie Goins, Jack Christian, Eugene Spivey, and Jimmy Coughenour.[2]

Stories of some of the boys who went away to war are shared here. As a number encountered friends from home around the globe, we visualize how extended was their world. No greater contribution, no greater sacrifice to the American war effort by the citizens of the New Hanover County area exceeded that service performed by its sons and daughters in uniform.

The Class of 1939

Bill Schwartz[3] recalled, "My vintage were one of the first groups that re-militarized the United States." A 1943 North Carolina graduate, he joined a navy officer program. Assigned to two YP patrol craft in Florida, for nine months he escorted tankers. "If we had ever fired one of our depth charges, I think we were the ones who would have sunk." Command of the YP-398 "taught me how indispensable I was."

As damage control officer on the destroyer escort USS *Oberrenber* (DE-343), he saw action at New Guinea, Lingayen Gulf, and Surigao Strait—

where the antisubmarine warfare ship "made smoke, fired torpedoes," and "got the hell out of there; that's all we could do." On May 9, 1945, while on radar picket station off northeast Okinawa, a Japanese suicide plane struck the ship, breaking the keel. "My job was to assess damage and report to the captain—he was dumbfounded, didn't hear a word I said." After dousing the fire, survivors and wounded scuttled and then abandoned ship.

On Manus Island Schwartz ran into classmates Preston Oliver and Carl Welker. Later in Hawaii he encountered Chestnut Street next door neighbor Catherine Craig working for the navy. In 1946 his final assignment was releasing men from the navy at Charleston, South Carolina, including Julien K. Taylor and Charles Graham.

Jim Stokley[4] earned a radio repairman's certification and technician 4th grade stripes with the 191st Signal Repair Company. "I was concerned that I wouldn't get overseas" because of all of the time he had spent at North Carolina and North Carolina State in the army's specialized training. In early 1945, stationed in Kunming, China, he watched Nationalist Generalissimo Chiang Kai-Shek take over the provinces, fighting feudal lords right outside their compound in his internal war against the Communists. As the Communists won, Americans prepared to evacuate. "How disturbing our letters must have been to the people back home, because we didn't know what was going to happen to us."

In 1940 the army activated local Battery A of the 252nd Coast Artillery, including Carl Welker,[5] Bobby Myers, Bill Eason, and Peter Brock. When promoted to sergeant, Carl sent home some chevrons. "Mom was so proud I had made sergeant. She sent me my shirts [back] with the chevrons sewn upside down." He didn't have the heart to tell her. His mother visited Private Carl at Camp Stewart, Georgia, before the war, but he was performing disciplinary KP duty. The guard house referred her to headquarters. "That made her as mad as a barrel of hornets." There

Sgt. James B. "Jim" Stokley, *rear*, with friends in China, 1945.

James B. Stokley

she asked for the commanding general, who sent her in a staff car to see her son. He got three days off.

Commissioned at Camp Davis in 1943, Carl saw action in New Guinea with the 470th Antiaircraft Artillery Battalion defending airfields. At Lingayan Gulf, Philippines, he downed a Japanese plane by himself. That was "my contribution to winning the war." Later as part of the 1st Cavalry Division he fought with the 37th Infantry Division into Manila. "Such confusion, such firing, such devastation, the stench of the dead was unbearable around the walls of the city." Mortar fire put him out of action two days. He later served as a career officer.

Stanley Rehder and fellow North Carolina State ROTC members entered together. Following commissioning, in November 1944 he joined the 66th Infantry Division. He was aboard the SS *Leopoldville* en route to England when it sank, losing 800 men, and later served in France and Germany. Dan Retchin, a company clerk with the 385th Infantry, 76th Infantry Division, advanced to Czechoslovakia at war's end. He crossed the Rhine River on a bridge built by Fred Shain's combat engineer company. In Nuremberg Dan ran into Bernard Davis, a cousin of Dan's wife. Ben D'Lugin and Babe Briskin served in the 800th Tank Destroyer Battalion. Dan and Babe found each other in Luxembourg.

* * *

The Class of 1943

To Pat Warren, "They ran us through the induction process and it scared most of us to death. When I was examined, they said my blood pressure was so high that I couldn't pass. It was the excitement of the exam and being 'run through like cattle.'"[6] The navy threatened Warren, nearly flunking radio school, with landing craft coxswain duty. "Nobody ever worked harder to pass radio school." Late in the Pacific war he was a PBY *Catalina* patrol plane crewman.[7]

The army sent Burney, Byers, Bell, Godwin, Council, Goins, and a few other boys to Mississippi, Nebraska, and later Louisiana. Most of Burney's Wilmington group, including Byers, remained in ordnance, but Burney volunteered for the infantry ("I didn't know what I was getting into"[8]). Burney and Jesse Byrd bought officers uniforms, wore them downtown, and drew salutes from unsuspecting soldiers. At home before going overseas, his mother told him to get his picture taken. "Mama, I'll go get it, but I'm not going to get killed."[9]

As the Battle of the Bulge began, some in the gang went into the infantry, but Byers, Bell, and Council stayed together and received discharges on March 6, 1946. On a wet, muddy day in Germany, Byers met Godwin stringing communications wire. Then a jeep containing General George S. Patton drove up. Byers said, "Let's get out of here."[10]

John J. "Johnnie" Goins.[11] "Dear Katharine [Harriss]," wrote her boy-
friend Byers on November 15, 1943. "I guess you have heard the news by
now about Johnnie. He died Sunday night....

> Sounds hard to believe I know, because I can hardly believe it my-
> self. He got up Saturday morning and said he wasn't feeling good....He
> went over to the hospital and they looked him over but couldn't find any-
> thing wrong....They sent him back to the barracks and told him to go to
> bed and they gave him some medicine....C. F. [Bell] and I came in from
> school about 4:30 and he was in bed and I could tell by the way he looked
> he was pretty sick.
>
> About 6:30 I walked up to the PX and got a milkshake and some
> aspirins for Johnnie. He had said something about his head hurting. I
> kept noticing that Johnnie was getting restless....[About 8:30] I asked
> him how he felt and he said that his head felt like it was going to blow
> up....In a few minutes he began tossing around in his bed so I went to
> him and tried to hold him. I finally got him still and he said that he
> just couldn't stand it any longer so I went to a phone and called the
> ambulance.
>
> ...By this time he was practically crazy. I finally got his clothes on
> him and the ambulance came up. He put his arm around me and walked
> to the ambulance....They put him in the ambulance but they wouldn't let
> me go with him. I said, 'Johnnie I'll see you in the morning,' and he said,
> 'all right Burrell.' That was the last thing he said to me.
>
> I came on back and went to bed although I didn't sleep very well
> because I had an idea what was the matter with him. Sunday morning
> I ...[saw] the C. O....He kept stalling me off so I said, 'Sir has he got
> spinal meningitis?' and he said 'yes.' Right away they sent me to the
> hospital to take some sulfur drug....[They] said that Johnnie had been
> out of his head all day but that he still had a good chance to live. This
> made me feel much better because I was about to go crazy myself....They
> didn't want it spread around camp because it would scare so many
> people.
>
> Monday morning we had to go over to the hospital to take some more
> sulfur drugs....[We] asked about Johnnie. The doctor said, 'He died last
> night.' I thought somebody had hit me in the face with a baseball bat....I
> still can't believe he's dead....Last night they took us into town to see the
> body. They certainly had him fixed nice. He looked almost as though he
> were alive.
>
> I guess [girlfriend] Margaret is taking it pretty hard. They really
> loved each other. I know I'm going to miss him because he was almost
> like a brother to me....We have been taking that sulfur drug and there is
> no danger of getting it.

Later Byers wrote Harriss, "...Since Johnnie died I just can't get him
off my mind....I was talking with him one day and the next day he was

gone."[*] Byers and Bell were slated to escort the body home but regulations prohibited a non-Catholic (Byers) from escorting a Catholic (Goins).

Haskell Rhett[12] entered navy college V-5 flight training in 1944 but "flunked out on purpose and went to boot camp." As an aviation ordnance man at the Washington, D.C., bomb disposal school, "we took all our meals at the WAVE barracks nearby, spent all my savings my dad had sent me, never had so much fun in my life. There were too many distractions. Went to cocktail parties as a young sailor." His aircraft carrier was at Okinawa in 1945. Haskell ran into Bill Burns in California, "the last person I wanted to see."

Gene Edwards[13] remembered, "Everybody in our graduating class went down and volunteered." While waiting, he worked at the Atlantic Coast Line, but after 20 days was fired. The railroad thought it unfair for him to stay beyond 30 days and gain seniority over those who didn't go. "If that's the way you feel about people going into the service, then I quit and I won't be back." In September he weighed only 120 pounds, two under the army minimum. After eating five pounds of bananas to qualify, he volunteered again. "Haven't I seen you before?" asked the officer. "Anybody who wants to get in that bad I'm not going to turn them down again." He fought with the 281st Field Artillery Battalion in France and Germany.[14]

Defending the Remagen bridge on the Rhine River in March 1945 stands out. Firing 105mm pieces, "we tore up a lot of small towns," and numerous one-man torpedoes the Germans floated down river to destroy the bridge. There he saw the German Me-262 jet aircraft. "They came in on us—we didn't know what they were—they were here and gone. We didn't know what was going on around the world. The Remagen bridge was just another day at the office."

Mitchell Saleeby, Jr.[15] was the only known Marine classmate. While working for his father's produce business, on a pickup trip to South Carolina he passed a Marine recruiting office, obtained enlistment forms (at 17 he was underage), and asked his father to sign. "His [father's] hand was shaking." Brother Emile (president of the NHHS '40 student body) was in the air force. The draft rejected older brother William in 1942. When William walked into Shepherd's Pool Room afterwards, Mitch saw his dejected look. "That opened up for me to take off into the service."

Saleeby fought on Iwo Jima, where as a corporal and 30-caliber machine gunner with the 2d Battalion, 27th Marines, 5th Marine Division, "I always did the shooting. I know I got at least seven [Japanese]. We didn't

---

[*] Private First Class Goins, 18, son of Mr. and Mrs. Julian Goins, died November 14, 1943, at Fort Crook, Neb. A popular classmate, ROTC captain and football player, he entered the army on August 13. Funeral services were held in Montgomery, Ala.

know what the hell we were doing...."
Replacing his mortally wounded section
leader, he covered the evacuation of
wounded, and received the Bronze Star.
He walked off Iwo unwounded, a
miracle. He proudly showed me his
Japanese .28 caliber rifle and Samurai
sword.

Ken Phelps, son of Mr. and Mrs.
Walter Phelps, went to the Pacific in
1944 serving on the submarines USS
Hardhead (SS-365) and USS *Piranha*
(SS-389). On returning home in 1945,
he visited our Forest Hills school. What
a treat! Brother Ronnie (my classmate)
wore Ken's white hat for days. Gleason
Allen[16] entered the navy's V-12 program in June 1943 at North Carolina.

Seaman 1/Class Kenneth Phelps, 1944,
Pacific submarine veteran of the USS
Hardhead (SS-365) and USS *Piranha*
(SS-389), brother of Ronnie Phelps.
Ronald G. Phelps

After becoming an ensign in May 1945,
he celebrated V-E Day in Chicago and
V-J Day in Georgia. Then "They just
shut the school down completely—
didn't teach us another thing."

By February 1943, Heyward Bellamy[17] was in the air force and later
received his diploma by mail from principal Thomas T. ("T-Square") Hamilton,
Jr. Preferring meteorology, he was trained as a bombardier-navigator because "the *Luftwaffe* was beating us up. They needed air crews." His parents wanted a weekly collect phone call until he convinced them "I was not
going to die. It was a sacrifice [expense] even though we were prospering at
the time. I never had the heart to tell Mother I could get chocolates at the
PX. Most of the men I was associated with had strong family ties. I saw
heartbreaks" in Wilmington, boys who went home to former sweethearts.
"Some of those faces still haunt me." The war ended while he trained in
Texas, living in tarpaper shacks waiting to be shipped out.

About the liberated Buchenwald concentration camp, Robert Hollis[18]
wrote, "'...The old hospital must have been the most crowded filthy place
you can imagine. Statistics show that approximately 60 persons died in this
hospital every day....I saw hundreds of living skeletons—almost starved to
death. But there was no fear in their eyes, only a joy that was apparent in
all for they were free men once more, and the way home beckoned.'"

Chapter 10
"Like Pieces of Steel"

Work at the North Carolina Shipbuilding Company began with employment manager Richard A. "Dick" Burnett. Until the U.S. Employment Service took over war industry hiring in February 1943, the Wilmingtonian was perhaps the shipyard's most visible figure. An instant "legend," he is fondly remembered by old timers.

Once Burnett, a fair and understanding man, had to lay off men to meet one department's requirements. "'You can't move people around like pieces of steel.'" He terminated them, then rehired them in other departments. He secured a crane operator position for his friend Jack Hart, who like the large majority of local men knew nothing about shipbuilding. Jim Stokley's father in the summer of 1941 obtained a job for him through friend Burnett as a welding school clerk. "My duties were to pass out welding rods to the students...and keep the records."[1]

* * *

The Nature of Shipyard Work

Employment office worker Betty Henderson[2] entered the yard only twice, the day she was hired and later substituting as the general manager's secretary. Riding public transportation home, "I would be so dead tired." Typical of both office and yard workforces, she packed her own lunch. Burnett escorted into her office Mayor Bruce B. Cameron, the only local man serving on the shipyard's board of directors. Her office was actively selling war bonds, and the mayor bought some from her. Burnett had no idea they were acquainted. His army son Dan Cameron was Betty's sweetheart. She kissed the mayor. "You can imagine the look on Burnett's face at that girl in his office." When Cameron died in 1944, Burnett gave her time off.

Allegations and rumors about excessive hiring ("padding the payroll") and favoritism in assignments surfaced, some undoubtedly plausible. Billy Humphrey heard of a man hired as a carpenter's helper who couldn't keep

Wilmington shipyard workers
North Carolina Shipbuilding Company

busy. After a few days on the job he noticed someone was following him, and thought he would lose his job. "The follower caught up with him and said he had been hired to help him help the first guy."[3]

H. G. Bryant[4] left his 13-year Coca-Cola Bottling Company job as an electrician and general maintenance man to work there for four years. "They doubled my wages." He worked on board the ships under construction doing general electrical wiring, pulling cables, and installing main panels and boxes. "It was a big operation. We were turning out two Liberty ships a week."

Normal working hours were 7:00 a.m. to 5:00 p.m. with an hour for lunch, some overtime, and occasionally seven-day weeks. Before electrical work began, hull sections were fitted together. After launching, the ships were towed to a pier for finishing. Much of the time Bryant worked by himself. He earned "top electrician's pay. If we could finish [the job] sooner we would get extra pay. Sometimes I made three times more than my regular pay. I then had to go somewhere else to work, or go somewhere to hide." Two months before the war ended he started his own electrical contracting business.

John Mintz[5] applied for work after the first ship, the SS *Zebulon B. Vance*, was launched on December 6, 1941. To him Burnett "was an outdoor man, rough and tough, but he had a heart of gold. He would do a man a favor," and knew first names. After giving Manette Dixon a ride home from church, Burnett hired her as a timekeeper. She lived next door to Mintz but they barely spoke during the war. (After the war Mintz and Dixon married.)

Mintz welded in the tough steel inner bottoms of hulls. Later Burnett assigned him to the north yard steel storage department to supervise several Negroes. This department was one-half mile long on both sides of the railroad track in three steel storage bays. Promoted to quarterman grade, he took the night shift at $5 extra pay for married shift leaders C. G. Smith and Nelson O'Quinn, and worked 10 hours, seven days a week.

Mintz' shop sent steel on railroad flatcars for processing to the mold loft building which housed the boilermaker shop and erectors. Shipways were on south yard. Fifty-seven Negroes performed hard manual labor on five gantry cranes on his shift. Throughout the yard no Negroes supervised whites, and only a few supervised other Negroes. One Negro missed two days of work, said he had been sick and could not notify Mintz, and was told to bring a note from his doctor. He brought back a piece of tablet paper with a note, "I have been sick. Signed, 'the doctor.'"*

The Atlantic Coast Line ran in trains every day loaded with components. One time the yard had 105 railroad cars loaded with steel. "The mills were pouring out steel," Mintz recalled. Cars were in short supply and were

---

* In a workforce that large, new excuses were being concocted daily. A shipyard worker staying with Jack Hufham's family got off work by lying that his grandmother just died, and faked temperature readings playing sick. She had been dead for 10 years.

supposed to be turned around quickly, but unloading time depended upon what their contents were and how difficult they were to handle and unload. Most steel came on 65-foot gondolas, similar to coal cars.

The rush to produce hulls heavily impacted every aspect of shipyard worker life. Old school buses brought in workers from nearby counties. Riders cut holes in the roofs and put in stove and pipes for heat. Workers learning of family deaths had no way to get home until their daily or weekly bus left the yard. Mintz "had to go home and get some rest and fix your lunch and go back to work the next day." With a brother "over there," this became his contribution to the war effort.[*]

Mintz stayed on as a quarterman until the yard closed in 1946 and then took a job with the Maritime Commission. The War Assets Administration assumed surplus property, and he helped sell it off.

HULL 204
NO LOST TIME
ACCIDENTS
KEEL TO LAUNCHING

Launching the SS *American Ranger* at the Wilmington shipyard, March 3, 1945.
North Carolina Shipbuilding Company

Emerson Willard,[6] placed on hold a year for the Navy V-5 pilot program, worked in the riveting department on December 7, 1941. The next morning soldiers moved in swiftly everywhere. A member of the tank-testing crew,

---

[*] First Lieutenant Victor Lee Mintz, veteran bomber pilot, died in an accident over Duxford, England, on July 19, 1944, returning from a mission. Recipient of the Air Medal and three Oak Leaf Clusters, he rests in Wilmington's Oakdale Cemetery. In 2004 I found his name on the 8th Air Force memorial display at the American Air Museum at Duxford.

"the lowest of the low," Willard checked for and caulked leaking rivets. He rode ships down the ways at launching and checked inside the hull for leaks. For this he was "paid the top dollar in those days. They were happy to get anybody."

Fred Day[7] was a shell welder under department head Red Adams, worked hard, and lost a lot of weight. With one-half hour for lunch, he had no time to go to the cafeteria. "It was for supervisors and big shots." Some workers drank beer outside the gate at lunch. Women did no heavy work. "They usually could get enough men" for those jobs. "I would just sleep and work" [seven days per week]. Day never sought a deferment, only the navy, but was refused. He was in essential work. Two months later the army drafted him.

Phil Dresser's[8] first job after finishing NHHS in 1942 was constructing three additional shipways and additional pre-fabrication facilities in the North yard. After on-the-job training, Dresser "installed and operated shipboard machinery outside the main engine room. This included the ship's rudder, the steering engineer that turned the rudder, the anchor windlass used to lift the anchor, and the deck winches that were used to lift cargo out of the cargo hold." His brother was a supervisor in the Layout Depot (Shapes and Plates) and his brother-in-law a welder. When the shipyard began operating plywood-bodied buses from New Hanover, Brunswick, and Pender Counties, he rode the bus.

"Based on my experience installing and operating shipboard machinery as an outside machinist, I was granted a deck engineer's license in the merchant marine and was an occasional member of the yard crew that sailed the completed Liberty ship in a sea trial." Until German U-Boat activity posed a risk, ships steamed past Bald Head Island lighthouse on their shakedown cruises, then returned to the shipyard.* Harbor pilots out of Southport conned the ships in and out of port. "We then turned the ship over to representatives of the Maritime Commission which assigned a shipping line and a civilian merchant marine crew."

Dresser remembered the trial trips to Southport as "memorable events" but "hated the cold, damp night work, no heat on ships, lack of transportation, overcrowding of Wilmington."[9] For excitement, occasionally an alligator got caught up in a ship's propeller during testing.[10] Dresser worked at the yard seven days per week for two years before entering the navy.

When Newport News Shipbuilding established the Wilmington shipyard, Virginian apprentice Rob Pollock arrived here for duty in December

---

* The sinking of the tanker SS *John D. Gill* off Southport on the night of March 13, 1942, a blaze seen by many for miles, dictated a change in testing procedures. Ships remained within the Cape Fear River thereafter. See *A Sentimental Journey* for *Gill* details.

1942. He returned to Newport News in May 1943. "Frozen" to an essential war job, his appointment to the Merchant Marine Academy was delayed until 1944.[*]

The North Carolina Shipbuilding Company (NCSC) administrative and apprentice dormitory buildings were right outside the main gate. A dormitory resident, Pollock ate at boarding houses. "Often it was a mob scene trying to get breakfast." Boarding houses packed lunches. On site in the yard, one company controlled vendors who used carts. Long lines for service formed. A few apprentices owned cars, but people walked everywhere.

The dormitory was only a place for sleeping with parlor, showers, and a record player, and radios for listening to the "Hit Parade." For recreation, residents spun yarns into the night. Apprentice school consisted of one day in class and four days on the job. They saw each other in the dormitory but went separate ways once they entered the main gate.[†]

Pollock worked as a machinist in the testing and steam engineering departments. "Never picked up a tool thereafter." On the eight-hour round trip trial runs he tested engines, anchors, and calibrated compasses and degaussing systems. During the shipbuilding record-setting month of May 1943, he experienced three exhaustive trial trips back to back. "The yard would see that it was feasible, so they set out to do it [setting the record]." Harry Payne, a night shift administrator and later ship purser, after the war opened a men's shop.

Soldiers and sailors felt animosity toward shipyard workers because they were not in uniform, and "yard birds" stayed on the defensive. "When a beer bottle was broken, then the fighting would stop." One of Pollock's buddies wore pink pants and provoked reactions. "He was straight," but that didn't matter. Pollock sometimes went to the movies and ate at the Crystal Restaurant. Workers qualified for ration books. He didn't buy much and sent money home for his mother to deposit into a bank. To pay for a Christmas trip home on leave he hocked his watch in Finkelstein's pawn shop, eventually reclaiming it.

From March 1942 to August 1944 when he entered the navy, Clayton Smith[11] worked at the yard. His friends were either in college or the service. "I was looking for something to do. The purpose for me was nothing but work and sleep and work, no middle life, no social contacts. You were with the mass focusing on just one thing—production, getting it done."

Beginning pay was 60 cents an hour, then $1.14. "I was making big money" for a 19-year-old. Smith worked mostly the swing and graveyard

---

[*] In 1992, the state unveiled a historical marker to the WWII shipyard at the corner of Shipyard Boulevard and Carolina Beach Road. Pollock was a principal speaker, along with Dick Burnett, ABC sportscaster Jim McKay, and Henry B. Rehder, purser on the SS *Nathanial Alexander*

[†] The apprentice dormitory is now the Marine Corps Reserve Center.

shifts, the latter at $30 per week. The switch "pretty much demanded you get eight or nine hours of sleep." With only two pairs of work pants, he lived in coveralls.

Jobs broke down into gangs, each with a leader. Workers clocked in and out at the main gate. Smith's gang met daily where they left the day before and received instructions. Picking up from the off-going shifts, they completed the previous job and turned over work to next shift. "It was my introduction to working with women. We were trying to rape them, as every 17-year-old kid thought in his mind. You learned a work ethic right quick."

Smith roomed at the 3rd and Market YMCA, taking the bus to work ("standing room only"), occasionally carpooling. Usually "it was buses or walk." Eventually he moved into his grandmother's house. He often ate meals at the Saunders Drug Store lunch counter and café. You stood behind a stool at the counter until it was your turn to eat. "For 45 or 50 cents, it was more than you could possibly eat." He divided his dirty clothes between Ideal Laundry and a downtown Chinese laundry.

"Everybody was trying to get out to the shipyard" when Ray Funderburk[12] began in mid-1941. He drilled holes so that sides of the hulls could be riveted together. Red-hot rivets were placed from inside and a jack hammer flattened them outside. He became a supervisor with a night-shift gang. The drilling department was just about all Negro when he started. Whites and Negroes mixed well and sang songs together. "Blacks were good workers," and "I got along fine with them. They accepted me as their supervisor; they knew I was their boss."

"We were making ships faster than [California shipbuilder Henry J.] Kaiser was." Watching Camp Lejeune being built, and impressed by a Marine in dress blues, he knew that was what he wanted. After his NHHS '38 classmates began leaving for active duty, in early 1943 he resigned and offered himself.

High blood pressure almost stopped him. A doctor told him to get a good night's sleep, drink lots of milk, and return tomorrow. Originally in a replacement draft for Iwo Jima, he was commissioned in 1945. "I regret it to a degree [missing Iwo]. I lost some friends over there." He retired in 1970 after commanding a company in Korea and battalion in Vietnam.

* * *

Training and Safety

Formal pre-job shipyard training was inconsistently administered and mostly acquired on the job. Shipbuilding required establishing welding schools, which turned out 7,247 certified graduates and other trades such as driller, reamer, riveter, burner, steam engineer, plumber, and sheet metalman. The experience of supervisors from Newport News proved valuable.

Yet, Jack Hart remembered "no one working there knew anything." He trained for two weeks before being responsible for a 12-ton crane which hauled sheet metal and hull plates. On its side he scribbled "Dive Bomber."[13] All crane operators were white. Oscar Buck, deferred at 33 with three children, began as a crane operator in late 1941. "He didn't mind heights. Some people were afraid of heights," his wife Bertha Buck remembered.[14]

The Federal Government had no regulatory agency such as the Occupational Safety and Health Administration to inspect working conditions in firms performing government contracts. Under present standards, physical working conditions in the shipyard appeared a bit primitive. The NCSC talked "safety first" but failed to plan or oversee adequately basic safety rules or initiatives, despite being awarded a National Safety Council award.[15]

"They claimed they had 700 days without an accident, but I know better than that," H. G. Bryant[16] stated. Ambulances ran around picking up injured workers. "With that many people working in that little space someone was bound to get hurt." As was customary with most yard workers, Bryant wore safety steel toe shoes, but not a hard hat. He saw a man get his foot cut off when an overhead steel load was dropped from a crane. "The report was no accident that day. I didn't feel that I was in much danger. You could fall down in one of the holds in the ships."

The first worker killed on duty (September 1941) was Negro Ellis Joseph "Buddy" Quick, Cornelia Haggins' uncle. A crane operator picked him up by mistake and then dropped him. "He had just graduated from Shaw University and this was just something for him to do while waiting to hear from his application to teach." He was a piano player, tenor, and married. "My grandmother never got over it."[17]

Shipyard management downplayed injuries and deaths. In August 1942 a 19-year-old electrician electrocuted himself while changing a bulb on a ship, and a below-decks explosion, "which apparently resulted from a spark from a welder's torch setting off a quantity of gas which had accumulated," injured four others.[18] Three days later, "Another Killed," an electrocuted 18-year-old welder.[19] "They would carry people out of there every day with injuries," Emerson Willard confided. "Everybody was behind everything trying to get the ships out of there."[20]

The central shipyard infirmary treated emergencies without regard to race, but, as James Whitted recalled, "they didn't do nothing together. Treated you in a different room."[21] Its staff of seven physicians and 17 nurses administered a minimum form of health care through the infirmary and first-aid stations. Two prominent physicians, Dr. Joseph W. Hooper and Dr. Donald B. Koonce, served as medical director and assistant chief surgeon.

Elizabeth Bell Day declared that her husband Fred Day's entering the service "probably saved his life." He worked around a lot of asbestos, a common building material during the war. "It was very dangerous work for a year."[22] Her father sold safety shoes. The company did not provide them. Scaffolds were without railings to catch workers if they stepped back, and men fell off and injured themselves.

In 1942 "the number of accidents was very low," the newspaper reported. "The rumors of high fatality and permanent injury rates are untrue....They constitute the sort of information subtle enemy agents and thoughtless citizens enjoy spreading."[23] Wow! I must have thought as I heard this. Real enemy agents in Wilmington? What do they look like, and where do I find them? This of course magnified rumors of German spies coming ashore in rubber boats from submarines off Carolina Beach. But the paper says they must be here, more exciting stuff to feed a boy's imagination.

Management *sloganeered* safety.* Workers received pamphlets and regulations, and "all over the yard they are greeted by posters with reader appeal." The catchy slogan "'Be Careful' is everywhere in evidence."[24] The yard provided neither uniforms nor hard hats, but did provide safety goggles and offered protective items for sale. Few workers wore hard hats. Asbestos floated through the air. Wearing safety glasses was not compulsory. No one person assumed responsibility for safety, only each supervisor.[25]

"That shipyard was a dangerous, dangerous place," Clayton Smith remembered. One night a man burning on deck caused his own injury by lowering welding equipment into a hold where he was working. "I think he lived about 11 hours" from the burns. "That place was so miserably hot in the summer from welders' smoke, burners' smoke choking you—heat from steel sitting in the sun all day."[26] Looking at a welder's arc would burn the eyes, "like sand being poured into your eyes," Smith said. Treatment was a cloth soaked with cool water placed over the eyes, and ointment from the infirmary. Once he was sick with walking pneumonia but was expected to work through it.[27]

Safety gradually improved. It had to. The 199th hull, a C-2/AKA-type ammunition ship named the USS *Paricutin* (AE-18) after a Mexican volcano, was launched January 30, 1945,† built "without a single lost-time accident....We also believe it is a national high mark in accident prevention in shipbuilding for a vessel of this type...."[28]

One of the most grisly deaths occurred in September 1944. Negro Zachariah Simons, serving as a flagman on a shifting engine, "caught his head in a turntable," crushing his skull. "He later fell off the platform onto an angle iron where he sustained additional head injuries, and died

---

* A worker's attitude toward industrial accidents was different than today. After all, if you despised your job you could always join the army at $21 per month.

† My first duty station after commissioning 11 years later was on board *Paricutin* for 18 months, with two deployments to the Far East.

immediately,"[29] at least death No. 7. Two worker suicides in housing projects were discovered during four days in December 1941. The company's final report lists neither the number of accidental deaths nor suicides. No one locally knows for sure.

*   *   *

A City Itself

The shipyard was almost a city within. Its newspaper, *The North Carolina Shipbuilder*, called attention to all manner of yard activities such as ship contracts, management announcements, sports and recreation, war bond drives, employees in uniform, construction progress, and what happened to their ships.*

"Your Camels were opened by us on Tarawa on the third day of the [November 1943] GI campaign," a Marine medical officer wrote the paper, thanking employees for the cigarettes. "I passed them around in an aid station I had in a captured Jap dugout....They came in so good" with Thanksgiving dinner.[30]

A local baseball legend grew larger. In September 1945, the *Shipbuilder* reported that Augustus "Shuney" Brittain, former Erectors Department worker, led the International League with .389 for the Montreal Royals. "When 'Shuney' was very young in baseball, he'd fight on a diamond, or off, at the drop of a hat. That made him good, but he was hard to handle. Maybe he

Augustus "Shuney" Brittain, New Hanover High School graduate and later wartime baseball coach, and former shipyard worker, led the International League in batting in 1945 with the Montreal Royals.
The North Carolina Shipbuilder,
September 1, 1945

developed that fiery temperament down on the beaches. That was back when young people (and old) drank too much white corn liquor, too often getting

---

* An assistant editor was Al G. Dickson, after the war the *Wilmington Star-News* editor when I worked in the sports department after school, on weekends, and during the summer for three years.

out of bounds. 'Shuney' grew up on the beaches. He was always big and husky, with a pin-up physique, and afraid of nobody." He was on New Hanover High's 1928 state championship team, and later "had a whirl with Cincinnati" in the majors.[31]

Toward a Union?

Absenteeism joined safety as a major problem. The locally recruited labor force "became renowned for its 'permitted' absenteeism, although it was usually that these workers were still assisting the war effort elsewhere, for at certain seasons they stayed at home to help on the farms." Still, "'enough manhours were lost in the yards of NCSC here in January [1943], ...to have built another Liberty ship.'" Officials appealed "to public understanding and employee patriotism,"[32] and further indicated "strong measures" might be taken.[33]

An editorial condemned. "It is as serious a problem in Wilmington's major war industry....Workers, receiving more money than ever before, have been laying off at will, ignoring their obligation to work to the limit....If they won't work, make them fight."[34] Absenteeism fluctuated throughout and to a degree influenced the community's response to the war effort.

For the most part, yard and shop employees worked well together toward common goals driven by a mixture of patriotism, high pay, and a desire to postpone or preclude military service. If there were a divisive issue, it manifested itself through vituperative attempts in 1942–43 to unionize. Three unions recruited members and sought recognition from NCSC management: the International Union of Marine and Shipbuilding Workers of the CIO (Congress of Industrial Organizations, the largest); the American Federation of Labor; and the United Shipbuilders of America. They soon muscled out a local organization, the Cape Fear Shipbuilders Association.

The National Labor Relations Board became involved early, holding hearings into unfair labor practices in the fall of 1942 which intensified the rancor. One supervisor greeted another with "'Hello, Communist. How is the Communist Industrial Organization, CIO, getting along?'" Workers spoke of fights, overturned vehicles belonging to organizers, and job-loss threats for either joining or failing to join a union. The rank-and-file were between a rock and a hard place.

By March 1943, the NLRB ordered management to "'cease and desist' from discouraging membership in the CIO or any other labor organization..." and prohibited the NCSC from negotiating with the CFSA.[35] Joining a union was permissible, but no union enjoyed bargaining power. Organizing efforts failed on September 4, 1943, when the employees "voted overwhelmingly in favor of 'no union'" by 6,628 to 4,582.[36]

"Those things didn't interest me," one worker said of the union efforts, reflecting worker opinion. "I used to envy the crane operator sitting up there, and here I am down here breaking my balls."[37] Public sentiment seemed to favor management. The *Star-News* recognized a sweet settlement. They blamed the CIO as "a disturbing element in Wilmington ever since the first workers were assembled...."[38]

In January 1944, the U.S. Circuit Court of Appeals enforced an NLRB order enjoining the NCSC from interfering with all labor activities of its employees, requiring it to reinstate eight employees.[39] After this, the labor issue never resurfaced.

Of passing consequence was the navy's decision in December 1946 to decommission the USS *New Hanover* (AKA-73), launched in October 1944. County citizens presented the officers with a customary silver service "as a token of their pride in her." The ship logged more than 75,000 miles and participated at Okinawa. The July decommissioning was "received with a feeling of regret by many here who hoped that the name of our county would continue on the high seas for years to come." But the navy reactivated her as a merchant marine vessel,[40] thus extending another link to the yard a bit longer.

The Record[41]

North Carolina Shipbuilding Company
Opened February 3, 1941; Closed October 9, 1946

Parent Company:
Newport News Shipbuilding & Drydock Company,
Newport News, Virginia

Ships Built and Delivered

Liberty ships (EC-C1 types, Maritime Commission), 1941–43	126
C-2 types, Maritime Commission, 1943–44	*
C-2 derivative/AKA-type ships[†] (Navy), 1944–45	53
C-2 derivative/passenger-cargo ships (commercial lines), 1945–46	64*
Total	243

Liberty ships	
First order, 25 Libertys	March 18, 1941
First 2 keels laid	May 22, 1941
First Liberty launching, SS *Zebulon B. Vance*,	December 6, 1941
First Liberty delivery	February 17, 1942
Final Liberty launching, SS *John Branch*,	August 21, 1943
Final Liberty delivery	August 27, 1943

---

* 64 total C-2s for Maritime Commission and commercial lines
† AKA attack cargo, AE ammunition, AGC command

Liberty specifications
 Length 441.5', breadth 56'; 11,000 tons dwt, 7,177 tons gwt, draft 27'; 3-cylinder triple expansion engine of 2,500 hp for 10 kts
 dwt—deadweight tons; gwt—grossweight tons; hp—horsepower; kts—knots

Average Liberty launchings per month	11
Average Liberty ship cost	$1,543,600
	(U.S. record low for 1943)
Average man-hours per Liberty	403,400
	(U.S. record low)
Miles in U.S. "bridge of ships"	21

C-2 ships

First C-2 launching, SS *Storm King*	September 17, 1943
First C-2 delivery	December 3, 1943
First C-2 passenger-cargo delivery, SS *Santa Barbara*	March 1946
Final C-2 passenger-cargo launching, SS *Santa Isabel*	April 16, 1946
Final delivery	October 9, 1946

C-2 specifications
 Length 459', breadth 63'; 10,660 tons dwt, 8,258 tons gwt; double-reduction geared compound turbine engine of 6,000 hp; single screw at 92 rpms for over 14 kts
 rpm—revolutions per minute

AKA-type ships

First AKA-type delivery, USS *Torrance* (AKA-76)	June 20, 1944
Final AKA-type delivery, USS *Taconic* (AGC-17)	March 6, 1945

AKA specifications were similar to the C-2s with certain naval modifications

The Yard

Groundbreaking	February 3, 1941
Ultimate cost to construct	$20,393,358

Site on 160 acres of swampland with 9 shipways, 3 piers, 67 cranes, 19 miles of railroad track
Profits: $22,701,229 (before taxes), on a capital investment of $3 million.
Awards (partial list):
 U.S. Maritime Commission "M" Pennant for productivity, with subsequent stars for its continued record;

Treasury Department "Minute Man" Flag for maximum war bond
    drive participation;
Army-Navy "E" Award for speed and efficiency.

Employment

Peak employment   21,000 on March 11, 1943
    (approximately ¹/₄ of New Hanover County's population at the
    time)*
Women in production departments   >1,200
Entered armed forces/merchant marine   Approximately 6,813
Number who died in service   At least 33
Gross peak payroll (1943) $52,390,140

---

* Sources disagreed on the peak number employed. One claimed 25,000, four-fifths of all
county manufacturing, [Alan D. Watson, *Wilmington: Port of North Carolina* (Columbia:
University of South Carolina Press, 1992), 154], as did the *Wilmington Morning Star* of
August 6, 1946. The figure 23,000 is also used.

A Lost Voice for the War Effort[42]

"One of the less dramatic and more subtle losses of the war...deals
with my father (stage name of Bob Page) having to give up show business to work in the shipyard just when Broadway-type success was
becoming a real possibility....Following the war he was never able to
fully recover emotionally and otherwise. He did on occasion share his
wonderful baritone voice in more modest settings...[including] a rather
impressive vaudeville show was presented by the workers entitled 'Hi
Mate!'...[he sang] a soul stirring rendition of 'The White Cliffs of
Dover'....Hopefully, Dad's little part played some role in bringing that
terrible conflict to a successful conclusion."

—Earl M. Page

NCSC Ships Lost

Twenty-eight ships built by the NCSC were lost: enemy action sank
23 Libertys, and three were scuttled to form the Normandy, France,
invasion breakwater. One C-2, a navy ammunition ship, exploded in
the Pacific. Libertys included (numbers of lives lost is partial):[43]

Nathanael Green (NCSC hull #2, built February 1942), after damage by
    German submarine (U-boat) and aircraft (a/c) torpedoes, towed to
    Algeria and beached, total loss, February 1943.

Virginia Dare (3, March 1942), after repairs from minefield damage, broke up at sea, beached Tunis, March 1944, total loss.

William Hooper (4, March 1942), disabled by a/c torpedo in Barents Sea, abandoned, sunk by U-boat, July 1942.

Charles C. Pinckney (7, May 1942), damaged by U-boat torpedo off Azores, abandoned, re-boarded, abandoned, finally sunk by U-boat torpedo and gunfire, January 27, 1943, 2 lives lost.

Jeremiah Van Renssalaer (11, June 1942), sunk by U-boat torpedo off Greenland, February 1943.

Artemus Ward (12, June 1942), sunk as "Gooseberry 2" at Mulberry Harbor A, Normandy, 1944.

William Gaston (15, July 1942), sunk by U-boat torpedo in South Atlantic, July 1944.

Richard D. Spaight (19, August 1942), sunk by U-boat torpedo and gunfire off South Africa, March 1943.

Benjamin Smith (25, November 1942), sunk by U-boat torpedo off Africa, January 1943.

John Penn (27, June 1942), damaged by German a/c torpedoes in Greenland Sea, sunk by convoy escort gunfire, September 1942.

John Drayton (34, September 1942), damaged by Italian submarine torpedo off South Africa, sunk by sub gunfire, April 1943.

Paul Hamilton (36, October 1942), sunk by a/c torpedoes north of Algiers, April 1944.

Henry Bacon (40, November 1942), sunk by a/c torpedo in Barents Sea, February 1945.

James Iredell (45, December 1942), sunk as "Gooseberry 2" at Mulberry Harbor, Normandy, 1944.

Penelope Baker (46, December 1942), sunk by U-boat torpedo in Barents Sea, January 1944.

Richard Caswell (48, December 1942), sunk by U-boat torpedo off Brazil, July 1943.

John Harvey (56, January 1943), hit by German a/c bombs and exploded, Bari, Italy, December 2, 1943, 10 lives lost.

Robert Howe (57, January 1943), lost May 20, 1944, 1 life.

Flora MacDonald (63, February 1943), damaged by U-boat torpedo off Sierra Leone, gutted and reported as a "distorted mass of scrap," May 1943.

James Sprunt (64, February 1943), sunk by U-boat torpedo southeast of Cuba, March 10, 1943, 2 lives.

Matt W. Ransom (65, February 1943), sunk as "Gooseberry 1" at Mulberry Harbor A, Normandy, 1944.

Edward B. Dudley (67, February 1943), sunk by U-boat in Atlantic, April 1943.

Robert Rowan (82, April 1943), damaged by a/c bombs and artillery fire off Gela, Sicily, abandoned, blew up and sank, July 1943.

Cornelia P. Spencer (89, April 1943), sunk by U-boat torpedo in Indian Ocean, September 1943.

Lee S. Overman (65, June 1943), sunk by mine off LeHavre, France, November 1944.

The SS *Walker Taylor*[44]

Distinguished citizen Colonel Walker Taylor founded Wilmington's Brigade Boys Club, participating until his death in 1937. As a reward for exceptionally active service in the war effort by collecting enough scrap metal to build a ship (1,418,974 pounds), the club got to name a liberty ship. They chose Colonel Taylor. Three granddaughters christened her on March 28, 1943: Rosalie Oliver, Virginia Oliver Tinga, and Frances Taylor Thornton. Grandson Walker Taylor III served in the merchant marine.

Chapter 11

"Smokey Joe" and Upholding Law and Order

Besides Police Chief Charles H. Casteen and Sheriff C. David Jones, the best-known member of local law enforcement was "Smokey Joe" Flowers, the prototype hard-nosed state highway patrolman. It seemed like he investigated every highway accident and wrote every speeding ticket. When we boys obtained drivers' licenses a few years later he became our nemesis, and we avoided confronting him like the plague.

Did criminals get revenge amidst the exploding crime spree? Judge John J. Burney, a tireless Superior Court circuit rider, gained fame for his no-nonsense deliberations and exacting judgments. A wrongdoer, you did not want the World War I veteran on the bench. In 1943 he sentenced J. J. Schmidt to 12 months on the roads simply for stealing 11 cases of cigarettes valued at $700 from P&F Motor Express company. But while the family was away on February 25, 1945, a thief broke into the Burney home at 1704 Orange Street through a rear window. He ransacked every room after shades were lowered to prevent detection, and heisted $2 in cash. Infantryman John, Jr., was then fighting in Germany.*

Judge H. Winfield Smith, the most visible member of the judiciary who presided over the lesser Recorder's Court, in August 1944 also stood firm.

> From now on there are going to be fewer fines and more prison sentences....There are no figures to compare New Hanover County's crime rate with that of other war-stimulated areas...but it is a safe guess to say that the rate is unusually high....The length of that crime parade is attributable largely to the free flow of money in the community, and the operation of "juke joints," where illegal whiskey is dispensed, and where beer is often sold during forbidden hours. The ample payrolls of wartime Wilmington have heretofore made it possible for offenders to pay the heavy fines....Swift, severe judgements should greatly help law enforcement.[1]

---

* Judge Burney covered 52 counties, driving his 1941 Chevrolet (provided by dealer W. A. Raney) at a speed limit of 35 mph.

The newspaper encouraged and applauded efforts to curtail law and order under drastic conditions. Some worked; some didn't.

* * *

Numerous Untimely Deaths

Ruth Starling of Winter Park died "less than an hour after she had been crushed between two automobiles which collided head-on on the Wrightsville Beach highway" at night. One operator, Negro Thomas J. Williams, was held without bond for improper brakes. After getting off the bus and holding a child in her arms, Starling was sandwiched between Williams and another car. She threw her baby to safety. Witness Faye King said "she stopped to adjust her purse while Mrs. Starling started across the highway...and saw Williams' car and cried 'Look out, Ruth!' just before the accident."[2]

The army took over the case of air force Captain Chic E. Smith, Jr., in the hit-and-run death of Robert Shawon on the Wrightsville Beach highway. An ice cream truck driven by an unlicenced operator struck an MP's jeep, severely lacerating Corporal Joseph Curcia's head. Military police arrested Private Henry Hertch on charges of driving under the influence of whiskey after his weapons carrier hit a commercial bus.

Lonnie Manning, Negro railway expressman, drew 2–3 years in the state prison for manslaughter by killing Negro iceman Herbert Singleton. Manning's landlady, Lela Smith, said, "Manning came into her kitchen where Singleton had come to collect for ice. The two men called each other liars whereupon Singleton picked up a chair and Manning a butcher knife with which she had been cleaning fish." In the ensuing scuffle, Singleton was fatally wounded.[3]

The most tragic drowning occurred in May 1944 at the Snow's Cut bridge on the Inland Waterway near Carolina Beach. Norlene Holt, 12, attempted to rescue her brothers, Jimmy, 4, and Ray, 5, who fell from the bank. Seventy-five soldiers camping nearby joined the search. Officials recovered her body but not the boys. Her father, C. G. Holt, was the bridge tender.[4]

Shirley, 8, the daughter of Mrs. W. B. Darnell, accidentally fatally shot her mother in April 1944. "Muttering her last words from a hospital bed, Mrs. Darnell completely vindicated her small daughter of all blame of the affair." Coroner Asa W. Allen stated it was "'purely an accident.'" "The child...is in a near hysterical condition....Sobbing wails of 'I want my mama' were heard." Her army sergeant husband was stationed at Fort Dix, New Jersey.[5]

In 1944 a Tide Water Power Company bus struck 11-year-old Robert Branch crossing an intersection on a green light with his sister. The bus' left side knocked them down, the rear wheel killing him. Witnesses and the coroner's jury agreed the accident was "unavoidable."[6] Construction worker

E. B. Fraley died in the hospital "after having slashed Mrs. Juanita Byrd to death" in front of her home. He "repeatedly stabbed and slashed" her, a mother of four, "one of the most brutal killings to be recorded in the city in many years."[7]

Alfred T. Surles shot and killed his estranged wife, Gladys Surles, at 132 Colonial Village. Judge Burney sentenced Surles to 20–25 years in the state penitentiary for first degree murder after telling Surles "he was a 'lucky man' to escape capital punishment for the murder of his wife. Surles said she had invited him over to discuss "'our future happiness.'" But "his mind 'went blank' a moment before the shooting...."[8]

* * *

Running Afoul of the Law

Police in November 1943 arrested an unusually large number of downtown jaywalkers. "Officers had been warning the public for months to obey traffic signals without obtaining cooperation."[9] A Negro girl, recruited to work in the federal labor camp but not needed, was arrested for trespassing on government property. "As proof that judges, lawyers and policemen are not so 'hardboiled' after all, a contribution of $5.10 was collected" to send her home to Charlotte.[10]

A growing group was "made up of men and boys who haunt alleys and back yards at night to peer through slits below window shades....We call them Peeping Toms...frightening women...so much that rest and sleep are out of the question...."[11] "Police are on the search for another 'meanest man'—the one who stole $29 from St. Paul's Episcopal." Rector Alexander P. Miller said the money was taken from a side door where two members left pocketbooks.[12]

Nick Lee, 63, tried slashing his throat with a pocket knife. He was treated and released. Sanford Prevatt attacked his wife, Florence, with a hatchet and then cut his throat and arms with a pocket knife. "...He met his wife on the street and told her that, if she would go with him to his room, he would give her some money for the children, police said, the oldest of which is seven."[13] His sentence: 7–10 years on the state road gang.

Crowded buses incited conflicts. "One [altercation] almost turned into a riot...." Alex Pridgen and James Lumpkins were admitted to James Walker Memorial Hospital with stab wounds. Pridgen said it "began when he asked the Negro to move further back in the bus and the Negro jerked out a knife and slashed him...."[14] For disorderly conduct and resisting arrest, the court ordered Wilmington sailor James Williams, home on leave, out of town. He and wife Laura "used vile and abusive language to a woman bus driver...and she cut the hand of officer W. J. Millis."[15]

Kure's Beach asked the county for additional police protection "on the basis of alleged disorder among civilians and soldiers that 'is growing unbearable.'" Defense workers "'all have too much money and they are spending it on whiskey and beer.'" Beach housewives made "their second appeal for adequate protection from lawlessness and rowdyism." County commissioners ordered an investigation.[16]

"Because he had told the truth," Judge H. Winfield Smith was lenient with Luther Craven, a Negro Wilmington Hotel porter charged with liquor law violation by possessing 120 cases of South Carolina whiskey. Craven had been selling it at the hotel for two years. "'As long as I am on the bench, I don't intend for any bootlegger to bring liquor from any other state.'" Craven got a $1,000 fine and a two-year suspended sentence.[17] For robbing Britt's Donut Shop of $400, two Negroes in March 1944 received sentences ranging from 2 to 5 years in the state prison. (A white received 12 months on the county roads for stealing $250 in cash and a $50 pistol from Boots Café.)

The county Bureau of Identification in December 1943 cautioned "to be on the alert as the number rises in robberies and sneak thief operations....The safest thing for a woman to do, besides leave her pocketbook at home, is to carry one of the smallest type practicable...." A. W. Wheeler, "who allegedly 'has papered this section of the state with worthless checks, and who is listed under various addresses and occupations,' pleaded guilty to four charges of forgery," drawing four months on the county farm. "The public has been warned time and again that a Social Security card is not proper identification."[18]

In 1944 a rash of flower and shrubbery thefts from cemeteries and Greenfield Park broke out. "Considerable public indignation has been aroused...." Two women were fined $50 each plus court costs, their attorney adding, "'Flowers and women are the two most beautiful things in the world...[and] naturally associated together....'"[19] "Thieves are again active in Oakdale Cemetery...a desecration [that] brings genuine grief to the loved ones of those who sleep there."[20]

"Parents of scores of youths who have been 'seriously interfering' with the movement of Atlantic Coast Line troop trains out of Wilmington for the past six months face indictment for neglect and contributing to juvenile delinquency...," a judge warned. Approximately 100 boys "have been hindering progress...by swarming over the switch tracks near Love's Grove." In February 1945, children threw a switch on the Seaboard Air Line on 6th Street causing a locomotive to derail with considerable damage.[21]

Negro Ben Kornegay "will not soon forget the good trimming he got at the Boy-B Barber Shop" on Castle Street. Before getting a haircut and shave, he took a drink with the barber. "'I got sleepy all of a sudden and just sat down and went to sleep.'" He awoke to find "he had been clipped of $45." The only man in the shop when he dozed off was the barber, "Tony."[22]

In 1943 the court fined the Manor Theater manager $50 for "showing a movie after midnight Saturday, in a test case of the city's ordinance banning Sunday movies prior to 2 p.m."[23] On a February 1943 day when the court fined 29 persons one dollar each for parking meter violations, it sentenced James Whitted to two months on the roads for assault. "Wait, I'm not the man," proclaimed another James Whitted to the newspaper. The positive reputation of the second Whitted, a Negro Castle Hayne shipyard worker, remained intact.

Authorities booked numerous violators for "immoral purposes." In 1943, three women received sentences for occupying a trailer near the shipyard for that crime. A white man got six months for "aiding and abetting in prostitution by allowing his trailer to be used for the purpose."[24] "Fornication," another frequent charge, sent May Hook to the Raleigh women's camp for 12 months. Partner Welmer Wright pulled a year on the county farm. Suspending both sentences, the judge likely admonished, "don't end up in my court again."

"For the purposes of prostitution," the charges read against six arrested cab drivers. Also booked for "vagrancy and charged with profligate living and prostitution" were Susan Baker, 18, and Sarah Lee Reaves, 19. The drivers allegedly transported the two in the cabs, but went free on insufficient evidence since the crimes happened in Brunswick County. The prostitutes previously had served time, and each, admittedly having venereal disease, received 12 more months.

The judge "[Believed] they would have ample opportunity to learn a trade and reform...." Baker confessed to recent "immoral relations" with cabbie L. B. Pollock and ten other men, including drivers and others shipyard workers. Pollock stoutly denied the accusation. Yellow Cab manager Julius Wenberg said it is "not within the province of cab drivers to inquire of passengers for what purpose they wished to be taken to any particular place."[25]

What if an "immoral" act involved only the telephone? Police arrested Negro Elliott Bethea, 15, "for allegedly making repeated telephone calls to white women in which improper advances were made" from a drug store phone. Officers said it "'breaks up a case we've been working on for months." Bethea selected random numbers, "often soliciting dates....He told the women he would meet them at certain places and would be driving a black Pontiac sedan. Police said 'he never showed up.'" Juvenile court issued a suspended six-month sentence upon condition he leave town.[26]

In December 1942 Carolina Beach police closed the Pot O' Gold club as a "game of chance." Owner Mal Franklin strongly objected. "Bingo and other 'games of chance' had been allowed in Carolina Beach for 12 years, and no fights or disturbances had occurred there," he claimed. After the manager was acquitted of carrying a concealed weapon, and an employee for selling beer to a minor, the club eventually reopened. But it was marked.[27]

In April 1944 Recorder's Court quickly cleared "the 20 [high school] boys from South Wilmington who boarded a Tide Water bus and invaded Maffitt Village last night with vengeance in their eyes were found not guilty of assault....The wholesale fight was said to be 'a return engagement.'" The Maffitt teenagers had beaten up five Wilmington boys a few nights before. "Fists were flying....This...has been going on here for generations. Old timers will remember 'the days when the South Side boys and the Brooklynites used to fight it out hot and heavy.'"[28]

Frequent shootings occurred in war housing.* Lester Dawkins, 16, shot his girlfriend Arline Yopp, 15, with a 22-caliber rifle "after loading it with what he thought was an empty shell." While playing, he loaded the rifle, pointed it at her, and jokingly said he was going to shoot her. X-rays showed approximately 75 non-serious shots in her neck.[29]

Officers arrested Banks Funderburk in 1942 for wearing a Coast Guard chief petty officer's uniform without authorization at the Wrightville operating base and ordering enlisted men around. Stripping him of the uniform, they released him to Coast Guard authorities.[30] Other cases of impersonating military personnel were reported or rumored.

Finding some old city ordinances in 1945, the city attorney informed Council of violations for appearing in "indecent dress or in dress not belonging to his or her sex." Councilman Walter Yopp said that made it against the law for women to wear slacks! "Women in Wilmington, however, who like the freedom that they claim is afforded by slacks, can rest easy, at least for a while, for no action was taken by the council towards enforcement...." Councilman J. E. L. Wade reported people were appearing downtown in scanty beach attire. Regarding "indecent exposure," the attorney said "'it's a relative term and hard to define.'"[31]

* * *

Numbers for the Record

By August 1942, the yearly 1,231 arrests included 11 for prostitution, five for robbery, three for indecent exposure, two for "jack peeping," and 58 for jaywalking.[32] In March 1943 police arrested 778 more persons than the same time the year before, and revenues for the Recorder's Court hit $10,092, the largest ever. Fines went into school and pension funds.[33] Police hammered motorists for traffic violations and over-parking, 864 in April.[34] By

---

* Kids liked toy air rifles called "BB" guns. The police chief asked for parental cooperation "in preventing wholesale destruction of street lights throughout the city" and promised to prosecute. [*Wilmington Morning Star*, December 30, 1941]

Mrs. Wilbur D. (Viola) Jones, my mother, who maintained the American Legion Post 10 wartime scrapbooks of area persons in military service, and served as Auxiliary president in 1943.

Author's collection

June, city arrests had dipped to 715, including 103 for breaking into stores. Automobile accidents continued to rise with the corresponding number of cars on city and county roads, 89 in June, 34 more than June 1942.[35]

The 40 holiday weekend arrests in 1943 marked "one of the quietest, most orderly Christmases on record in recent years." Most "partook of too much liquid cheer, a few traffic violations, and the usual minor cuttings that make the record on the weekends."[36] With food and supply price increases, maintaining a prisoner was costing $1.26 per day vs. $1.09 the previous year.

The city had almost 1,000 fewer arrests for fiscal year 1944 than for 1943, "a peak year for crime in the city" with its 7,613 arrests.[*] Murders dropped from 24 to 11, drunkenness from 2,226 to 1,599 ("perhaps attributable to the decline in...whiskey available in local ABC stores"), prostitution from 215 to 160. Even parking violations waned. Deaths from auto accidents, auto thefts, and reckless driving increased. Police returned 191 of the 198 stolen cars to owners.[37] City robbery cases dropped by about one half during 1945 from 1944 (54 vs. 103), and over half the 1945 cases were false alarms or baseless, and warrants issued, 9,936 vs. 13,951.[38]

* * *

A New Enemy—Fire

Jacqueline Moore, 2, died a fiery death in November 1944 in the Carolina Beach Road dwelling of Wade Pierce, just south of the city limits.[39] Owner Mike Patellis of the Famous Grill, 100 yards south, called the Wilmington Fire Department station six blocks from the fire scene and was informed the city required a $100 guarantee to attend a fire beyond the city limits. "Patellis said he volunteered to stand good for the money, but the fire department failed to appear...."

A woman across from the Pierces' phoned the WFD three times saying a child was in the burning building, "and each time she was told they could not come." An assistant chief tried to contact the city manager. Jacqueline's navy father, a former local police officer, was stationed in Florida. Her mother, who with Mrs. Pierce went to buy soft drinks, went to the hospital in shock.

City Manager A. C. Nichols said "firemen were free to use their own judgment in answering outside calls, when such authorization was not forthcoming from him or the mayor." Firemen notified Mayor W. Ronald Lane two hours after the fire. County commissioners then guaranteed $100 for every such WFD response.

---

[*] The 1945 report on the chief classes included: larcenies, 722 reported; burglaries, 276; auto theft, 102; robberies, 47; assault, 708; and murders, 6.

The city's 1944 fire losses totaled $124,649, about $2.06 per capita, and compared favorably with 1943 fire loss figures of other large North Carolina cities. Much of the losses came from the St. Luke's AME Zion Church blaze on January 1 ($50,000), and the People's Furniture Store and Elks Club ($25,000). Two deaths resulted from the fire at 1007 MacRae's Alley in December. The most dangerous fire of 1944 occurred July 27 when lightning struck a river gasoline barge, completely covering the river with burning oil.[40]

Wrightsville Beach fires razed a number of cottages in 1943. In April, three burned to the ground, including Solomon Sternberger's where the blaze apparently originated. Rebecca Sternberger's house next door was destroyed, and Mrs. E. I. Bear's and Thomas H. Wright's cottages were damaged. On October 24, fire leveled the 11-room Stone Street house of Wilmington Mayor Bruce B. Cameron, severely damaging the next-door structure of E. B. Bugg. Mary Armstrong, wife of renter General Claire H. Armstrong of Camp Davis, suffered from shock and smoke inhalation.

Officials blamed the War Production Board for the beach's inability to fight those fires by denying it the right to buy a capable pump, stating "the community does not serve essential war plants....Because of the housing shortage in Wilmington many scores of war workers...and army officers...dwell there....an indispensable part in this area's war effort."[41]

Larceny, Inc.[42]

"Larceny, Inc....appeared to have been dissolved here yesterday [January 9, 1944] by police with the arrest of five local white men, accused of being the principals and participants in a series of major robberies extending over the past two months." Booked were Robert Rising, Bill Rising, Roy Hendricks, Richard Crocker, and Emory Sloan, all with prior criminal records. Charges included store-breaking, larceny, receiving, and violation of the narcotics law. "...All of them reportedly had a hand in one or more of the crimes. The chain of evidence against them is long and securely forged."

They stole $300–400 in morphine and a pistol and sundries from Southside Drug Store. "The men reportedly used the narcotics obtained by giving each other vigorous shots of the drug" through a hypodermic needle. The case-breaking evidence was Hendricks' footprint. The crew also entered Todd Furniture Company, Batson Motor Company, Saunders Service Station (stole a 22-caliber revolver), and Long Motor Company (eight crates of Coca-Cola).

In July 1944, police arrested Bill Rising and Charles Blair for a $6,500 jewelry theft of Kingoff's Jewelers on Front Street during July. In September, Rising, free on $5,000 bond, was arrested again for breaking into the Carolina Furniture Company. For the Kingoff's job, he received 8–10 years in the state penitentiary. Blair, found not guilty, was held as a Texas fugitive. Aaron Goldberg and David Sinclair served as defense attorneys.

In October, authorities apprehended shipyard employees Sam Lineberry and John Robert Stroud in the Kingoff's robbery. Lineberry, out on parole for second degree murder, posted bond. Stroud, unable to post bond, remained in jail.

Chapter 12

"Those Incredible Doctors" and Other Combat Experiences

A fascinating story unfolded as Wilmington doctor R. T. "Tom" Sinclair, Jr., and his chief nurse, Myrtle Reynolds, served over the battlefields of Europe. Before being activated in the Army Medical Corps Reserve a year prior to Pearl Harbor, Major Sinclair had practiced with Dr. Ernest Bulluck at Bulluck's Hospital. Sinclair organized and later commanded the 51st Field Hospital unit. Once he was the flight surgeon for a B-17 squadron at Hickam Field, Hawaii, commanded by Wilmingtonian Lieutenant Colonel Brooke E. Allen.[1]

At Camp Bowie, Texas, in 1943 Captain Reynolds was among 18 nurses forming the unit. Reynolds, younger than most surgical nurses, "had not the vaguest idea what a field hospital was when I received orders to become chief nurse of one. We sort of knew that once we got a promotion we would be sent overseas."

The mobile hospital concept was simple enough. As battle lines advanced, three small tent units followed by leapfrogging. While one unit was processing wounded for shipment to England, another moved forward. "The idea was to have a front line surgical hospital for definitive treatment of seriously wounded that could not be moved to an evacuation hospital," he stated. In Germany his unit utilized buildings.

The 51st consisted of three platoon teams each with a surgeon, anesthesiologist, one or more surgical nurses, and several enlisted technicians. Treatment of wounded began with a medic on the field, then to the battalion aid station, then evacuation by jeep to the division clearing station a mile behind the front (within enemy firing range). The hospital set up next to the clearing station for the most serious cases: chest, belly, head, and severe leg injuries.

For the invasion of Normandy, France, on June 6, 1944, personnel and equipment boarded three ships. Scattered components exacerbated the chaotic landing on congested and deadly Omaha Beach. Sinclair came ashore on D+2, the nurses on D+4. Getting the necessary supplies in England had been difficult. "We reused everything except the bloody bandages...and very little was thrown away."

A German bunker on the bluff overlooking Omaha housed the initial aid station. "Sixty hours after landing...the 51st Field Hospital handled more than 1,000 casualties," an official report read. "It was a woman's war, too, because nurses came with them." The 51st moved more than 30 times, mostly with the VII Corps in First Army.

After the Falaise Pocket breakout, the 51st encountered prisoners of war. "They dumped hundreds of German prisoners in that place" without any guards. Americans dispensed sulphur pills, morphine, water, and rations, and treated minor wounds. "It was hard to be awfully nice given what had happened, considering what had happened to our boys," said Reynolds. "Later we realized they didn't want to fight; they had been made to fight." The 51st lost one member to a mine, and a nurse and chaplain to severe stress.

The February 1945 issue of *Women's Home Companion* featured Reynolds in an article, "Those Incredible Doctors." "'When we remember this afterward...we'll think of being in tents. Tents are important.'" She also remembered the cold, mud, snow, and ice as causing the most discomfort. Their hospital tents were heated with pot-bellied stoves. "Often it was so cold the drainage from the patients' bodies would freeze before entering the bottles." Having more operating experience than most nurses, she rigged plasma to prepare wounded for surgery in the "shock tent."

She saw few men die, but one patient stood out, "a handsome blond fellow fighting so hard to live. Just couldn't save him." He talked about his wife and family. The first thing they all said was, "nurse, I'm going to get well, right?" They showed photos, if they could talk. "Many of them had a good sense of humor, which was remarkable." This man smothered in his own blood from a chest wound.

"I could have had a C. O. who couldn't handle the job, but he was mighty good to me. I had had good nurses training but not for that sort of thing." A lieutenant colonel arrived to replace Sinclair, who then commanded a sub-unit. Both received the Bronze Star, Reynolds for her overall performance and being the first nurse ashore, and Sinclair for establishing the unit. He believed the 51st was the first across the Rhine River at Remagen.

They endured more than the war experience and fell in love. "It was very unsettling getting that discharge [March 1946] and back into civilian world, making the transition" to her home in Richmond, Virginia. He returned to Wilmington in late 1945, joining Dr. Carter Mebane in partnership (they later established Cape Fear Memorial Hospital). Not long after the two veterans were married.

* * *

Ship Sinkings and Decorated Aviators

Ship sinkings always made the news. Former Wilmingtonian Henry Gore, rescued after 38 hours in a life raft when his merchant ship was torpedoed, visited his brother in 1942. "After I spend a few weeks here, I'm going back again."[2] • "'The first one picked me up off the deck about two feet,'" is how Yeoman Third Class Walter Musial described torpedoes that sank the carrier USS *Wasp* (CV-7) on September 15, 1942, near the Solomons. In the water for three hours, he swam four miles. "'The crew was nice and calm. The last I saw of the *Wasp* she was all afire but the flag was still flying.'"[3]

The destroyer USS *O'Brien* (DD-415) went down with *Wasp*. "I'm glad to be here, but I'm ready for another crack at the Japs," said Boatswains Mate First Class Walter H. Meshaw. When the torpedo hit, Meshaw said, "'It's time we got started, boys.' The whole crew wanted action and 'prayed' to get another chance in the battle....Every man was rescued at sea...one of the miracles of World War II...."[4] • Some men coming home hesitated to talk about combat. Clyde Potter, on furlough in June 1942, when asked about his ship, the carrier USS *Lexington* (CV-2), sunk at the Battle of the Coral Sea, replied, "there's really not much to tell....We simply abandoned and then watched it go down from the deck of a destroyer."[5]

Aviators, particularly fighter pilots, reaped considerable glory, local recognition and the bulk of decorations awarded to area men. Former Atlantic Coast Line employee Captain Roland Wooten, "one of America's most distinguished fighter pilots now," scored a number of firsts in 1943.[*] He was (1) among the first all-American fighter squadron to fly over France and the Low Countries; and (2) among the first Americans to engage the Germans in aerial combat. He was the first American pilot (3) to make a safe return to his base after being shot down by ground fire (North Africa); and (4) "to use the magic of gold in bribing Arab tribesmen to take him through the German lines back to his base." After 130 missions, he spoke here in 1944 for the Fourth War Loan Drive.[6]

By June 1944, my neighbor, Lieutenant James F. Hackler, flying P-47 *Thunderbolt* fighter "Tar Heel Tornado," had flown more than 40 missions over Europe escorting heavy bombers and dive-bombing, including the D-Day invasion. A year later he had received the Croix de Guerre, the Distinguished Flying Cross and Air Medal with 20 Oak Leaf Clusters.

Winter Park resident Captain James R. Starnes, 21, destroyed 12 enemy aircraft in his four P-51 *Mustangs* nicknamed "Tar Heel," flying more

---

[*] In July 1944 Bluethenthal Field ceremonies, three pilots received the DFC: Captain John M. Winkler, and First Lieutenants Duane A. Marshall, Anthony Evans, and Harry W. Tyler. Winkler, Wooten's wingman for 131 missions, already had 14 OLCs. Evans had 12 in P-38s (destroyed four German planes), Marshall seven for 300 combat hours in B-24s.

than 500 combat hours in Europe with the 339th Fighter Group.* He wore
the DFC, Air Medal with 12 OLCs, and the French Croix de Guerre signed
by General Charles DeGaulle. In the New Hanover High School '42
Hanoverian, only the word "ROTC" is listed beside his senior picture. Saving his achievements for after graduation, he retired in 1974 as an air force
colonel jet pilot.

"With the AEF",† a newspaper column in 1944–45, noted James T.
Johnson in January 1944 at Anzio.

> "You can't land a P-40 *Warhawk* on the little airstrips designed for
> the artillery's tiny *Cub* spotting planes. But Lt. Johnson did. You cer-
> tainly can't take a *Warhawk* off from such a field. But Johnson did." And
> who is Johnson? He's a '23-year old Wilmington, N.C., boy who became
> "the first fighter pilot to land on the new Anzio beachhead south of Rome."
>
> His flight had just bombed Nazi troops and come over to patrol the
> beachhead when his engine began to sputter. He spotted the tiny tempo-
> rary strip...."I had just stepped out of the plane when guns started open-
> ing up all around me....It seemed like a good place to get out of so I
> borrowed a screw driver and a pair of pliers and fixed up that coolant
> leak...." By practically lifting her off the end with his hands he got the
> plane into the air and back to base.[7]

"In Wilmington, Johnson's relatives were delighted to learn [this]
news...." The NHHS graduate "was a popular youth in local social circles."

By August 1944, First Lieutenant Pelton W. "Mickey" Ellis, 23, had logged
50-plus missions in his P-38 *Lightning* fighter, over Hungary, France, Rumania, Bulgaria, Italy, and Yugoslavia. Ellis enjoyed bombing and strafing more
than aerial combat, although he got an Me-410 over Austria one day when his
formation downed 21 without a loss.[8] ● From the "Trouble Shooter Squadron"
of the 9th Air Force Hun Hunter Group: "It took a call for help from a fighter
pilot over Caen [France] to lead him to the enemy, but a 'flash of a ship in the
clouds' was enough to insure Captain Maurice L. Martin a 'kill,'" an Me-109.
Flying his P-47 "Turbo Second" he heard his buddy radio, "'Help me. There
are four on my tail and I'm out of ammunition.'"[9]

Captain Victor N. Curtis and fellow pilots of his P-47 group "blazed a
trail of destruction behind enemy lines in France recently as they carried out
a daring low level attack on a German airfield and transportation facilities."

---

* Starnes killed six Focke-Wulf Fw-190 and Messerschmitt Me-109 fighters in the air, and six
  aircraft on the ground, qualifying him as an "Ace." His achievement is honored at the Mighty
  Eighth Air Force Museum in Savannah, Ga. A member of my church, Starnes supported the
  Normandy landings but mostly escorted bomber missions. The most memorable: a May 1944 B-
  17 run to Pozen, Poland ("as far as Wilmington to Boston and back, and the nearest place you
  could land would be Wilmington"), where he snuck behind and downed an unsuspecting Fw-190.
  [Interview with Starnes, November 28, 2003]

† Allied Expeditionary Force in Europe.

Curtis and company destroyed nine enemy planes, 60 army vehicles, 39 freight cars, nine locomotives, and an electric power plant. They damaged 125 freight cars, 31 trucks and 21 locomotives."[10]

Aviation Radioman Second Class George A. Fowler received the DFC for action in the Philippines' Sibuyan Sea in October 1944 when his SB2C *Helldiver* pilot scored a direct hit on an IJN *Atago* class cruiser. Fowler flew 36 combat missions off the carrier USS *Essex* (CV-9). ● Marine Captain Howard M. Conner, husband of Mary Sell Conner, in 1943 was stranded on top of his crashed plane submerged on a reef for 10 days in the Solomons. The Guadalcanal veteran survived on two chocolate bars, but suffered from malaria and exposure.

Major John A. Carey relayed a fighter pilot's viewpoint from Supreme Allied Headquarters in England over NBC's "Army Hour" radio show. The squadron leader fought in the North Africa-Mediterranean theater for two years and was in four invasions, and earned the Purple Heart and Silver Star for landing behind enemy lines in Tunisia and capturing 97 Germans and Italians. ● Airman Staff Sergeant S. Davis Polvogt received the DFC and Purple Heart during the capture of the Marshall and Gilbert Islands. Although hit by flak over the target, he reassured his wife it was "'nothing but a bad bump and cut on the ear drum'...'fine and still flying, so don't worry.'"[11]

When Cliff Morris, Jr., received his army wings and commission in February 1943, his choice was medium bombers.[12] But "Once I got into [a B-17] I fell in love with it. If I was flying some other aircraft I probably wouldn't be alive today. It could take a lot of battle damage and come back." Cliff flew the refurbished and famous *Flying Fortress* "Memphis Belle" after its war bond drive.

Morris' real test came with the 32nd Squadron, 301st Bomb Group, 15th Air Force, from 1944–45 in North Africa and Foggia and Luchera, Italy. The target of his first mission from Italy, on June 4, 1944, was a railroad bridge viaduct at Anthera in Southern France to deter the Germans from moving troops to the Normandy beachhead. After a December 11 mission, his flak-crippled plane made an emergency landing in Rumania on a Soviet airfield. The bomber was so badly damaged it couldn't be flown again, but no one was injured. The Soviets turned him over to the U.S. military mission in Bucharest which was repatriating POWs and air crews, and flew them to Foggia. Called an "evadee," he spent Christmas day with Rumanian King Michael IV.

Morris flew 50 missions. "I had some real characters but they were good." Once he and crew reached their base on December 27, "they had a crop of stories to tell...." He neither lost a crew member nor had one wounded, and received the DFC and Air Medal with two OLCs.

Dangerous Episodes

Fred Sternberger was drafted in January 1944. Brother Solomon closed his law office, volunteered, and became a military policeman. Brother Harold entered the draft at 38 in 1942 but stayed in only six months. Lawyer Bill Rhodes went with him, was rejected for OCS, and reopened his law office. The draft got him later.

A loader/cannoneer in Company D, 24th Tank Battalion, 13th Armored Division, Fred landed in France in January 1945.* Through the battles of Rhineland and Central Europe, his unit drove M5 Stuart and brand-new M24 Chaffee tanks. Once his machine ran up on a German 88mm antitank gun at point-blank range. "Oh my God, this is it." But it had been knocked out. Accompanying several others on a souvenir hunt, Fred encountered about 250 Germans waving a white flag. "They didn't give me any trouble," and he released them to MPs. His tank commander nominated him for the Silver Star but it didn't go through.[13]

Frederick B. Sternberger and his M24 tank, "San Joachim," Germany, 1945.

Frederick B. Sternberger

Jim Stokley, serving with the 191st Signal Repair Company in India and China, in 1945 wrote:

> I have not seen war but I have seen the aftermath of war and it isn't pretty. Towns here leveled to the ground, nothing standing but a few charred sticks....Great holes showed where the shells had fallen....Unexploded shells...a few dead Japs were lying around, a booby trap went off nearby and blew a car all to pieces, and the road was torn up....We saw what used to be a large temple. Standing in the middle of the temple with the roof scattered around her feet was a huge statue of Buddha about 20 feet high with the bright gilt head shining in the sunlight. The only remainder of the temple was the statue and the scattered roof....We took a break near a hillside where the Japs had dug in....It looked like it took years to get them out of their holes.[14]

---

* Sternberger's car bears the North Carolina plate "24THTKBN."

Three Wilmington area men "played roles in one of the most romantic and dangerous episodes of the war against Japan." Yeoman First Class Marvin B. Murphy, Jr., brother of schoolmate Kenneth Murphy, W. S. Rourk, Jr., and Boatswains Mate First Class G. C. West belonged to a group of navy guerillas, intelligence agents, and weather observers behind the lines. They supplied Allied commands with weather reports and intelligence on movements of ships, troops, and supplies. The SACO group (Sino-American Co-Operative Organization) became a "fighting unit, killing Japs, blowing up trains, raiding Jap outposts....Adept at Chinese disguises and aided by Chinese assistants, [they] slipped through enemy lines when they chose."[15]

"Along the roads we could see German graves with their helmets on a cross," wrote Sergeant John Burney, Jr., of Company A, 254th Infantry Regiment, 63rd Division. "Some were not even buried for there were booby traps on them. I have a German helmet I am going to send Louis [his brother] if I can.* The people in the U.S. don't know how lucky they are. They should kneel down once a day and kiss the ground."[16] Later, "I led the first patrol that went out from our company. I was not scared while I was out there. When I came back and thought about it, that's when it scares you."[17]

Later, "I am now in a general hospital. You don't hear any artillery or machine gun fire....I have a light case of trench foot. We were pinned down in a ditch filled with water and ice by a Jerry machine gun. We stayed there for 8 hours. I have never been so cold in all my life. I [*sic*] fingers got so cold I threw away my rifle for I couldn't fire it."[18] (Also seriously wounded earlier, he failed to tell his parents.) "I can't see how the scrapnal [*sic*] did not break any bones. I kinda wish I did have a broken bone so I would be able to come home. I hope I have fired my last shot. I have the Purple Heart and two clusters."[19]

Brothers Nichalos "Nick" and George Fokakis entered the army together in August 1943. Sergeant George served in the 127th Infantry Regiment, 32nd Infantry Division, the unit receiving General Tomoyuki Yamashita's surrender. Sergeant Nick received the Bronze Star with the 63rd Infantry Regiment, 61st Infantry Division. Both fought in New Guinea and the Philippines.[20]

"Besides having to worry about the Japanese," George recalled, "you had to worry about the chiggers, bloodworms, leeches, diseases, varmints,

---

* Neither can remember if Burney, my hero and dear friend, sent Louis the helmet. But John's home is loaded with memorabilia including his M1 rifle and German pistols. John fought against Werner T. Hessen three times, finally meeting him at the unveiling of a joint German-U.S. memorial to the Battle of Jebsheim, France. Burney fought alongside the French artist and armored soldier Jean Suard, who later painted several paintings of John's unit, which he displays. Dedicated to his comrades, he decorates self and vehicles with 63rd Division reminders.

and having food. The only way we got food was by plane." Oppressive jungle heat, high humidity, swamps, jungle rot, frequent rain, caused constant sweating and wet feet. Water purification tablets purified stream water. Rats, snakes and wild boars created fear, havoc and noise, especially at night when sounds resounded.[21]

Lacking smokeless powder, U.S. forces did little night fighting, but not the Japs. Fighting was man-to-man as mortars and artillery proved ineffective in thick jungle. Nick remembered, "the kuna grass was so high and tough it would take sometimes almost eight hours to go one mile. You had to go by compass. You could have Japs in one end of the field and us in the other and neither knew it." George contracted malaria and Nick typhus fever, hospitalizing him for a year. "Leyte was hell," but "not much different from fighting in New Guinea."

George Fokakis (hatless), *center*, 127th Infantry Regiment, 32nd Infantry Division, on the Villa Verde Trail on Luzon, Philippines, summer 1945.

George Fokakis

Flight Officer John A. Gorman, 22, "Wilmington's glider pilot hero," landed in France on D-Day, "eluded the Germans only to be forced to surrender, later escaped and returned to the beachhead with 30 Nazi prisoners...." On June 24, 1944, his parents learned of his exploits when they received recordings of his NBC interview in London. The "handsome young gliderman," when asked about being the pilot of the eighth glider in the first squadron to have landed in France, replied, "'I guess it was quite an honor, but there were a few times when I had rather have been in Wilmington, North Carolina.'"[22]

Former shipyard worker Staff Sergeant George Browder, 11th Airborne Division, "is one of the reasons why Japanese commit *hari-kari*. They can't kill him." The squad leader in early 1945 "was the first American soldier on Nichols Field [Philippines] when his unit led the advance....A 20mm Japanese gun promptly pinned him down. Then the Japs hit him the first time...near his left eye." Patched up, he returned to lead action against a pillbox and was hit by shrapnel. After medical attention, he went back again.[23]

"Bhamo, Burma, Easter 1945. I was in the battle to take Bhamo from the Japs. Dec 1944 was a nasty affair. The Chinese 38th Div lost 231. I counted them."—Jack Hart's handwritten notes on a faded photograph. Arriving in the United States, he had lost 40 pounds after almost 18 months of jungle fighting.[24] • Friends of medic Private First Class George Tilley saw him in a 1943 theater newsreel on the Sicily campaign with recuperating wounded soldiers. "The newsreel proved prophetic," for shortly afterwards Tilley was wounded.[25]

The June 4, 1942, *Morning Star* page one headline "Alaskan Naval Base Twice Bombed by Japanese" added, "Wilmington Boy at Dutch Harbor." He was navy yeoman Thomas Cowen James, 23, previously employed by the Atlantic Coast Line.[26] • Flying out of Bluethenthal Field, Sergeant Robert Edwards crewed a B-24 bomber that sank an enemy submarine off the Atlantic Coast in 1942. The pilot said, "The first two were direct hits on the conning tower. It looked like a clay pigeon."[27] • Two riflemen of the 337th Infantry Regiment, 85th Infantry Division, drew commendations for taking the 3,000-foot Mount Pratone in Italy's Gothic Line: Privates First Class Hilbert V. Hayes, and James M. Hemminger, Jr. They "dug German soldiers out of elaborate concrete pillboxes and earthworks...overcoming great obstacles made of mud, rain, wind and cold, and living and fighting on the meager supplies mules and men carry up to them on their backs."[28]

Ensign Robert E. Calder, Jr., served with underwater demolition teams at Normandy, southern France, Anguar, Peleliu, Iwo Jima, Lingayen, Zambales, Okinawa, Tsugen Shima, Kerama Retto, Saipan, Tinian, and in the occupation of Japan. The casualty rate for his "sailors in trunks" unit was 40 percent at Normandy. • "Two of the 11 German planes destroyed by American airmen over Italy yesterday [January 26, 1944] went down before the guns of a Wilmingtonian, Lt. Gaston Ward Callum, a member of the famous Flying Skull Squadron," reported the Associated Press.[29] • Kwajalein Atoll, AP: Marine Tech Sergeant Albert B. Haynes, five minutes after landing on Namur, built a communications center "over the bodies of dead Japs."[30]

While walking down Front Street in June 1946, Hugh M. Morton spied the Royal Theater's marquee message: "Combat Scenes from the Pacific War—Fox *Movietone News*," accompanying the documentary *Appointment in Tokyo*. A combat newsreel cameraman with the army's 161st Signal Photo Company attached to the 25th and 37th Infantry Divisions, Morton shot pictures of the Philippines Campaign on Luzon, Leyte and Corregidor, and earlier on Bougainville. He bought a ticket to see what he had filmed on March 18, 1945, the day he was wounded on Luzon. "He was one jump ahead of other theater-goers," the newpaper stated, because "he took a good portion of the battle action." A comrade had brought him mail in a field hospital. The first letter read to him was his mother's report that his father, Julian W. Morton, died of a heart attack on March 1. "It was the low point of Hugh's life." Still bandaged, he flew home on emergency furlough.[31] ● Lieutenant Commander Benjamin E. Adams, Jr. Skipper of the submarine USS *Rasher* (SS-269), received the Presidential Unit Citation "for sinking or damaging 'thousands of tons' of shipping in Japanese-controlled water."[32]

Warrant Officer Aaron May, 14th Armored Division, fought in the Battle of the Bulge and helped liberate the Dachau concentration camp, and was ticketed for the Pacific when the war ended. ● Jack Hufham enlisted in the navy "underage" at 17.* "I got one day of vacation, Monday." His brother-in-law Billy Spencer, a B-24 *Liberator* pilot, advised him to join the air force. Jack's assignment was the USS *Cross* (DE-448) which reached Okinawa on June 1, 1945.[33] ● North Carolina student Leon Stein was commissioned while in college in 1944. For action on the USS LST-703 at Balikpapau, Borneo, in 1945, he received the Bronze Star. He also participated in landings on Leyte, Mindoro, and Luzon, Philippines.[34]

Fletcher Taylor found this magazine photograph of North Front and Grace Sts. before landing on D-Day in Normandy. He considered it a good omen and kept it throughout his European battles. Note creases where he folded it.

Undated *Wilmington Morning Star*

---

* Jack's grandfather was a Confederate soldier, his father was in the navy in WWI, and his son served in the navy during the Persian Gulf War.

The night before landing at Normandy on D-Day, Fletcher Taylor wondered about his chances. "Then homesickness struck. It was quiet, and in an effort to distract himself, he picked up one of several magazines lying around. It opened to a picture of a bustling downtown scene. Taylor was stunned. 'I said, My God, this is my hometown.'" The photo was of Front Street in Wilmington. "Taylor decided the picture was a good omen. He ripped out the picture, took it to shore, and carried it through France, Belgium, and Germany to home." He didn't recall the magazine's name but it was in a feature "Our Main Streets."[35]

Skinny Pennington, whose family owned the Flying Service at Bluethenthal Field, became an air force civilian ferry pilot in 1942. In May he married Anna Feenstra and took her with him around the country. When he left for China as an active duty major she returned to Wilmington in January 1945 by train with her new son. Skinny flew C-54 transports over "the Hump" in the Himalayas from India, then was stationed in Kunming. In good weather he could fly at 12,000 feet, in bad the flying altitude was 18,000 "or you hit a mountain, the aluminum trail." The China wing lost 40 percent of its aircraft. "You could see them plastered on the side of the mountains."[36]

One of the few in the Coast Guard was Johnny Van B. Metts, whose father headed the state's Selective Service.[37] "My father wanted to draft me No. 1." In October 1941, with small boat experience and competitive examination only, he departed for a ship without training. His first was the USCGC *Dione,* a small rum runner. Promoted to lieutenant commander, he served on the USCGC *Menhadin* escorting cargo ships and tankers in the Caribbean, the USCGC *E.M. Messick*, and the frigate USCGC *Dearborn* in the North Atlantic. *Dearborn,* homeported in Argentia, experienced a high suicide rate sitting on station in the middle of ocean and sending weather reports. "The only reason we weren't attacked is because the Germans probably had our weather codes and were using our information."

Sailor Carl J. Cunningham in August 1942 wrote "a graphic account" of the ongoing Solomons Campaign. "I was lucky enough to survive without a scratch the big battle....The ship I was on shot down five Jap planes....Boy, was I scared—and how!....I have seen the Jap reports of the battle. Do not believe them...."[38] ● After landing in the Solomons on August 7, 1942, Sergeant L. B. Harper of the 1st Battalion, 2d Marines, 2d Marine Division, earned six campaign and service bars and the Purple Heart. Snipers, his main worry, "'...nearly blew my head off when I lighted a cigarette on the island one night,'" his "'closest shave. I picked off six myself,'" four in the trees and two on the ground.[39]

* * *

"This One Last Glimpse of War"[40]

While at North Carolina, Allan Strange got his draft notice on Christmas Eve, 1942. He joined Battery C, 358th Field Artillery Battalion (105mm-howitzers), 95th Infantry Division fighting with General George Patton's Third Army in France, the Rhineland, and Central Europe. "When you are winning the way we were, morale was way up." Strange moved into the line on October 20, 1944, before Metz, France, "the most heavily fortified city in Europe," advancing on the Maginot Line.

His memoir continued. "Of course it was raining which it was every night, but we had boiled chicken that night and the rain would replenish the gravy when it got low." In Altforweiler "we fired over the Saar River and into the town of Saarlautern. It was in this position that we lost three of our forward observers....The enemy had railway guns, emplaced 88s [88mm], and self propelled guns with which they bombarded us constantly. One day they threw 6,000 shells and we were given the order to throw back five times as many."

[About December 12] "They threw in a terrific barrage and our position was bracketed....Two American P-47s came over and dropped two 500-pound bombs about 300 yards from our gun. The explosion killed five men....That sort of accident makes a guy a trifle mad. Our captain would stand up and shake his fist and curse the American planes as they came over....We learned not to trust any plane and hit the mud when any came over.

From left, soldiers Samuel N. Sprunt, Charles Johnson, and Allan Taylor Strange with Mrs. J. Laurence Sprunt, 1943.

Allan Taylor Strange

"While we were in this position the Ardennes Bulge started and we had to displace to the rear or just bluntly retreat....[The 95th] had about 60 percent casualties and couldn't be sent....Our commanding officers had chosen men to stay and fight to the last and also the men to retreat and form a new division when we were wiped out. We were thankful that the expected attack never materialized."

January 29, 1945, near Bastogne, Belgium—"The coldest night I ever spent. The temperature was -4 degrees and there was a foot of snow....By morning we were about frozen. And the doughboys moved up in open trucks. How they stood it I'll never know." Then came his first time off the line in 103 days. At the Roer River, "it was about this time I heard that

[Wilmingtonian] Harold Alexius was missing and his name went out on many a shell when I was firing. I started looking at all the dead doughboys to see if one could be Harold."

After crossing the Rhine, Strange wrote, "in about two weeks of the toughest fighting we had yet encountered we swept through the cities of Hamm, Dortmund, Soest, etc. We were going rapidly now and the end was in sight....We moved positions every day and liberated at least half a million slave laborers....The slaves would stand around while we ate and what we threw in the garbage can they would go after with both hands flying....We were in the center of Nazi land now and even the 15-year-old kids would shoot at you from the windows....When someone shoots your buddy you don't think about age, sex or health, and we put them to the sword.

"...The German army is a looting, pillaging army but they can't hold a candle to the army of the USA. When we got through with their houses there just wasn't anything left to loot....We then kicked the folks out into the street and slept in their beds. The old women would run around calling us swine and dogs. But they asked for it....The doughboys were even worse....After a certain period on the line against the *SS* troops they just forgot to take any prisoners.

"Our loudspeakers would tell the German soldiers to lay down their arms and we would treat them fairly. The doughboys' idea of fairness is something they didn't expect....The snipers would dress like priests and stay behind and shoot our doughs....The only difference between our soldiers and any others is that once a prisoner is in a prison camp he is treated fairly decent.

"We fired our last shot in combat at Applebech near Dortmund on April the 14th. We then moved into Munster for Allied military government work." The 35th Infantry Division relieved the 95th at Roxel, and then from Le Havre on June 22, "with this one last glimpse of war at its worst, we slipped into the twilight and the English Channel bound at last for home."

* * *

Wilmington's 252nd Coast Artillery, and Company I of the 120th Infantry[41]

Fuller Sistrunk was one of many boys with pre-war service in the local 252nd Coast Artillery Regiment of the North Carolina National Guard or Wilmington Light Infantry. Dry-Ponder Fuller, who hung around Hall's Drug Store owned by Mike Hall, his company executive officer, drove a heavy prime mover (for towed 155mm guns) in the 136-man Battery A of the 252nd.* Other units were located throughout Southeastern North Carolina. The

---

* The 252nd's pre-war headquarters is now the Cape Fear Museum. Battery A's headquarters was at 5th and Market in the old WLI building.

252nd consisted of three battalions, with one (Battery A) of the 1st Battalion's two firing batteries in Wilmington and the other in Lumberton.

The WLI served in the Civil War and World War I, but by the late 1930s its military functions had disbanded. Members continued it as a social club and civic organization, membership in the 252nd a prerequisite. Virtually all Battery A men belonged. "They had no idea in the world they were ever going to war." Activated on September 16, 1940, the 252nd trained for more than one year at Fort Screvin, Georgia, setting up their 155mm's on Tybee Beach. Each firing battery, augmented by reservists, now had 253 men.

In February 1942 Battery A, commanded by Wilmington Colonel C. D. Cunningham with First Sergeant Sistrunk, protected the world's largest oil refinery on Aruba in the Caribbean. German submarines set the refinery afire. Battery A fired back and is credited with sinking two.[*] Fuller became sergeant major of the headquarters battalion. In 1943 the 252nd was disbanded "and the individuals shipped wherever the whims of the army have determined." Some had been killed. About half of the battalion became officers. Fuller was reassigned to lead a battery in the 199th Field Artillery Battalion, which landed on Omaha Beach on D+2 and fought to Salzburg, Austria, with the 4th Armored Division. In August 1945 he transferred to the air force and completed his career.

The National Guard 120th Infantry merged into the 30th Infantry Division, praised by General Lawton Collins for holding the line of the German Seventh Army near Mortain, France. He singled out the 120th's action, as did the August 21 issue of *Time* magazine.

The 120th had fought in Italy and later landed in Normandy several days after D-Day. With the VII Corps, they helped capture Cherbourg, spearheaded the Normandy breakout, broke through the Siegfried Line, captured Cologne and Aix-la-Chappelle, closed the pincer from the south around the industrialized Ruhr, and then met the Soviet forces (the first corps to do so) on the Elbe River.[†]

First Sergeant John I. Kelly reported the whereabouts of Company I men in France, and others kept in touch later from Okinawa. In May 1945 army First Lieutenant James H. Morse wrote, "'I am in a cave in the front line on Okinawa, just outside the city of Naha. We are really giving the little

---

[*] Fuller displays a lithograph by German artist Oskar Dolhart of the U-boat firing on Aruba. He found it in a drawer in Nantes, France. The 252nd has annual reunions here.

[†] At least four Wilmington 120th men were killed in action. Private Vivian G. "Biddie" Brown, in Italy in 1944; First Lieutenant Porter Lee Hufham, in France in 1944; Private John T. Jordan, in Germany in 1944; and Technical Sergeant Grover D. Watson, in Belgium in 1945. At least four from the 252nd died: Private First Class James Carr Saunders, in Aruba in 1942; Master Sergeant Emmett Allen, in South America; Second Lieutenant Leroy C. Robertson, Jr., in Surinam in 1943; and Private Ernest L. Rogers, in Germany in 1945.

yellow devils a fit, and hope before too long we can finish them off....Miss Wilmington and hope soon to be on Front Street again.'" Originally activated with the 120th, James assaulted Okinawa on April 1 after combat on other islands.[42]

Army First Lieutenant Leon F. Andrews led a tank column against Yonabaru on Okinawa, "in some of that campaign's hardest fighting," reported a United Press dispatch. NHHS graduate and ACL employee Andrews served in the 252nd and on Leyte. He had not been home in two and one-half years. His brother, First Lieutenant James L. Andrews, received the Bronze Star and Purple Heart for New Guinea and Luzon.[43]

* * *

William G. "Billy" Broadfoot, Jr.
459th Fighter Squadron, Burma-India[44]

Billy flew the twin-engine P-38 *Lightning* out of Chittagong and Rumkhapalong, India, from late 1943 to February 1945. The 459th, mostly under British command, maintained 20 pilots, but lost 30 in combat. Most of

Capt. William G. "Billy" Broadfoot, Jr., in cockpit of his P-38 *Lightning* fighter "Hell's Belles," India, 1944.

William G. Broadfoot, Jr.

his 125 combat missions were over Burma. His four P-38 machines each bore the nickname *Hell's Belles*.

"I had gotten good at what I was doing. I knew where all the ack-ack nests were. I didn't want to go back to the States." This determination was emphatic in a May 1944 letter to his parents about requesting to remain. "First, I know that I shouldn't be going home. I haven't even hit my stride....Second, you don't jump off a sure-fire winner in the middle of the race. This is the hottest squadron in combat....Each time you come back you have more reason to go back again, usually a grudge against some guy that came too close."[45]

The "Twin Dragon" squadron's history book recorded a number of Broadfoot-led missions, including the March 17, 1944, mission of 12 planes escorting B-24 bombers to Chauk and Lanywa oil installations. On April 15, "[He] indicated 450 mph on his way down [to target], and the other pilots stuck close to his tail. With the stick in his lap, he whizzed across the field, guns blazing, and was rewarded with seeing an *Oscar* in flames." The book concluded,

> It has been many years now, almost a lifetime....There seems to be a lingering sentiment that brings on memories: of hot, steamy days when one could almost fry an egg on the runway; of monsoon seasons with rains that fell unabated for weeks...of showers made of 55-gallon drums filled with rainwater or by bearers with water from nearby brackish pol-luted ponds; and of mosquito nets hung over wooden-framed cots strung with tough hemp rope, the nets to be drawn religiously each night to prevent that scourge of malaria which almost grounded a squadron....
>
> Members of the "single-engine club" [home on one] will never forget their special experiences, particularly Broadfoot who had three...from air battles deep in enemy territory....During squadron reunions when they gather to fight the Burma Campaign once again, they realize that they, particularly the pilots, were bonded together forevermore during the greatest adventure of their young lives.

The toughest Japanese fighter Billy faced was the *Tojo* (built like the P-47). "One day I never will forget. I was flying along and there dead ahead of me was a *Tojo* headed for me. I maneuvered out of the way, and saw it was a P-47 with a *Tojo* on his tail. The Japs were good airmen, but not as well trained as our pilots" by then. One day on patrol his flight came across a formation of single-engine planes painted all black. After maneuvering and gunfire, no hits were confirmed, and both sides broke off. "We looked for them when we went out, but never saw them again."

My neighbor, Lieutenant Colonel Broadfoot, came home to Forest Hills in March 1945 with an array of medals after 22 months in India-Burma: Silver Star ("for gallantry in action on fighter raids deep in enemy-held territory in Burma"), DFC, Air Medal, and British DFC ("for his leadership in American air attacks against the Japanese").

"Twin Dragon Victories: Broadfoot, William G."

Date	Confirmed		Probable		Damaged	
	Air	Ground	Air	Ground	Air	Ground
2Apr44		1 *Lily*				
15Apr44		1 *Oscar*				
16Apr44		½ *Betty*				
10May44				1 S/E		1 S/E
18May44		1 Bomber				
23May44						2 *Oscar*
6Jun44						3 *Oscar*
20Oct44	1 *Oscar*					
4Nov44						2 *Oscar*
13Nov44	½ *Tojo*					

Total confirmed 6 (4 solo, 2½)

Lily = Kawasaki Ki-48 twin-engine bomber
Oscar = Nakajima Ki-43 Hayabusa single engine fighter
Betty = Mitsubishi G4M twin-engine bomber
Tojo = Nakajima Ki-44 Shoki single engine fighter
S/E = Single engine aircraft

While away, some men tried maintaining interest in family business to feel needed and comfortably pull the umbilical cord. From India, Billy offered advice or responded to suggestions. In December 1943 he was involved in selling his car and decorating his parents' house. "You folks go right ahead and manage my affairs. I don't believe I will ever suffer for it."[46] By May 1944 his Buick was still unsold. "Make sure that it doesn't depreciate at the rate you enter on the books or I'll owe you money...." Business included his St. James Episcopal Church. "I took the Easter contribution envelope that Daddy sent me and sent Morty [Reverend Mortimer] Glover a five rupee note 'to use as he sees fit.'"[47]

No matter how distant, they cared not to be *that far* from business-as-usual on the home front.

Chapter 13

The Worthiest of Intentions

Early in the war the Wilmington Star-News *staked out an ambitious wish list for peacetime, reiterating the program periodically until overtaken by the war effort.*[1] *It included:*

—*Consolidated city-county government under council-manager administration*
—*Public port terminals*
—*Seaside highway from Wrightsville Beach to Bald Head Island*
—*Extension of city limits*
—*35-foot Cape Fear River channel, widening turning basin, with ship lanes into industrial sites along eastern bank south of Wilmington*
—*Paved river road to Southport*
—*United industrial and resort promotional agency, supported by one county-wide tax*
—*Shipyards and drydocks*
—*Negro health center for Southeastern North Carolina, developed around Community Hospital*
—*Adequate hospital facilities for whites*
—*Junior high school*

The worthiest of civic and economic intentions, this list represented serious progressive thinking and grew into lofty community goals for the postwar era. Each required governmental action or encouragement. Some took longer than others to be accomplished, if they ever were.

The impression was thinkers looked backwards to create that which never existed, as if to mollify past neglect, or reconstruct on old foundations that time, technology, and natural growth had swiftly passed.

* * *

Local Government

Hargrove Bellamy, who took office in May 1941 as the first mayor under the city's council-manager government, resigned to accept an army major's commission in November 1942. Mayor Pro-tem Edgar L. Yow became mayor until replaced by Councilman Bruce B. Cameron in March 1943. Cameron died suddenly on a trip in Philadelphia, Pennsylvania, on July 17, 1944, and was succeeded by Ronald W. Lane, owner of three drug stores.*

The city in 1942 bought $550,000 in war insurance to cover city-owned property. The 1942–43 city budget reflected "some idea of Wilmington's improving economic situation" and "because assessable valuations have advanced so greatly the council has been able to reduce the tax rate 10 cents," plus providing a $20 per month city employee pay raise.[2] At mid-1943, the county's assets totaled $5,910,604, half being the school system. With revenues exceeding expectations substantially, "New Hanover County is in the best financial condition it has enjoyed in many years."[3] At the same time, because of "war-born prosperity," the city "'is definitely passing the corner which prosperity was just around the Depression years.'"[4]

Mayor Cameron in 1943 named a committee "to work together to further harmony and promote cooperation between the white and Negro races here," consisting of chairman Reverend Sankey Lee Blanton, Dr. John T. Hoggard, A. C. Nichols, Wilbur Dosher, L. J. Poisson, and John E. Hope; and Negroes Dr. Foster F. Burnett, Reverend R. Irving Boone, E. M. Butler, Dr. L. W. Upperman, Reverend H. B. Shaw, J. Otis Smith, and L. C. Berry.[5]

The April 1943 city primary election drew only 5 percent (411) of registered voters, "conceding that no vital issue was at stake....Perhaps the best way to arouse the people to their obligation to participate in war activities would be for an enemy bomb to drop at their busiest intersection...."[6] By May 1944, 13,841 Democrats and 410 Republicans had registered, a gain of approximately 2,000 to 100. That year President Franklin D. Roosevelt topped Republican Thomas E. Dewey in the county 9,431 to 1,820, a record turnout. Both Southeastern North Carolina and the state went heavily for Roosevelt.

The county's 1944–45 budget of $1,214,204 included a higher amount for schools caused by the elimination of federal assistance and an increase in Negro teachers' salaries. The 1944 county value of real and personal property climbed to $74,955,941, up $4.47 million from 1943. Holdings of white citizens were $54,760,383; Negroes, $2,809,558; corporations, $13,160,818. County residents owned 202 horses and 359 mules, 946 milk cows, and 9,596

---

* "In the passing of your distinguished husband, Camp Davis mourns its best and staunchest friend....Hearts will be saddened all over the world" by servicemen who trained near Wilmington. [Colonel Adam E. Potts to Mrs. Bruce B. Cameron quoted in the Camp Davis *AA Barrage*, July 22, 1944] Nearly 1,000 persons attended his funeral.

cars. The September 1945 property valuation was $77.8 million, including $62.6 million in real estate. The January 1944 article "War-Boom City Strengthens Finances" in *The National Municipal Review* complimented Wilmington for "reserving its war-boom surpluses for post-war needs."[7]

County commissioners rejected a 1943 proposal for Sunday horse racing at Legion Stadium after the Ministerial Association strongly disapproved. Public welfare aid increased from an average of $14.10 to $17.50 monthly per recipient. In the 1944–45 year the number of needy receiving benefits rose from 496 to 513. The 184-year-old Wilmington library's book circulation for 1944 was its heaviest ever: 167,216 volumes. The library, located in City Hall, contained 37,572 books. The Negro branch library of 4,500 books moved from 8th and Princess to 6th and Red Cross in February 1945.

Unhesitating in tackling heavy wartime issues, the city warned in 1945: The city dog catcher began his annual rounds looking for dogs not wearing rabies tags, banishing to the pound those without.

* * *

Principal Wartime Officials

Federal

U.S. Senators: Josiah W. Bailey (–January 1945); Clyde D. Hoey (1945–); Robert D. Reynolds

U.S. Congressman: J. Bayard Clark, Graham A. Barden

U.S. Employment Service: Felix A. Scroggs

Postmaster: Wilbur Dosher

State of North Carolina

Governor: J. Melville Broughton (1941–45), R. Gregg Cherry (1945–)

State Senators: Rivers D. Johnson, Warsaw; J. E. L. Wade, Wilmington

State Representative: R. M. Kermon, Wilmington

Wilmington

Mayor: Hargrove Bellamy (–June 1942), Edgar L. Yow (June 1942–June 1943), Bruce B. Cameron (June 1943–July 17, 1944); W. Ronald Lane (July 1944–)

City Manager: James G. Wallace, A. C. Nichols (August 1942–45), James R. Benson (acting 1944–45; 1945–)

Fire Chief: Ludie Croom

Police Chief: C. H. Casteen

Director, Office of Civilian Defense: C. David Jones

Housing Authority, City of Wilmington: Henry R. Emory

City Attorney: W. B. Campbell

City Council (besides the mayors)

Robert Legwin, Garland S. Currin, Robert R. Romeo, Walter E. Yopp, J. E. L. Wade

New Hanover County
Chairman, County Board of Commissioners: Addison Hewlett
Clerk of Court: August L. Meyland
Register of Deeds: A. B. Rhodes
County Sheriff: C. David Jones
Treasurer, Auditor, County Accountant: John A. Orrell
Tax Supervisor: Addison Hewlett
Tax Collector: C. R. Moore
Coroner: Asa W. Allen
Superintendent of Health: A. H. Elliott, MD
Superintendent of Schools: H. M. Roland
Superintendent of Public Welfare: J. R. Hollis
Home Demonstration Agent: Ann Mason
Farm Demonstration Agent: Robert W. Galphin
Chairman, Board of Education: Dr. John T. Hoggard
Chairman, Board of Elections: H. G. Carney
Game Warden: Edgar Nicholson
County Attorney: Marsden Bellamy
Judge of Recorder's Court: H. Winfield Smith
Solicitor of Recorder's Court: J. A. McNorton

Commissioners (besides the chairman)
Harry R. Gardner, George W. Trask, Louis J. Coleman, James M. Hall, L. W. Todd
Greater Wilmington Chamber of Commerce, executive secretary: F. O. Fockler, Walter J. Cartier

* * *

Transportation

Supporting the war effort often boiled down to asking citizens not to do things to which they were accustomed, or where common sense would dictate denying oneself. City bus operator Tide Water Power Company asked "pleasure" riders to stay off the buses during hours when they were needed to transport war workers. Officials on December 1942 asked motorists to pick up soldiers looking for rides. "There is no perceptible increase in gas consumption with an additional passenger or two aboard...."[8] Two years later the situation remained. With Camp Davis closed, more Camp Lejeune and Cherry Point men visited the area even with inadequate transportation, forcing long hours waiting for a bus or thumbing a ride.[9]

The newspaper in January 1943 editorialized against the "grievous bottlenecks" of transportation, acknowledging attempts to acquire buses (blame the bureaucrats) and rolling stock (unavailable). The situation by March 1945 was "growing no better fast." Workers heading home between

4–6 p.m. "seldom find standing room on buses, because available space...is occupied for the most part by women...shopping and marketing...."[10]

The Atlantic Coast Line Railroad realized an 89 percent increase in passenger miles over 1942, and the city bus line averaged more than one million riders per month for its 60 buses in 1943. People were urged "To Help Shorten the War...Travel Sparingly. Save all the Pullman and coach space you can for the men and women in the services or for people engaged in war work."[11] In 1944, "With the Battle of Europe underway wounded men will be coming home in greater numbers...."[12]

By 1943, "Wilmington's traffic signal system has been synchronized....Now all that is needed is for drivers and pedestrians to obey the signals and for the latter to stop jaywalking."[13] In two days in 1945 police arrested 16 drivers for faulty brakes from improper maintenance. Aging cars benefitted from low speed limits and fewer on the roads, and wrecks dropped in 1945.

Police in 1942 issued instructions on using the downtown parking meters which monopolized 12 column inches of newspaper space. Not long after, motorists were slugging and jamming the meters.[14] By June 1945, the meters, diligent enforcers, and over-parkers remained irritated. (Some attempts at progress grip us in the past.)

A new highway (Shipyard Boulevard) built with federal funds officially opened in November 1942 between Winter Park and the shipyard and "is destined to relieve much of the congestion..." and facilitated shipyard traffic. A shortcut (Military Cutoff) between U.S. 17 and Bradley Creek, allowing expedited traffic from Camp Davis to the shipyard and port, opened in June 1943. A new hard-surfaced road opened in January 1944 between Hampstead (Highway 17) and Castle Hayne (Highway 117) allowing drivers to avoid downtown. Military, civilian, and commercial vehicles pounded streets and county roads. Only three could bear heavy traffic: 3rd, 5th, and Market. Intolerable noise and frequent accidents resulted. Unlike some other boomtown problems, this one bore directly on tomorrow.

* * *

The Constant Demand for Housing

"Wilmington must face the fact that it has not grown with its opportunity. Lack of vision has stood in its way since the city became a defense center," the newspaper chastised in December 1942.[15] It cited "failure to provide accommodations for large numbers of young women and girls drawn to the city by the many jobs available...." Two years have passed since Wilmington began to grow by leaps and bounds....Yet we have [not] opened a single girls' hotel....The time has come for Wilmington to wake up...and to recognize its obligation...."

Vehicles leave Washington, D.C., en route to Wilmington pulling trailers for use as temporary housing for shipyard workers.

Wilmington newspaper clipping, ca. late 1941

The problem remained, but the War Housing Center, headed by Louie E. Woodbury, Jr.,[*] persisted in placing female renters.[16] A number of civic leaders volunteered in housing capacities, including Frederick Willetts, Harry M. Solomon, Dr. W. Houston Moore, Dr. John T. Hoggard, and Ranald Stewart. "'Think it over if you and your wife live alone in a house which could accommodate 10...Do you feel any responsibility?'" asked Woodbury.[17]

Owners carved up historic downtown homes such as the DeRosset House into rentals. A 6th Street carriage house, "disused since the horse and buggy disappeared here," was the first building converted.[18] But renovations fell short of need.

A March 1944 "Can't Wait for Peace" editorial attested,[19]

...Some structures occupied as homes would be tenantless but for Wilmington's over-size wartime population, but the present housing situation does not relieve owners of ramshackles from responsibility to keep them in repair....In their present state of dilapidation at least 150 buildings...[are] hovels no self-respecting farmer would use to house his hogs....It will not do to say improvements must await postwar planning.

---

[*] Mr. Woodbury, a successful businessman with a lifetime of public service, performed perhaps his finest contribution in this job.

In one, "40 shipyard workers are living with but one flush toilet and a single bath tub....People are being forced to live in attics, basements, hallways and parlors...."[20]

The Liston W. Humphreys next door rented a room to Camp Davis Lieutenant Vern and Mary Louise Eckstrom and stayed in touch until about 1996.[21] She drove Billy Humphrey and me to Davis several times. Some six families lived there, often in two rooms simultaneously. Harold Laing's family ran the Powers rooming house on Market Street.[22] After dinner, folks sat on the porch telling stories "from all over the place." Military husbands joined their spouses on weekends.

"Chateau Bethell"

The W. C. P. Bethell family of Oleander opened their home to Camp Davis officers. Some became "regulars." Mary Eloise Bethell recalled her mother turned over three of their four bedrooms "to use when they were in town.[23] They'd come in on Friday night with steaks to barbeque on the grill in our yard, or they might take us out to the airport...where we ate dinner with soldiers. Sometimes we went to Uncle Henry's....For $1 you ate all [the oysters] you wanted."

Mary wrote, "I especially liked Captain Burrows who was good looking, interesting, and one of the nicest people I've ever known." She accompanied him as he studied local tidal creeks. "Some time later Mother told me that Captain Burrows, out in the Pacific, had been seriously injured. That brought the war closer to home."

The rental money allowed Mary to return to Converse College. "For those of us in school the war seemed pretty remote most of the time except when someone we knew was missing or killed in action. I'd been sort of going steady with Tommy Jenkins, so when he was killed in the early days of the war it was a terrible shock...." Mary and her mother worked at the filter center spotting planes. "All those single men under her wing brought out her mother hen instincts. She arranged parties and introduced them to 'nice girls.'"

Friend Mildred Harris said,[24] "So it happened that officers from Camp Davis, eager to get away from 'Splinter Village,' found a weekend retreat in a two-story brick home located on a large lot at the northwest corner of Park Avenue and Windsor Drive [it still stands]....The officers christened it 'The Chateau Bethell.'" Their 1943–45 letters further the story:

> As members of the original "Bethell Gang" were posted from Camp Davis to other areas, new ones took over their rooms. Some absent ones wrote only occasionally; others kept up regular correspondence...[giving] us a snapshot of Wilmington people and places as well as some idea of the effect at home of disruptions, large and small, caused by the distant war. They wrote about mail never received; they thanked [Mrs. Bethell]

for the boxes of goodies she kept sending them—whether they wanted them or not; they hinted at the grimness of war; they recounted amusing incidents; they passed around news of other members of the gang, of family, and friends. In cold huts on the Western front and on sweltering islands in the Pacific, they reminisced about the food and other comforts of their home away from home....

Early on, Davis commander Major General Frederick H. Smith recommended priorities for occupying the new Lake Forest quarters. Priorities should "go to civilians permanently employed as 'key personnel' at military reservations in the vicinity of Wilmington," then enlisted men of the first three grades[25]....Lake Forest's masonry apartments cost from $35.50 to $40.50, and Hillcrest (for Negroes) $22 to $26, based on approximately 20 percent of income.

Wilmington war housing projects included:

Nesbitt Courts	215
Taylor Homes (Negro)	246
Lake Forest (Greenfield Lake)	1,057
Hillcrest (Negro)	216
Vance Section*	800
Hewes Apartments*	720
Raleigh Section*	1,286
Hewes Dormitories*	356
Worth Section*	599
Total	5,495 units[†26]

In January 1944, 75 percent of Lake Forest, Maffitt Village, and Hillcrest tenants responding to a Housing Authority of the City of Wilmington (HACOW) questionnaire asking where they intended to live postwar replied they hoped to stay in New Hanover County, "provided suitable employment is available."[27] Most of these tenants claimed North Carolina home, and indicated their housing was suitable for permanent living. Liking the housing or not, the masses moved on.

* * *

Public Health

Although local government aggressively pursued a rat control program, typhus and typhoid fever increased in August 1944. Vaccines and cures were unknown. "'There is no cause for alarm,'" said health director Dr. A. H. Elliott. By mid-September, authorities recorded 26 cases, but no deaths.[28]

---

* Maffitt Village (one of these sections was for Negroes)

† Most units are still occupied as public or private housing except for certain portions of Maffitt Village. Nesbitt Courts and Taylor Homes were constructed right before the war.

Ten months later the rat control fund was exhausted. Water from the new King's Bluff project on the upper Cape Fear River began flowing into Wilmington in April 1945, culminating a four-year program. "The new service represents one of the greatest forward strides Wilmington has taken in many years."[29]

" 'The most crowded conditions I have ever witnessed...exist at James Walker Memorial Hospital,' " reported a state official in February 1943, urging locals to "learn nursing and first aid methods that will take some of the load off the local hospital." Completion of the nurses annex* would "only partially alleviate the situation....Persons are being sent home constantly in conditions far from recovered."[30] The nurses training school operated continuously, graduating 27 in May 1943.

Registered nurses, hospital doctors, and the JWMH Board of Managers stalemated in 1944 over staffing. The board (J. C. Roe president) issued an urgent appeal for volunteer nurses and announced " 'luxury nursing'—or private duty nursing except for extreme cases of illness—will be discontinued....' " The facility admitted the most patients ever, 282, since opening.[31]

Charging the board with failure to oversee hospital administration, the *Star-News* stated, if unresolved "the welfare of the community and of a large area beyond its borders will remain in jeopardy....[Meanwhile] People continue to get sick and need hospitalization...."[32] Small Bulluck's Hospital, upstairs in a North Front Street building, closed after the 1944 death of founder Dr. Ernest Bulluck.

Becoming "untenable by expansion of the airport and efforts to obtain federal financial assistance have so far been unsuccessful," the county's Red Cross Tuberculosis Sanatarium closed in 1943. The 31-year-old institution had helped reduce the incidence and mortality of TB. The commissioners soon approved construction of another unit, but none replaced it during wartime.[33]

I remember the periodic skin tests for tuberculosis given in school, and follow-up x-rays for those who showed positive. In March 1944, officials pinpointed approximately 208 county TB cases. Area deaths in the past three years were 12 whites and 70 Negroes, but 24 died during 1944 alone. By the end of 1945, the county recorded 20 deaths ("the dread disease from which no race, color or creed enjoys immunity....").[34]

The County Home, a major health and human rights concern and political whipping boy, remained an issue "for more than 30 years...the subject of hot argument and debate."[35] In February 1944 the institution was labeled a "home of prisoners...juvenile delinquents, the aged and decrepit, feeble

---

* The wartime nurses annex, now a housing unit, is all that remains of JWMH.

minded and mentally afflicted persons." A year later, inspectors found "inmates drinking from jars and cans (with ragged edges)....Inspectors uncovered dirt, grease and grime that must have been years old....Trails of rats, mice, and roaches were traceable...."

Government inspectors declared it "unfit for human occupancy." Mayor Bruce Cameron and local organizations attacked the Consolidated Board of Health and the home's administration, threatening personnel changes. Board member Dr. B. M. Morrison resigned in "'vehement protest'" of the manner in which Mayor Cameron "criticized the Health Department."[36] The problem dragged on. Commissioners approved the recommendations of "a stinging indictment" by a 1945 grand jury, but tabled new construction until "such time as it seems opportune."

By January 1943, the county had 30 white and five Negro doctors—only one physician for every 3,000 persons against a goal of one for 1,300. Of the whites, three were pediatricians and four treated eyes, ears, nose, and throat exclusively. George Koseruba was among three newly arrived physicians.* Those serving in uniform by mid-1942 included: D. B. Rodman, Victor Sullivan, Samuel Warshauer, Paul A. L. Black, Fred Fay, Fred Barefoot, Charles Graham, E. C. Anderson, and Robert Fales. Gasoline restrictions and patient volume made house calls difficult, requiring patients to visit their offices.

Ten million units of the "miracle drug" penicillin, "the drug that doctors say will cure many of the ailments potent sulpha drugs will not," in 1944 was released to JWMH patients. The hospital became a state depot for the drug.[37]

The YMCA at 3rd and Market formed a health club for businessmen and military officers to stay "physically fit and mentally alert during these abnormal times especially." It offered masseur services, vibrating machines, an indoor pool, weights, and medicine balls,[38] and was the center of many kids' activities. The staff included general secretary J. B. Huntington, Adam Smith, and Russell Caudill.

Daddy belonged to the health club, essentially using it for the steam room, and I spent mostly pleasant hours in the gym, social room, and pool—where everyone had to take a soap shower and swim naked. Boys and adults had different pool hours. Other memories stuck: We boys completed Saturday activities before heading to the movies, the chlorine-doused locker room odor, and chugging Royal Crown Cola or Pepsi bottles filled with salted Toms peanuts.

* * *

---

* This amazing pediatrician and Rotarian still dabbles in practice today.

Community Organizations

Civic organization members individually and collectively advised and influenced local government. Valuable catalysts in the war effort, they provided volunteer leadership and coordination, forums for information exchange, and rallying points for drives. The Greater Wilmington Chamber of Commerce, actually representing the entire county with its full-time paid director, took the lead. Together with the all-male Exchange, Rotary, Civitan, Lions, and Kiwanis Clubs, the American Legion, and the Junior Chamber, they mustered a formidable force. Women participated in the American Red Cross, United Service Organizations, Legion Auxiliary, Salvation Army, churches, and war-relief and social-welfare groups.

Wilmington Rotary Club 1943 president Gene Edwards recognized members in the service: navy, Lennox Gore Cooper, Charles P. Graham, M. Hall Lander, Peter Browne Ruffin; army, Emil Engel, John Bright Hill; and Marines, George A. Gary. The Wilmington Lions Club in 1941 passed a resolution that the club "fast" at one meeting a month and buy a $25 defense savings bond. Kiwanians in 1943 heard soloist Hannah Block "in songs distinctive for their war motive: *Coming in on a Wing and a Prayer*; *As Time Goes By*," and more. "There a contagious element in Mrs. Block's voice, capable...of rousing male audiences to raucous cooperating in choruses."[39]

The ACL Employees Service Club, which had shipped 5,000 packages of cigarettes to servicemen, elected Liston W. Humphrey president. Clubs often listened to rousing, patriotic, and inspirational talks by military personnel. In 1944, Bluethenthal Field Lieutenant Eugene Johnson told Rotarians of his "rugged" experiences with the Flying Tigers in China when the Japs outnumbered them 15 to 1.

On June 18, 1943, president Richard Dunlea and the Exchange Club "romped through a special Father's Day program [arranged by Wilbur D. Jones] with their sons...ranging in age for two years to army-age." Guests included "Happy" Lee of station WMFD and sons Terry Ronner, C. S. Lowrimore, Private First Class Ray Brindell, Jr., Clayton Holmes, Jr., Charles Brindell, R. A. Dunlea, Jr., J. H. Fussell, Jr., and myself.[40]

The Brigade Boys Club served primarily underprivileged boys from Dry Pond and The Bottoms emphasizing religious, physical, mental, intellectual, and spiritual development. It became heavily involved in the war effort. The Senior Fraternity of businessmen provided its backbone.[41]

W. Elliott O'Neal replaced John Sheehan as Jaycees president in 1944, "pledging to better the communications for the men who return from war."[42] The Chamber's 1944 directors included J. Kyle Bannerman, E. Blackwell Bugg, Bruce B. Cameron, W. A. Fonvielle, N. L. Foy, A. E. Jones, Emsley A. Laney, H. A. Marks, F. P. O'Crowley, E. R. Toms, Dan H. Penton, L. A. Haney, James G. Thornton, E. L. White, and Frederick Willetts. Members of its

Wilmington Exchange Club honors fathers and sons, June 19, 1943. I am in front row on left (dark pants), my father directly behind me (crossed hands). Photo taken at Front St. post office, downtown's central meeting place.

Author's collection

influential Military Affairs Group included chairman O'Crowley, Wilbur R. Dosher, J. L. Duffy, J. H. Gerdes, and Wilbur D. Jones.

The International Order of Odd Fellows owned their own building at 3rd and Princess. Daddy served as a local and state officer, and Mother loyally in the women's division, the Letitia Rebekah Lodge. Mother, sometimes dragging me along, loved to socialize with Rebekah buddies including president Margaret Mintz, Lois Albright, Nell Dicksey, state president Elsie Burke, Bertha Skipper, Mabel Garrison, Florence Tiencken, Etta Craig, and Leona Matthews. Other active women's clubs included the Wilmington Business and Professional Women's Club (1944 president Louise B. Polvogt) and the North Carolina Sorosis.

In January 1944 the American Legion bought the Bridgers' house at 3rd and Dock as their post home. "Legionnaires have heartily agreed that boys returning home from the war should have a place where they can go and be among each other; a place where they are free to fight the war again,"[43] and mix with the World War I old-timers. Governor R. Gregg Cherry dedicated the $50,000 home in March 1945. In 1944 the post reelected commander Norwood S. Westbrook. Army dischargee Chesley D. Harris was the first WWII veteran to join (1942). Daddy, post commander in 1929–30, worked on several committees, occasionally taking me. Mother stayed busy in the Auxiliary.

Chapter 14

"Khaki Uniforms" and "Sweeping Evening Dresses"

*Southeastern North Carolina supplied a steady stream of dance part-
ners for officer and enlisted socials at Camp Davis, Camp Lejeune,
Fort Fisher, and Bluethenthal Field. In February 1944, 400 girls de-
scended on Davis for the grandest of all. "On the dance floors khaki
uniforms and the bright colors of sweeping evening dresses moved
rhythmically as festivities continued until 11:30, to end with the tra-
ditional playing of the national anthem....The soldiers and their guests
crowded soda fountains for cold drinks and refreshments. Reluctantly
the dancers ended their celebration...buses waited to take the girls in
their party frocks back to their homes. Men in uniform dispersed in
the direction to their barracks and the gala affair ended."[1]*

Oh, what a night it must have been. And there were many more almost
matching it, so many attempts to please the GIs.

To Lottie "Clara" Marshburn and friends, the United Service Organizations' formal dances were "really something" for borrowing or making
dresses. "We were poor." Sometimes army trucks drove to Castle Hayne to
pick up her and others. With strict rules and a minimum age hostessing of
16, "What you did after leaving, you were on your own." You could go anywhere with soldiers, but took the same bus home.[2]

* * *

To Davis and Lejeune

"Girls get your best dance frock in readiness, for this week a 'big dance'
is to be given for the Marines at the Jacksonville USO" on April Fool's Day
1943. Supervised by Mrs. Carl (Ethel) Powers, Woodrow Wilson Hut director, several hundred members of the dance club went along. Buses left the
hut at 7:00 p.m. with chaperones.[3] Six buses transported 400 young ladies
to a formal reception and hop given for Military Academy cadets at Davis in
June 1944.[4]

Davis' final open dance attracted more than 1,000 people to Farnsworth Hall on October 21, 1944. Its on-again, off-again activation and closing, however, precipitated a June 1945 call for 1,000 more hostesses for buffets, dances, and skating parties.

"We were so busy trying to have a good time we didn't have the same feeling our parents did about the war," said Emma Mitchell, "being high school students—a lot of volunteer work—that was also our social life. We [girls] were not affected by the war as the boys."[5] My across-the-street neighbors, both Mitchell brothers, served. Mrs. Powers "had a list of girls who were approved" for Davis. At officer candidate school graduations, "part of the graduation experience was knowing social graces. They had us girls line up on the balcony with OCS candidates lined up below. We went downstairs and met [paired up] with the officers below." Emma also went to Lejeune to entertain the Dutch marines, "but we couldn't communicate."

North Dakotan Percy Hedquist, stationed at Davis, visited the 2nd and Orange USO.[6] The only vehicle he and his lieutenant found in the motor pool for carpooling was a 2½ ton truck. Percy met Josie Henry and took her home. The lieutenant rode in the back and she rode up front. "You can imagine how the family reacted when they saw that truck driving up in front of their house," friend John Clayton recounted. Percy married Josie.

The Travelers Aid main office, chaired by Mrs. Herbert Bluethenthal, operated at 2nd and Orange. In three years it provided 350,000 services for the city's 425,000 strangers. In May 1942, "Mrs. Walter Sprunt offered her beautiful home on the [Greenville] sound" for a USO wiener roast and games.[7] Besides Hannah Block ("on hand when music is needed"), the Wilson Hut's leading volunteers included Irene Rich, Mrs. Louis Goodman, Lucille Sternberger, Maud Davenport, and Mrs. Lester Preston. The Hut furnished multitudes of young ladies for Davis.

Mary Belle and Lewis Ormond and other couples hosted there, once taking home two OCS candidates.[8] "The minute any of them entered my door, rank stops. You're all buck privates to me." One pair was John White and Snowden T. Herrick. Long after the war every Christmas John called her, and Snowden every December 7, until they died. "It meant a lot to the boys to have a home to come to."

"I had to go out with 17- or 18-year-old women in Wilmington" in 1943, recalled OCS candidate Justin Raphael.[9] He did not know his future wife, Wilmingtonian Shirley Berger, only 13 then. Until he danced with Manzette Peterson at the USO, he thought little about home. With her "it all came rushing back—thoughts of home, Mother—Manzette's smile gave me one of the biggest thrills of my life."

Justin befriended the family of Lila and Matthew Peterson, a rural mail carrier, and three daughters. "They took me in—chicken every Sunday dinner." Although Jewish, Justin accompanied them to First Baptist Church, and reciprocated with dinner trips to Davis and Fort Fisher and picnics at Greenfield Park. "They treated me like one of their sons." Once Mr. Peterson gave him the keys to his car to use to take out the girls. The girls were excited because Justin brought GI friends. Growing up in New York with no car, he couldn't drive. "The girls' faces just dropped." Once he invited the Petersons to Fisher and feared his men would whistle and go berserk over the three girls. They acted like gentlemen.

The Camp Davis newspaper's 1944 feature column "GI SASSIETY" headlined Wilmington events, such as the gala Mid-Summer Street Dance on July 28.[10] "There'll be partners for all." The previous week Fisher hosted the "Shellsapoppin" variety show. The Famous Club "housed one of the most rollicking events of the season...[in July] as members of the Headquarters Battery (137th Antiaircraft Artillery Battalion) bathed in the SASSIETY spotlight....Plenty of gals were there...." On July 20 at Lumina, the 793rd Battalion "gathered to indulge in a fine swimming-dancing-partying fest...." As Davis shut down in September 1944, the girls bid farewell to the 424th Battalion at Lumina. "Girls in the city are cordially invited to attend."[11]

* * *

Principal New Hanover County Service Clubs

The USO eventually operated 13 county clubs and a 14th in Southport. From 1941 to 1945, Wilmington hosted approximately 35,000 service personnel per week. On weekend nights, 600 men crowded into the 2nd and Orange basement dormitory. The lobby canteen "dispensed the two commodities for which the USO was most renowned—coffee and doughnuts."[12] Some other clubs were:

—National Catholic Community Service, Club House for the Colored, 9th and Nixon Streets

—National Catholic Community Service, 215 South 4th at Ann

Thomas C. Wheatley, *left*, director of the 9th and Nixon Sts. Negro USO Club, with Fr. Thomas J. Honahan, 1945.

Wilmington newspaper clipping provided by George N. Norman

—Travelers Aid Service, Union Bus Terminal

—Women's Division, 124 South 5th at Orange

—YWCA, 223 North 3rd at Grace

—Carolina Beach, Cape Fear Boulevard, second floor

—Salvation Army unit, Harbor Island (Wrightsville Beach)

(—Woodrow Wilson Hut, on City Hall grounds, community-operated, unofficially referred to as a USO)

Wilmington had several other service clubs unaffiliated with the USO. They included the officers club in the Revolutionary-era Cornwallis House at 3rd and Market, and the civilian war workers club upstairs at 221 Princess which opened in 1944. "A colonial air pierced the atmosphere when Matilda Austin, an old Negro woman nearing her hundredth birthday, beamed her smile at the guests." The North Carolina Society of Colonial Dames, Chamber of Commerce, and City Council supported the Cornwallis club, which contained a game room, snack bar, kitchen, dining room, dormitory, breezy piazza, and bridal suite.[13] Its lounge and bridal suite were refurnished during Wartime Wilmington Commemoration, 1999.

* * *

The Beach People: "Mr. Carolina Beach," Carl Winner, Jr.[14]

Who better to tell the story of Carl Winner than his daughter Pearl Winner Fountain and husband Jim. A Carolina Beach icon for decades, Carl built boats and houses, including his own, and buildings at Fort Bragg and Camp Davis. When Pearl was 12, her parents were divorced. Before Carl entered the merchant marine, Pearl handled his businesses while he was away and often walked home at midnight with money from the establishments, the police accompanying her home safely. The next day she was up early selling tickets for the fishing boats. "I didn't have time to get in trouble."

Carl served in the invasions of Italy and Normandy, and returned home occasionally to the businesses and six children. Siblings included Jeanean W. Wiggins, and brothers Chubby, Skippy, Skeets, and Tuttle. Bobbie, later Carl's wife, stayed with the kids and assumed many of Pearl's responsibilities. Carl's primary business was head boats taking fishermen across the surf to bigger boats off shore. Selling tickets, Pearl "could see a lot going on" including fireballs of burning ships. Walter Winner owned the fishing pier at Fort Fisher.

Carl was absolutely an amazing person, "an all-American guy," Jim recalled. "He believed in our country." Pearl added, "He believed in Carolina Beach. He knew how to make a dollar." Carl shared his family ration coupons with other beach families. His friends included Negro fellow businessmen Harper McQuillen and Benny Ross at Seabreeze. Every Thanksgiving and Christmas "Dad piled us all in the car with food and took it to poor families at

Carolina Beach. He always shared." But he also "was gruff, unpolished, and a soft touch."

Jim's grandfather, W. G. Fountain, ran Fountain Oil Company in Castle Hayne, with storage facilities at the oil terminal just south of the shipyard. W. G., elected Carolina Beach mayor in 1945, owned the upscale 55-room Royal Palm Hotel. Jack McCarley, living at Echo Farm on the Carolina Beach Road, spent time with grandparents A. O. and Minnie McEachern. She enjoyed boardwalk bingo. After bingo closed, Jack walked her to her oceanfront house.

Carolina Beach oceanfront and boardwalk, 1945.

Hannah Block

The beach had some rides but mostly slides and swings.* The Plummer family store sold hotdogs, hamburgers, Cokes, sunglasses, and bathing suits. GIs loved the place. Next door was a bingo parlor.[15] Catherine Solomon's family owned the boardwalk's Beach Shop on the land side. She and sisters Marie and Jean sold beach wear there. You walked beneath Batson's Bath

---

* A visitor can visualize what the wartime oceanfront boardwalk looked like. Many of the structures remain in use, although concrete long ago replaced the boardwalk itself and constructed dunes buffet the ocean view. The Royal Palm is the Astor, appearance hardly changed. Even the old electric bumper cars are still there.

House on the boardwalk "to see how much money you could find."[16] Gil Burnett ran a snowball cone stand on Carolina Avenue at the Ocean Plaza Hotel corner. Hannah Block taught him how to swim when she was the head lifeguard.

"It was a favorite spot for soldiers from Fort Bragg, which had an 'R&R' (rest and relaxation) camp at Sugarloaf on the back side of the beach," remembered Frances Wagner. "Also there were those...further down the beach at Fort Fisher. We could see their planes flying up and down the beach for target practice during the day. In the evenings at times we could see their searchlights....Seeing the fires of the burning ships and oil slicks in the days that followed was a reminder that American lives had been lost."[17]

Remembering Wrightsville[18]

Eva Sanders Cross, a Wrightsville Beach fixture at Roberts Grocery for 56 years, died in 2000. Whatever was happening on the Island, she probably knew about it. She and shipyard-worker husband Bill Cross moved there in October 1942 with 8-month-old Sandra, renting the Tar Heelia Cottage. Bill was subject to the draft unless he took a defense job, and among the last to leave when the yard closed in 1946. Their friends included Elaine Creasy and the Creasy parents.

Eva shopped at Roberts Grocery because of convenience, and in 1944 began cashiering there. Charlie Roberts opened the store in 1919, and it remains the beach's oldest business. Charlie and wife Dorothy lived over the store then across the street from its present location. "If we got busy Mrs. Roberts would come out of the office and help." The Roberts special was "always the meat." They dressed chickens (kept live behind the store) to order by phone. Hearing about a shipment, customers stood in line.[*]

Rufus Benson was town manager and Riley Wiggs police chief with five officers. Wooden boardwalks ran along the Station One area on entering the island. Prisoners helped construct concrete sidewalks to replace some wooden ones. Babies Hospital pediatrician Dr. McIlvoy accommodated. "I'll stop by on my way home." Most visitors and renters were officers. "The finer people went to Wrightsville. We never had any problems with any GIs."

Prominent shoppers included Mrs. Hargrove Bellamy, Mrs. P. R. Smith, Mrs. J. D. Taylor, and the Bruce Camerons. Volunteer fireman Bill helped fight the 1944 fire that destroyed the Cameron cottage. White's Ice Cream Company supplied milk, W. H. McEachern's Sons and Saleeby's sold them produce, and N&W Grocery provided wholesale items. The smaller Rogers Grocery on Harbor Island was "a real nice little grocery store."

---

[*] By 1949, both Crosses were working at the store, the year that Charlie died. Everybody liked Eva.

Harold Laing's family often stayed at the Hanover Inn ("wonderful meals"). Parents dropped off kids for the evening in the "porpoise room."[19] Kentuckian Buddy Adkins, Camp Davis soldier, enjoyed Lumina but never learned to dance. "I would stand and chat with the girls while my buddy danced." He never "messed around" Carolina Beach. "It was rougher."[20] Catherine Russell and Laura Roe ventured onto the beach at night flirting with soldier guards. Virginia Harriss spent summers at her grandfather John T. Hoggard's North Lumina cottage. She remembered "being scared to death" in blackouts and during air raid drills. "I thought they were getting ready to bomb us."[21]

John Debnam's family rented their beach house first floor to a couple ("they were just desperate"). Most owners usually occupied their cottages in summer and rented them in winter. The James G. Thornton family never charged servicemen rent for using their Wrightsville house. Like other houses, the Debnams had no central heat. He watched AAA firing at

Marie Burgwin at Newell's store and soda shop at Station One, Wrightsville Beach, 1943.
Eleanor "Elkie" Burgwin Fick

towed targets on Figure 8 Island and collected shell casings. Wrightsville had no theater, so John walked to Harbor Island's "pink club" USO for movies. Civilians paid 25 cents.

Sergeant Harry Mann played the saxophone and clarinet in the Fort Bragg dance band. In the summer of 1942 he joined a civilian gig at Lumina with other soldiers. Not allowed out of uniform away from the base, for this event he wore a tuxedo. Later he changed into sports clothes on leaving the beach.* Guards allowed him to proceed because a girlfriend accompanied him. Later he served as a Signal Corps officer at England's Bletchley Park.[22]

* * *

From Society to Lady Wrestlers: Wilmingtonians at Leisure

One of the society set's top annual Christmas events, the Cape Fear Country Club's 1942 L'Ariosa German Club dance, distracted attendees from

---

* "The beach" usually meant Wrightsville Beach. If Carolina Beach specifically, it was so spoken and written. Wrightsville had the "upper set" Yacht Club, Surf Club, and Hanover Seaside Club, and generally attracted military officers and people of means. Carolina became the "enlisted" and "Coney Island" beach.

the war news. Club officers were president Frederick B. Graham, secretary-treasurer John D. Taylor, and leader Lemuel L. Doss. The 45-member Spinsters rang out 1943 with their annual Country Club dance, with music by Key Scales' orchestra. Betty Henderson was Spinsters president, Mary Davis, secretary, and Julie Worth Sprunt, treasurer. Louise Hooper and Louise Wells organized the event. The April 1944 Cape Fear Horse Show saw Louis B. Orrell defending last season's championship.

Still going strong in 1944, female wrestling at Thalian Hall featured world champion "attractive" Mildred Burke. Other "name" grapplers performing between 1942 and 1944 included Chief Little Beaver (most appearances), Milo "The Muscle" Steinborn, Cowboy Luttrell, "Georgia Charlie" Harben, Strangler White, and the Masked Marvel (another favorite).

The hillbilly carnival "Naughty But Nice" played at Legion Stadium in March 1944 to "Whites Only." The Wilmington Co-Operative Concert Association in 1944 presented Czech pianist Rudolf Firkusny in the New Hanover High School auditorium as one of its four concerts. The newspaper bemoaned the lack of a hall with twice the seating. "The city's rapidly growing musical community deserves more adequate accommodations...."[23] The auditorium was suitable for the high school's operetta "HMS Pinafore" in March 1944. The Wilmington Museum closed during the war, leaving the city without an exhibit gallery for the paintings of Wilmingtonian Claude Howell, on the road to fame. Jesse Reynolds, appointed city recreation director in 1943, in one year had "gone ahead to unprecedented heights" with strong community support.[24] His program helped curb juvenile delinquency.

Gasoline driving restrictions forced sports cancellations. Without enough quality players, Coach Rupert Bryan scratched New Hanover High's final nine 1945 conference baseball games, playing only smaller schools. Girls' softball teams fielded 10 players in 1944. Saffo's Café won the 1945 YMCA basketball league with a team of Weenie and Buster Brown, Clarence and Jere Hilburn, Fred Babson, Big Head Russ, George McLean, and George Saffo. In June 1945, NHHS Coach Leon Brogden awarded letter shirts to YMCA house champions, including Russell Clark, Jim Schulken, Charles Hunnicutt, Homer Bessant, Stacy Bragg, and me.

Nicknames for the 1942 NHHS Wildcats gridiron squad included John Burney (Judge), Dewey Hobbs (Grandpa), Jim Coughenour (Hero), Bill McIlwain (MacKil-Flip), and Randall Dyches (Piggy). The 1943 football squad improved over the previous season thanks to the running of Dyches and placekicking of back McIlwain. Starters included Dick Watts and Dick Piner at ends, John Hobbs and Red Holt at tackles, Jim Snow and Graham Barefoot at guards, Stanley Glines at center, and backs Jack Lowrimore and Johnny Symmes. They captured second place by defeating Fayetteville 7 to 6 for the second straight year. By December, the 6'4", 200-pound "giant luminary" three-sport athlete Watts left school for the navy.

The 1944 team closed its home season by losing to Hamlet 7 to 0. Highlights were the cheerleaders' bonfire rally at 13th and Ann the day before, led by Charlie Mitchell, and the snake dance and pep rally down Front Street. The Bryan-coached 1944–45 basketball team compiled a 5 and 7 conference record but included future stars Billy Mason, Johnny McKoy, Louis Collie, Toddy Fennell, and Tinky Rogers who in 1947 won Coach Leon Brogden's first state championship here.* Williston High's Tigers football team posted a 6-0-1 record in 1944.

Cape Fear League baseball teams represented the shipyard, Winter Park, Seagate, and other area communities. Standouts were local baseball legends Lefty Cheshire, Ed Urban, Ed Hobson, Roy Lamb, and Johnny Edens. A few teams played independent games with military or visiting squads. By 1945, manager Bert Kite's Wilmington Pirates semi-pro team prepared to play a normal schedule. The most notable local player was catcher Augustus "Shuney" Brittain, who coached NHHS in 1944 while a shipyard worker and player. "With the same old pepper," the *Morning Star* reported, Brittain "was blaring out with an incessant line of shouts and firing the ball around the bases just as in his heyday....'We'll give the Wilmington fans the best brand of ball they've seen here in several years.'"[25]

Fred Sternberger "didn't mess with girls until I got out of the service. Went to dances but not much else. Most of us boys just hung out together." From Jarman's Drug Store at 16th and Market they bummed rides to the beach. "There wasn't a whole lot to do."[26] Early in the war Joe Reaves joined the *Saus Fauties* male social, fellowship group, which met upstairs in the Odd Fellows Hall. Member John Burney sat near the window spitting out. "Footloose and fancy-free," Joe broke girlfriend ties when entering the navy.[27]

Isabel Russell's best friend at NHHS, Katie Gray, married a soldier and moved away. Isabel and Dorothy Kure liked to fish at the Kure's Beach pier built by her father, Hans. Their sorority met in the 3rd and Princess Odd Fellows building, and staged all-girl beach house parties, where they watched planes searching for submarines.[28]

Mannette Dixon's sister Elizabeth married a Coast Guard sailor stationed here, and another married a sailor from Virginia. "They were great USO girls, my sisters." Elizabeth "loved to dance and taught all the Yankees how to jitterbug." Dixon never went to the USO and dated few servicemen, mostly shipyard apprentices. "The boys [soldiers] were just like your brothers." Both remembered standing in line for movie tickets. The Bailey Theater line wrapped around to Market Street. She enjoyed seeing who was dating, calling friends about it the next day. The Peacock Alley drive-in restaurant

---

* Wilmington tired of losing to Wilson and hired their coach, Brogden, in March 1945. With numerous state championships and legions of star players his legacy, the late Brogden became one of the state's most successful and respected coaches.

sold hotdogs and hamburgers at 17th and Queen. Mannette, "Betty and all of us would get off work at three and go by there. You were safe walking down the street, never afraid," even when banks stayed open until midnight to cash workers' checks.[29]

All in the Day's Work[30]

"A soldier's sweetheart wants a home wedding—a frantic service-man seeks help in locating his wife—a soldier's baby on a visit gets the measles," reported the Camp Davis newspaper in 1944 as examples of Wilmington USO service. "Straightening out these human tangles is all in the day's work....The weekend tasks...are enormous...."

"When a Camp Davis soldier's bride-to-be came in for a justice of the peace," her father appealed to director Martha Ordway of the 3rd and Grace USO. "Ordway got a minister, searched for other USOs for a best man, bought a corsage for the bride, decorated the fireplace of the club with masses of dogwood, and the couple were married with all the atmosphere of a real wedding."

Each USO developed its own individuality, and soldiers usually returned to the same one. "The USO best known for its all-around services is at 2nd and Orange....Here soldiers can find almost anything desired from making a long distance call home to developing film in a fully-equipped darkroom. Over the weekend the club at 4th and Ann houses about 70 men."

At its peak in service (third anniversary) and usage, by January 1944, 2nd and Orange reported estimated attendance of 567,432; number of volunteers assisting, 4,390; dances, educational, cultural events, 59,448; movies, dramatic, musical programs, 17,293; religious programs, 10,296; miscellaneous service (showers, etc.), 131,701.[31]

Chapter 15

"Directing Their Children's Footsteps"

It never would have occurred to us kids, but the Board of Education mandated a plan for every elementary student: "Mental, physical, and moral growth...more thoroughness in the fundamental subjects....Exactness, and thoroughness in mathematics is imperative; a full knowledge of our democratic institutes and government...intensified study of geography, history and related subjects; the literature arts should be taught more thoroughly. Music and art are more important than [ever]....Character education....Understand the meaning and real value of the democratic way of life. Teach Americanism, Democracy and Patriotism...every day."[1]

The *Morning Star* in 1942 added its viewpoint. "At the risk of being accused of preaching, we feel it advisable to point out that with the world locked in war, with bewildering bypaths of conflicting and unsound doctrine too well trodden, parents have had no more baffling task since this country was born than that of directing their children's footsteps in the ways of our nation's fathers....that most clearly shapes his adult thinking and conduct."[2]

Our parents received advice on preparing us for school, all tied to patriotism and the war effort.[3]

"Fully as important as is the task of furnishing these boys and girls with clothes they will need, supplies they must have, care for their diet and health and home backgrounds, the job of sustaining their morale is equally important. This involves convincing them that their role as students...constitutes in itself participation of the Nation's War Effort....The obligation of the school child to his country is clear....

"While providing the wardrobe is a mother's job, keeping it in good condition should be a task shared by the little wearer....[First] is durability, which means quality." Makers have eliminated old favorites such as patch pockets, introducing "a brand new wartime styling for men's clothes, which patriotic youngsters should hail...," including new synthetic fabrics.

We kids received "no new bikes for the duration, so take care of yours now....For top performance the bike should be kept clean and oiled," and requirements for tires and brakes inspections. What, none for helmets and seat belts? One can imagine the delight of today's legislatures and watchdog agencies in protecting us from ourselves.

* * *

Applying the Standards

Our Forest Hills grammar school teachers over 1942–44 included principal Katherine Von Glahn,* Harriett McDonald, Miriam McEachern, Dessie Moody, Emma K. Neuer, Margaret Pickard, Caroline Newbold, and Regina Bischoff. Three were neighbors: too close, I thought. Mrs. Richard Rogers led our mother-dominated Parent Teacher Association in 1945.

Our school earnestly sold war bond stamps. Each class strove for 100 percent participation. Kenneth Murphy remembered, "Some of our classmates' parents did not have enough money to even let them buy a ten cent stamp. So Dr. [William S.] Dosher would buy stamps in their name so we would have 100 percent." For the 4th grade year Kenneth answered the school's phone. "At the end of the school year I was given a half day off. I went to the Carolina Theater and sat through *Sergeant York* twice."[4]

Classmate Evelyn Bergen switched from St. Mary Catholic School to Forest Hills when gas rationing began. "I was delighted to be attending school with my neighborhood friends."[5] Classmate Joe Knox moved here in 1944, greeted by the principal who "crossed her arms over her chest and stared down at the kids." Discipline was the rule. "Hattie McDonald was a very strict person. She would pound on the table with a ruler."[6] Bill Leeuwenburg entered our school in the 2nd grade under Mrs. Moody. She was "tough." "She and I didn't gel."[7]

Ronnie Phelps and trumpet started a school band. Navy brother Kenneth Phelps sent the instrument, "wanted me to be the local Harry James." The band, which included Norman Tyson, Bobby Hughes, Kenneth Murphy (clarinet), Joe Johnson (trombone), and Louie Woodbury (trumpet), played the entrance music at every assembly. "I'm not sure we didn't play the same song every time. *Onward Christian Soldiers* was one of our favorites. We were a religiously-integrated body—Jews, Christians, we were all alike."[8]

Dudley Humphrey transferred to Forest Hills in 1943. "I had one hell of a time catching up on 5th grade math because I had a constant procession of teachers at Sunset Park in the 4th grade. The kids did not have shoes until Thanksgiving. I would take off mine so I would not be different. Had a

---

* We kids knew Miss Von Glahn was <u>old</u>; her age was a military secret; mid-40s? That was <u>ancient</u>. She retired in 1957 when I was a new naval officer.

Medieval serfs? Waifs? No, my Forest Hills School fifth-grade class play, 1945. *Left to right*, Ludwig Leiner (black sweater), Lonnie Jones, John Blake, Louie Woodbury III, Walter Yopp (crown), Evelyn Bergen, Billy Dosher, Bobby Cameron, Tinky Milliken (headdress), George Rountree III, Joe Johnson, Gene Robinson, Mary Van Walbach, and Betty Buck.

Ronald G. Phelps

constant case of ringworm."[9] Betty Buck's younger brother Bob got into some trouble, distressed with his uncle's service death, and worried about his father possibly dying. Miss Von Glahn told his mother, Bertha Buck, "she would have to do something about it." He settled down.[10]

George Rountree remembered Miss Von Glahn swatting him with a ruler. "Once I carved my initials on my desk. Von Glahn called my mother, who came to school. Mother beat the living daylights out of me. Von Glahn also beat me. I had to sand down the desk but still didn't obliterate the carving." She even punished incidents happening on the way to and from school, like tossing firecrackers at girls.[11] Like me, Lucy Ann Carney went to Mrs. Hinnant's St. Paul's Episcopal kindergarten for two years and then entered Forest Hills in the 2nd grade. She remembered how tough Forest Hills was for Gibson and Mercer Avenue kids.

* * *

School Days Elsewhere

Right Reverend Monsignor Cornelius E. Murphy led the 75th anniversary celebration of St. Mary Catholic school on May 20, 1945. The Swart kids remembered all Wrightsboro School teachers were women, including principal Nell Fentress. Ed Swart said "they were like ministers and doctors, people you looked up to. They visited homes. They didn't put up with any mess."[12] Mary Cameron Dixon's mother, Mary Esther, taught at William Hooper School, which established at least three separate first grade classes. Hers totaled 55 pupils, not uncommon. Shipyard worker children heavily impacted the Hooper and Cornelius Harnett districts.

County grammar school football proceeded at the 13th and Ann field. By late October 1944, three teams were tied for the lead: Chestnut Street, Winter Park, and Tileston. Then Chestnut, coached by Robert Venters, defeated "heavily out weighted" Forest Hills 19 to 0, behind Charlie Niven.[13]

Chestnut's popular principal, Annie Wells Herring, married Elmer B. Snipes, Independent Ice Company manager, in June 1944. Those honoring the bride included Mrs. Q. B. Snipes, Mrs. J. H. Debnam, Mrs. E. I. Snipes, Jr., Mrs. Lucille A. Shuffler, and Mrs. Claude Efird. "She was treated like she was on a pedestal," Ann Williams boasted. "Every teacher, the way we treated them and the way they treated us, was a wonderful thing about Chestnut Street." Ann's buddies included Mary Fisher, Pat Poplin, Hazel Bonham, Nancy White, Charles Hunnicutt, and Jack Franks, some classmates for 12 years."[14] Nancy West recalled "the day they took my best friend out of math class to tell her that her big brother had been killed in the war."[15]

Negro students living in Love Grove north of Market walked two miles to Williston Industrial (High) School. Buses took those in the Wrightsboro area. Otherwise everyone walked. In 1943 "New Hanover school children made 5,040,000 crossings of busy streets and highways at school zones without a single accident of any sort last year," the police department stated.[16] Almost twice as many pupils were transported daily by school buses by June 1942 than in the previous year, and without an accident. When the 1945 school year ended, the influx of students "increased so greatly that the fleet of buses previously in use could not carry them all," forcing the county to "put up with vehicles the usefulness of which was limited."[17]

"Necessitated by the increase in population...the 11 new teachers [just hired] will make a total of 311 in the school system," Superintendent H. M. Roland reported in July 1942. "Despite vacancies...caused by the war and by teachers leaving for other jobs, the teacher standards in the county will not be affected...."[18] In May 1943 Maffitt Village's white and Negro schools opened.* By summertime, Assistant Superintendent J. W. Grise noted the system was "'having "the most difficult time it has ever had" in getting teachers....'"[19] At school year's end total enrollment was 14,846, a two-year increase of 4,466. "'Whooping cough, measles, chicken pox and other communicable diseases have taken their toll....'"[20]

---

* The Board of Education received approximately $550,000 in federal aid for public school construction during 1942–43, erecting nine new schools (*Wilmington Morning Star*, May 7, 1943)

Williston Industrial (High) School class of 1945.

Cornelia Haggins Campbell

Pupil numbers slumped significantly with the close of school in June 1944 when transient families relocated, but in late September climbed to 12,602. A few days after V-J Day, a survey found fewer poverty-stricken families had been enrolled during 1944–45 than previously, and 27 students participated in the free lunch program.

* * *

New Hanover High School

In December 1942 the population at NHHS included some 1,800 students, 78 faculty, and 10 cafeteria workers (feeding 1,200 daily). Non-traditional courses included: the Victory Corps; a nursery school of some 30 "academic babies" run by home economics students; mathematics and science courses taught with new methods; vocational programs; and new emphasis on health and physical education. "'Our activities have been redefined by the current emergencies. We take them from cradle to the job,'" Principal T. T. Hamilton stated.[21] Students also handled war bond and stamp sales and worked for merchants during the holidays.

Within one year at NHHS, vocational classes trained 13,000 as war workers, but in late 1943 only 5,000 as the labor supply dwindled.[22] NHHS enrollment was 75 percent of that two years before. An estimated 500 students quit school for military or industry service. "The problem [is] how to shepherd them back to their books after the war is over."[23] Even then Roland was looking ahead to postwar schools through sterner discipline and physical education.[*] By 1943, the business department assisted emergency agencies in grooming students for clerical jobs in government and industry. Faculty member Mary Elizabeth Hood taught my sister Elizabeth typing and shorthand for shipyard work after she finished college. By March 1944, special courses had trained 21,000 adults.

In writing *Gyrene: The World War II United States Marine*, I designated three periods in which men entered the Marine Corps.[†] One I tabbed "the Pearl Harbor patriots," or "class of '42," those seniors who left school to enlist or enlisted after graduation. I found little indication that NHHS or Williston students dropped out in 1941–42 to join. Some "drop-outs" appeared as members of later NHHS classes.

---

* In February 1944 the National and North Carolina Education Associations honored the "'beloved' superintendent" Roland, and Grise and Hamilton for their work. [*Wilmington Morning Star*, February 15, 1944] Roland "would go in in the early morning and last until late at night, nearly drove himself crazy." Wife Perida Roland recalled the expanding school system: if he had known it was going to be that hectic, World War I veteran Roland would have accepted an army commission. "It nearly worked my husband to death trying to keep the schools going." [Interview with Perida Roland, January 15, 1999]

† Wilbur D. Jones, Jr., *Gyrene: The World War II United States Marine* (Shippensburg, Pa.: White Mane, 1998).

Class of 1942

Janet Rabunsky.[24] One of the first classmates killed in action was "a guy I had a crush on, Cliff Owensby." She fondly remembered Jimmy Lynch, another classmate KIA. "He was very popular, very smart. He was headed for stardom." Her class of nearly 300 graduated in daytime at Legion Stadium because lights were forbidden.

Donald Blake.[25] "The class of '42 was not actually a class. Many were taking part high school graduate courses" in the senior year. "We were attending classes sometimes with people who were a year ahead or a year behind.* All of us knew where we were going. Norfleet Jackson was the only one I knew who wore a zoot suit." Swallowing gold fish was the thing, particularly Jack Nall on the senior steps. None of his buddies had gasoline for dating. Friends were Jim Starnes, Chick Mathis, and Jack Laughlin (who flew over "the Hump" from India).

Norman Davis.[26] His father insisted he enter North Carolina State after graduation. He did, but soon he requested army aviation cadet training to fulfill a dream. He admired his father's World War I service in the Wilmington Light Infantry. "I couldn't wait to get into ROTC. I always liked uniforms." Davis became a B-24 *Liberator* navigator in the Pacific.

ROTC Sergeant Lawrence Gruits "was by the book; you couldn't pull anything over on him. We appreciated that later on." Every Friday and Monday the ROTC paraded at 13th and Ann. Gruits later received a commission. Davis played football in 1940–41 weighing "120 pounds soaking wet," but only in a mop-up role for head coach former North Carolina All-American Paul Severin.

Frederick Sternberger.[27] He earned 30 cents an hour after school and all day Saturdays bagging groceries and stocking shelves at the Big Star Market on 3rd. An A&P store was across the street. Most of his contemporaries also had after-school jobs, as did his best friends such as Jim Lee, Ronald Walters, Leon Stein, Jack Christian, and Jack Bissette.

Class of 1944

James Lee.[28] Lee began NHHS in 1940. In 1943 he attended Augusta Military Academy in Georgia, along with Delmer Seitter and Archie Craft, "to try to improve our grades." NHHS academics were very demanding with tough standards. He took an aviation course, and lots of his classmates trained at Pennington Flying Service. Drafted after graduation, Jim received a Military Academy appointment, finishing in 1949. A retired lieutenant general, he served as both infantryman and aviator.

---

* Ruth Middleton ('44) remembered many boys returned to school after the war to get their diplomas and claimed NHHS '42, '43, '44—with whichever class they would have graduated. [Interview with Ruth Middleton Clayton, July 28, 1999]

"We were extremely proud of our ROTC unit, the first in the state." Every boy who wanted to be was in army Junior ROTC.* "We had sponsors, pretty girls, the days before feminism. We had excellent teachers who were admired greatly." Lee rose to sergeant major and flag bearer, and buddy Allen Spivey was battalion commander. When Colonel W. V. Ochs was called to active duty, his replacement was Major Emil Engel, "friend of MacArthur, squared jaw, Sam Browne belt, wore his leather boots, was armor—he was tough."

A football end and guard on the "C squad" for three years at 150 pounds under Coach Bumgartner, he never played varsity. He had to block big John Burney, who "chewed tobacco a lot, had quite a reputation," and spit at him. Lee's main girlfriend was Dorothy Romeo, "clearly the most beautiful girl in the class, a very

New Hanover High School JROTC Sgt. James M. Lee and friend Dorothy Romeo, 1944.

James M. Lee

popular girl." He also dated Virginia Oliver ("blonde, blue eyes"), Ida Jo Graham, and Betty Lou Morrow. "A lot of boys dated my sister Ann," whose buddies included Gretter Duffy and Dotty Southerland.

Mike Michaelis.[29] "I was an excellent student until my junior year, then I sneaked through," he said. "My senior year I knew I would have to serve, and I started to goof off." Until then he had "average grades." Mike spent three years in ROTC and played football his senior year as a 135-pound center. Coach Rupert Bryan made Michaelis wash his car for spitting tobacco juice on it.

Catherine Russell.[30] Some of Russell's male friends went to summer school for extra credit to graduate early and go to college before entering the service. She went through NHHS without a car and usually rode the school bus or city bus everywhere. For a 25-cents fare, she spent all day

---

* The Army Junior Reserve Officers Training Course, politely dubbed "rotten old tin can," began at NHHS in 1938. The course covered physical training, infantry drill, military organization, discipline, sanitation, first aid, customs and courtesies, leadership and command, and more. Every participant but one told me how valuable his experience would be on active duty.

swimming at the Carolina Yacht Club and visiting classmate Laura Roe. Russell and other girls flirted with soldiers guarding the beach at night.

Bill McIlwain.[31] McIlwain's older sister was an "achiever"; so when he reached NHHS he heard, "Oh, you're Isabel's brother." "Not that good a student," he felt pressured to produce. Eventually he rose to the top in his career in national journalism which he spawned as sports editor of the school newspaper, the *Wildcat*. Mrs. Symmes taught the journalism class, and Mrs. Burroughs Smith and Virginia Walsh heavily impacted him.

Jack Hufham.[32] Jack, a "B–C" student, never forgot his teachers. Geometry teacher Mrs. LeGrand: called "Itchy," always reaching up to straighten her bra strap. Short geometry teacher Polly Levine: "I did pretty good in solid geometry, about the best grade I ever got. She sat in the middle of the classroom, assigned students alphabetically to 'go to the board' to work problems. I could tell when her finger went past the 'H's.'" First year aeronautics teacher Tommy Brown: "He only had to keep a day ahead of us because we didn't know a thing about aeronautics." Mrs. Walsh: "She laid down the foundation right in English."

Dick Jones '45.[33] "I remember the night a bunch of us were out riding in his daddy's car," Dick Jones recalled about John Burney, "and he was driving too fast around a curve and turned it almost over." It landed on its side at an angle. The boys got out and pushed it back over upright. John said, "We need to concoct a story about what happened," so he could tell his district judge father. "He was in training then to be a lawyer." Dick quit school at 17 and joined the merchant marine.

Jack McCarley '47.[34] Before entering NHHS, Jack McCarley looked forward to the end-of-school outings at Carolina Beach sponsored by the Wilmington police for county traffic boys. The "prettiest girls" were Diane Costello, Patty Southerland, and Betty Walters. Too bad. "Dad would not let us use the car to date and drive around."

* * *

Would there be a "school for veterans"? In 1946, an item reported 25 discharged veterans had enrolled at NHHS "catching up on the education they missed while in the armed services....Naturally they are impatient...." In April the school opened a "special four-year course for veterans in which they may attend classes exclusively on their own and move from grade to grade as their work and proof of progress is demonstrated...." Basement classes convened after regular students departed.[35]

"Emergency conditions currently delaying college entrance to returned servicemen and recent high school graduates may be relieved by the establishment of a branch of the University of North Carolina in New Hanover County...." the newspaper divulged in 1946. Tentatively planned for 800–

1,000 students, the veterans school moved across into Isaac Bear School in 1947 to form Wilmington College, the forerunner of the University of North Carolina at Wilmington.[36]

Local boys back from military duty attending predecessor to Wilmington College (later the University of North Carolina at Wilmington), 1946. *Left to right*, Walter Powell, Charlie Jones, Mayo Holmes, James Godwin, Ed Lamb, Willie Hewlett, Burrell Byers, Tommy Jones, Gerald Conrad, and Clarence Council.

George Burrell Byers

The Board of Education and Principals, 1943–44[37]

New Hanover County Board of Education—Dr. John T. Hoggard, Chairman; members L. T. Landon, Vice Chairman; J. C. Roe, Mrs. C. L. Meister, Emsley A. Laney, J. S. Craig, Jr.; Cyrus D. Hogue, Attorney. Dr. Hoggard began his sixth consecutive term as head of the city-county school system.

Superintendent of Schools, H. M. Roland; Assistant Superintendent, J. W. Grise; Assistant Superintendent for Secondary Schools, T. T. Hamilton, Jr.

"Principals—White"

New Hanover High	T. T. Hamilton, Jr.
Hemenway	Sue Boon

Tileston	J. W. Grise
Chestnut Street	Annie W. Herring
Lake Forest	Mrs. Manley Williams
William Hooper	Arline Kimball
Sunset Park	Mrs. Lucille Shuffler
Washington Catlett	Mrs. E. R. Blakeslee
Wrightsboro	Nellie Fentress
Forest Hills	Katherine Von Glahn
Bradley Creek	J. W. Webster
Winter Park	C. G. Berry
Carolina Beach	Mrs. C. G. Van Landingham

"Principals—Negro"

Williston Industrial	F. J. Rogers
Peabody	C. H. McDonald
Williston Primary	Booker T. Washington
Acorn Branch*	William Blount
Castle Hayne*	Lucile Lofton
Wrightsboro*	Lula Cobb
Middle Sound*	Mary H. McFarland
East Wilmington*	Essie R. Miller
Kirkland*	Eliza Johnson
Wrightsville*	Annie Weber
Masonboro*	Ada McKoy
Oak Hill*	Isabelle Barnhill

* Rural Consolidated Schools (from 1 to 4 teachers each)

Senior superlatives, *The Hanoverian* 1943[38]

Athletic—Agnes Morton, Heatwole Thomas
Friendliest—Blanche Jacobi, Dewey Hobbs
Independent—Mary Elizabeth Toms, Charles Brindell
Intellectual —Eloise Smith, Heyward Bellamy
Popular/All Around/Personality/School Spirit—Dotty Southerland, Dewey Hobbs
Nonchalant—Elizabeth Goldberg, John Burney
Flirt—Pattie Darden, Billy Haas
Dependable—Dotty Cameron, Dewey Hobbs

Chapter 16

Hardships, Sacrifices, and Inconveniences

One year after the United States entered the war, the "ration situation" was this. "The average man finds many of the things that were commonplace in pre-Pearl Harbor days are now scarce, rationed or out for the duration. First it was tires...then cars...next metal objects....Some foods have become scarce because armed services and lend-lease are dipping deeper into our larder...[and] limited shipping facilities slow transportation of items...."[1]

Of all wartime hardships, sacrifices, and inconveniences, undoubtedly gasoline rationing manifested as the biggest headache for citizens and governments. By September 1942, it was "placed on a nationwide basis not only because the rationing authorities have failed to establish a distributing system...[to] give consumers in all sections of the country a square deal, but because tire conservation...can be accomplished by no other means...."[2] A system based on a vehicle owner's job requirements and normal driving habits authorized a windshield sticker denoting either the "A" (lowest), "B," or "C" (highest) level for that vehicle.

Rules changed, but you had to read the newspaper. Before February 1943, only a preferred list such as physicians and essential war workers merited "C" books. Afterwards, under certain circumstances, persons lacking adequate gasoline on a "B" book could be approved locally for "C" books. By late 1944, new "A" coupons were good for only four gallons weekly. Laura Roe's father, J. C. Roe, merchant and school board member, "For some reason seemed to get enough gas. Maybe because he was so civic-minded."[3]

Regulators' heavy hands held the public at bay one January 1943 day. "No Calls Answered: Do not call or visit the fuel ration department of the local ration board on Friday or Saturday of this week...." Therefore, apply through the mail, and anticipate gas needs 3–5 days in advance.[4]

In mid-summer 1943, 848 visitors faced charges from local ration boards for "pleasure driving" to area beaches. Even though no ban existed, boards found it was hard for many owners to explain how their "A-10" coupons for home driving leave enough gas for vacation trips. A survey of oyster roasts, night clubs, and other "amusement and eating places outside the city limits, [feel] the pressure of decreased business as a result of the pleasure driving ban....One popular night spot on the Carolina Beach Road"* considered closing down.

A popular oyster house nearby said regular customers and proximity to the shipyard prevented serious inroads. The Office of Price Administration permitted stopping to eat along a road where one's car is traveling on a "legitimate errand." "'People don't have to give up their amusements,'" OPA attorney J. Frank Hackler said.[5] Nice sounding, but the board revoked numerous permits: "No pleasure driving on war rationed gas."[6]

The *Morning Star* reacted to "another example of bungling by gasoline and fuel oil rationing authorities. The principle may be all right but the execution and enforcement is poor...."[7] Some 22,000 county motorists purchased annual tags, and some 25,000 had approval for gasoline and tires. Automobile drivers caught the brunt, but by 1944 the local Office of Defense Transportation cited commercial vehicle operators for "many abuses."[8]

One reason for the 35-mph speed limit was to save tire wear. Tires were rationed and retreading was difficult to obtain. People remember threadbare tires, and military personnel reported the anxieties of flats and breakdowns driving to duty stations. Midway through the war rationed synthetic rubber

Neighbor D. C. North at Camp Davis, ca. 1943.
Catherine Solomon

tires came on the market. Tire expert Gardner Greer stated, "'I believe synthetic rubber is here to stay.'" He was "affiliated with one of the largest tire concerns [MacMillan & Cameron] in the city...." The nation returned to pure rubber after 1945, and Greer later opened a tire and auto store.[9]

* * *

* The Plantation Club, the county's No. 1 night spot, closed temporarily in 1943 because of the driving restrictions, but reopened to "operate as in the past to serve our famous food....Entertainment discontinued—only dining—city prices." [*Wilmington Morning Star*, January 22, 1943]

Infamous Ration Books

Officials introduced point rationing, the most perplexing of systems, in February 1943 through War Ration Book #2, issuing one book to each household member. "You can buy unrationed foods meanwhile."[10] Shoppers learned to use points for fresh and canned goods. Many foodstuffs were interchangeable, "a matter of taste and convenience whether you have corn, peas, string beans...or some other vegetable." Scarce peas cost more ration points, corn less. "Let's give point rationing a fair try before we get excited about the irritations that will crop up."[11] By February 1944, citizens used red and blue one-point, thin-plastic ration tokens received as "change."* Ration books and tokens made good war mementoes. I still have several of my books.

In March 1943 OPA placed the retail sale of butter, margarine, lard, and other fats and oils under point rationing, and "Wilmington housewives responded quickly" by stripping stores of each.[12] Beef, veal, pork, lamb and mutton, cheese, and canned fish followed. A number of food products, particularly canned, moved on and off the ration lists.† "The whole program of food rationing has been typical of the waste that has characterized the bureaucrats' dictation from the time they came into power."[13] Inconsistent policies, indecision, and red tape produced equivalent results, and shortages in various foodstuffs fluctuated.

Wilmingtonians in 1943 developed numerous ways to misplace ration books, including War Ration Book #1 for sugar, coffee, and shoes. "Officials blamed 'carelessness'....Most books are left in grocery stores." Citizens had to file a new application, advertise in the newspaper (oh, sure), and then wait 30 days before warranting a new book.[14] People carelessly left books in clothes taken to the laundry and dry cleaners.

We Had to Have Shoes

Shoe rationing, a first-class unavoidable nuisance, required coupons, too. Trouble was citizens could purchase only two new pairs a year. In those days kids usually wore to school leather dress shoes with leather or hard rubber soles. Old pairs were for play. With normal activity, shoes scuffed and wore out. We wore "Chuck Taylor" or "Converse" "gym shoes" of light canvas and rubber soles, often outside. We waited for the summer barefoot season, but had to toughen feet for the hot pavement.

---

* "A Wilmington grocer swears the following happened...: A woman came in and purchased three pounds of ration-free lard....She returned and purchased three more pounds. That afternoon, she returned and a third time with six pounds of salvage fats, which she exchanged for cash, and 12 red ration tokens. She used the tokens and cash toward the purchase of a steak. The grocer is still wondering." [*Wilmington Morning Star*, March 8, 1944]

† In September 1944, point values on the following items were doubled or even more: all canned and bottled fruits, fruit and vegetable juices, tomatoes, catsup and chili sauce. Some processed foods were removed such as jams, jellies, fruit butters, various vegetables, and soups and baby foods.

"The [February 1943 rationing] order was issued without fanfare or build-up....Persons without ration cards whose shoes are about worn out may go barefoot unless they can persuade their local boards to issue them necessary credentials....The available stock...will be more equitably distributed than any rationed article in the past."[15] But not for Negress Bertha Patten and the six people in her dwelling who told police "that an enterprising person has stolen the No. 17 coupon from each of six War Ration Books No. 1...."[16] That same day, the Brigade Boys Club started teaching shoe repair fundamentals.

Officials modified the initial plan to allow citizens more footwear of certain types. Considered to be "non-rationed" were locker sandals; house, burial, and bathing slippers; shoes with a fabric upper and rubber sole ["gym shoes"]; wedge-heeled and platform shoes; sandals with a heel height of $1\frac{1}{8}$ inch or less; soft-soled moccasins, infant shoes; overshoes and waterproof footwear. Efird's Department Store at Front and Grace advertised:

1. Buy shoes as you have always bought them. Don't be rushed into spending more money for shoes than you need to.
2. Shoe stamps are transferrable
3. ...If an individual has less than two pairs of wearable or repairable shoes of the type he needs and has spent his stamp and cannot use a family stamp, he may apply to his local board for a certificate to purchase another pair.[17]

The Coast Guard Auxiliary issued Oscar Grant's father GI shoes with his uniform. He shared coupons with the family. Ronnie Phelps, like many of us, wore the durable Boy Scout shoes from Belk's, considered more rugged than Buster Browns or Thom McAns. The rest of Wilmington "have been rushing to buy non-rationed [light-weight soft-soled canvas sandals] 'play' shoes, as well as having all of last summer's footwear repaired....Shoe repair shops here [Big Ike's especially] have had their business increase twofold...."

You thought men didn't wear shoes. Women got the attention. In 1943, "Local women do not intend to be 'caught without footwear' as sales at Wilmington shoe stores indicate....One large store had 600 pairs of sandals last week which almost caused a stampede. [Customers] selected their own, scattering shoes about the department and leaving many 'mis-matches.'"[18] In January 1944, "thousands of Wilmington women flocked to the city's shoe stores to buy ration-free footwear....Shortages have resulted in one underlying rule—that persons stand in line and take their turn to make a purchase....[from] harassed clerks."[19] My slightly heavyset mother preferred lace-up pumps, but took what she could get.

My Forest Hills Parent-Teachers Association "found a remedy" to help our own. "Whatever statistics may show to the contrary, parents know their children's feet grow fastest....Keeping children in shoes is one of the little tragedies of this war." The PTA set up a used shoe exchange where out-grown shoes could be traded.[20] PTA president Mrs. Charles F. Jones an-nounced the collection "already available at the school has been disinfected, polished, sorted in sizes and types and labeled."[21]

* * *

The OPA and Black-marketeering

A few patriotic citizen groups rallied behind the U.S. OPA's effort, but not the agency. "'Rationing and price ceilings are our weapons,'" said Mrs. Julian Morton of President Roosevelt's pledge campaign, "'and they will be effective only if each and every citizen makes an honest effort to abide by the regulations of the OPA.'"[22] Rationing on meats and fats ceased in No-vember 1945. "During the ration period, counter service has been indiffer-ent. Here it is—take it or leave it...."[23]

Shortages hit restaurants hard. "Based on the pre-war population, the ration allowance was never adequate to meet the needs of Wilmington's wartime population...."[24] The OPA retorted, "'There is no more necessity for restaurants closing than for a housewife to close her kitchen.'"[25] Such word battles continued for the duration, but totally adequate allocation, supply, and distribution systems never evolved.

By April 1943, authorities made headway, but meat markets faced short-ages. "It would be a good time to turn vegetarian, if the vegetable situation were not even more acute....Accept the inevitable and learn to live on too little until some genius solves the farm problem, the distribution problem, the price problem, the help problem and sundry other little problems the bureaucrats are too busy to tackle."[26] The newspaper stayed on it.

Classmate Kenneth Murphy's family "would jump at any news about some merchant getting a shipment [of meat]."[27] He stood in line at 4:00 a.m. one day at the Broad Circle Food Store. Mr. Carnage, the butcher, had told customers he was getting a "beef." When Kenneth left for school, his mother replaced him. "All this for a small piece of beef."

The OPA tried to stop even trivial offenses. In September 1943 authori-ties lectured 25 retail businesses on overcharging, including for bottles of beer. In October 1943 a prominent local fruit and produce company paid $135 to settle an OPA triple-damage suit for alleged overcharging for cab-bages and onions. In some instances black-marketeering created shortages, such as the 1944 dumping of counterfeit gasoline coupons. Then black mar-ket meat hit town, "reprehensible on all counts...hurtful to the nation's war effort....To peddle meat of inferior quality is to commit potential murder."[28]

The fight against illegally selling meat over ceiling continued sporadi-cally, based partly on its fluctuating availability. As late as April 1945, "as

Wilmington Marine Sgt. Addis S. McGinn, Jr., *left*, with Jap booty on Guam, 1944.
Wilmington newspaper clipping in American Legion Post 10 Wartime Scrapbooks

point values rise and the nation's meat supply dwindles, Wilmington proudly reports 'very little' black market operations," the OPA stated.[29]

The OPA applied housing rules equally. "For the second time in less than two years OPA rent director George W. Jeffrey is about to be evicted from his residence here. In both cases the landlord was found to be within his legal rights....He had no idea where he would move...because of the housing shortage in Wilmington."[30]

The local headquarters closed in September 1943 without replacing Hackler. One year later, O. H. Shoemaker, the only New Hanover War Price & Rationing Board chairman, resigned. C. Van Leuven replaced him for the duration. By late August 1945, the board cut its staff by one-third, and only one OPA representative remained.

* * *

The newspaper column "Weekly Rationing at a Glance" reported on the status of commodities such as sugar, gasoline, coffee, fuel oil, rubber boots, tires, scrap; recent regulation and announcements; and what coupon stamps were good for what products, for how much, and when. One February 1943 item stated that applications for a baby must be filed within 30 days of their birth, and must include a birth certificate. Another rule, another restriction, another regulation. All were hardships or sacrifices—at the least inconveniences—to be endured until victory.

The Uncertainty of Whiskey Sales

The state and local governments divided rationed liquor sales receipts the fiscal year ending June 30, 1944, gross ABC store sales in New Hanover County were $2,325,268, a decrease of $897,600 under the previous year attributable to the liquor shortage. Disbursements made: State: $160,270; Wilmington, $160,000; County, $80,000; Wrightsville Beach, $15,000; Carolina Beach, $17,000; Wilmington port development, $9,289; law enforcement, $11,231. [For the 1945 fiscal year county sales rose 38 percent and profits 13 percent, although the population declined.][31]

The state ABC board's bottle-a-day plan lost money and presented Otis Benton a hangover. He gave an unidentified Negro a $20 bill to purchase a pint of whiskey from a Brooklyn ABC store while he waited outside. "The Negro came out of the store at a gallop and paused not to give Benton the whiskey or the change." Benton collared the man, but he broke the bottle over Benton's head and escaped with the change.[32]

Justice Was Served[33]

Schoolboy Earl Page lived in five different places, including Fort Fisher and Maffitt Village, and attended three county schools. For kids like me such instability was difficult to comprehend. "We had all toughened up a bit as we learned to eat within the limits of our ration books," my later NHHS classmate recalled.

We had no car so gasoline wasn't a problem. But then there was Mr. Boston, the family butcher who worked in the Groceteria on Market Street. He was able somehow to dole out to our family a "little extra something"....If we were truly breaking the rationing rules, what follows can now be put into proper perspective. Mr. Henri Emurian, the likable, rotund, eccentric, but superb organist of the First Baptist Church, paid us a visit....He let [grandmother] know that he was quite hungry and might he fix himself a little breakfast. Gentle sweet Tahi...[said] "go right ahead." Henri commenced extracting numerous eggs from the fridge and then proceeded to fry up our entire precious one pound of bacon as my poor grandmother looked on in silent horror and amazement....Justice was served.

Chapter 17

What if They Had All Come Home?

"Seventy-five of these men I knew, went to school with, went to church with, lived in the same neighborhood with, went into the army with," Harold Fussell *solemnly told me by the Hugh MacRae Park war memorial. Its names for World War II total 148. He proceeded down the list, pausing at familiar ones. Butler, LeRoy Cedric, New Hanover High ('39) classmate, they worked together at North-Smith Coal Company, killed in action in Italy in 1944; Combs, Seldon W., a Marine, would have graduated with him; Heustess, Talbert J., infantry, played baseball together; Waters, William S., Jr., classmate killed in an air accident in Asia; and so on....*[1]

The large majority of New Hanover County's men who died during service had been pre-war residents. My research indicates at least 187 county men died, as shown in Appendix B. My number includes men from the merchant marine, whereas the memorial, erected by American Legion Post 10 in 1988, omits them.

The dead came from varied economic, social, and educational levels and included the merchant marine and all armed forces except the Coast Guard.* All but four presumedly were whites. Most deaths resulted from combat or tragic accidents. The North Carolina Shipbuilding Company employed at least 33 before entering the service.

Because my research on this subject ends with 1948, I carry four men missing in action. Each likely was eventually declared dead. Had they been prisoners of war, liberation would have cleared the MIA tag. My MIA listings, therefore, may be a bit inaccurate, but presumably they died. That increases the total to 191.

---

* Actually the Memorial lists 149 names, but one is in error, Zora Aaron Sneeden. He is the father of Floyd Bagley Sneeden, who is correctly listed.

Additionally, I found 44 other dead having a direct county connection, and 13 such still listed as MIA. This 57 plus the 191, for all intents and purposes, allows the county to claim 248 men dead or MIA.

Selected representative cases follow.

* * *

Alvin Henry Allen.[2] The 15-year veteran chief metalsmith was killed in action when the destroyer USS *Meredith* (DD-165), bombed by 27 aircraft, sank off Guadalcanal on October 15, 1942. *Meredith* survivors, "many of them desperately injured, spent a nightmarish three days and nights clinging to rafts before being rescued. As men on the floats died, others in the water took their places. Schools of sharks added to the horror...."

John Richard "Dick" Garrabrant.[3] On December 15, 1944, at Wilmington's First Presbyterian Church, the Fort Bragg commanding general presented the Distinguished Service Cross to Emily Garrabrant, widow of Wilmingtonian Captain John Richard "Dick" Garrabrant. The DSC is the army's highest award for valor.

Citing "extraordinary heroism in action against the enemy on 10 June 1944, in France," the commanding officer of Company C, 8th Infantry Regiment, 4th Infantry Division "volunteered to lead a patrol to seek out and destroy a hidden enemy strong point which was holding up the advance and inflicting heavy casualties upon the men."

Exposing himself to fire, Garrabrant successfully assaulted the position while losing his life—four days after landing on Normandy's Utah Beach on D-Day. The widow's children, Edgar 3, and Margey, 19 months, accompanied her, along with his parents, Mr. and Mrs. Edgar Cornelius Garrabrant.

It took a long time for the family to learn of his death. By mid-July, brother Bill Garrabrant remembered, "We hadn't heard, but lots of other families had heard from their men by mail. Dick never wrote in those four days. He never wrote from France. You realize others are receiving mail and you're not, and you haven't heard from the War Department either. It was excruciating because it was such a protracted time."

Two soldiers delivered an official notification telegram on a weekend with the entire family at home on Mimosa Place in Oleander. The family was unaware that Emily Garrabrant already knew. She learned it from her friend, the wife of a major close to her husband in their unit, who had written with the news. "Emily was never able to bring herself to share this with the family. She just held herself together. In her mind she guessed it was wrong."

Born in 1916, Captain Garrabrant, a graduate of New Hanover High School and North Carolina State, worked for the Atlantic Coast Line before entering the army in 1941. Margey, now living near the old home, proudly

Edgar C. Garrabrant, *seated*, with his sons Capt. John Richard "Dick" and William "Bill," holding Dick's son Edgar.

displays the memorabilia of her father's service including a June 1944 *New York Times* photograph showing her father interrogating a German prisoner, probably taken hours before he was killed near Montebourg. His sister Betty Garrabrant Cantwell saw the picture in the *Times*, phoned them, and they sent her a print.[*]

Ernest F. Peschau, Jr., and Preston B. Bellamy. Margaret Bellamy Alexius experienced having a husband and brother declared MIA at the same time in December 1944. Germans breaking through at the Battle of the Bulge captured Harold Alexius of the 99th Infantry Division. An army B-24 *Liberator* bomber carrying bombardier First Lieutenant Peschau and gunner Staff Sergeant Bellamy went down in the Central Pacific on their 13th mission. Peschau had completed his requisite missions. Alexius was liberated, but the airmen were never found.

Victor Lee Mintz.[4] Already a veteran of 33 B-17 *Flying Fortress* missions over Europe, pilot First Lieutenant Mintz volunteered to fly again on July 19, 1944. Victor took flak over Hamburg, Germany, forcing a return emergency landing at Duxford, England. The crash killed everyone aboard. A letter to his parents, Mr. and Mrs. Daniel Mintz, indicated orders to rotate Stateside. Manette Dixon Mintz stated, "He always felt he was better off than those boys on the ground." In 1948 Victor was re-interred in Wilmington's Oakdale Cemetery.

Robert Rhodes "Bobby" Hatch.[5] Former North Carolina State student Lieutenant Hatch died in a B-26 *Marauder* takeoff crash in New Guinea in January 1943. In August 1942 while leading a formation forced down by weather, with his crew lost for 29 days in the jungles, he walked 150 miles to a U.S. base. His death merited a *Saturday Evening Post* picture and story on November 14, 1942, and the cover of the January 1944 *State College News*.

William A. "Billy" Brown.[6] A glider pilot with the 9th Air Force's 436th Troop Carrier Command, Major Brown, a neighbor and graduate of NHHS ('38) and North Carolina State ('42), was KIA in Germany on March 24, 1945. His glider landed first during the invasion of Southern France, and participated in strikes in Normandy, Holland, and the Rhine crossings. "Wilmington lost...another of the cream of its manhood. If it was necessary for Billy to die, we know he went the way he would have wanted: fighting for and defending the things he held dear....To his parents...you gave one of the

---

[*] "Colleville-sur-Mer, Normandy, France. I did not know army Capt. Dick Garrabrant. His brother Bill, of an Oleander family, was a Forest Hills schoolmate and comrade in arms in our neighborhood homefront battles helping the boys overseas win the war. On Wednesday, a lovely day beginning and ending in cemeteries of the Battle of Normandy, I met Capt. Garrabrant. He lies here with 9,386 other American service members." [Author in *Wilmington Star-News*, June 5, 2004, from the American Normandy Cemetery] See photo in *A Sentimental Journey*.

finest...." He held the Distinguished Flying Cross, Bronze Star, Air Medal with Oak Leaf Clusters, and Presidential Unit Citation.

Tebe DeWit Sanford, Jr.[7] Early in the war, Japanese captured Pharmacist's Mate 3rd Class Sanford on Corregidor, Philippines. The family received five postcards, the last in January 1945—an April 1944 card from a Manila camp saying he was alive. In June 1945 the word reached home. "To a hopeful mother...came the heart-rendering news that her son...had gone to his death on October 24, 1944 when a Japanese ship, on which he was a POW, was sunk by an allied submarine off Shoonan...China." Transferring prisoners to Japan, the ship allegedly bore markings indicating POWs were aboard.

Robert Aaron "Bobby" Goldberg, Jr.[8] To those who knew and loved him in school, he faced an unlimited postwar future. The son of prominent attorney Aaron Goldberg, he was an outstanding student and leader at NHHS and Wake Forest. Sisters Libby Goldberg O'Quinn and Frances Goldberg Walker recalled his interest in aviation. "This was a patriotic war. They all wanted to see action."

Goldberg received his commission as a Marine second lieutenant and wings in October 1943. In 1944 he joined squadron VMF-511 on the carrier USS *Block Island* (CVE-106), flying F4U *Corsair* fighters. During a mission on May 27, 1945, over the Ryukuyu Islands searching for his missing commanding officer, Bobby became MIA. The wing man saw him go down.[*]

Mr. Goldberg learned he was MIA after Western Union phoned and told him to wait for an important telegram. "That irritated him," said Libby, who was in Texas awaiting her first child. Frances went home from work and entered the kitchen where her mother was cooking. "She said when I walked in, 'I've lost my boy.' Daddy started calling people to find out something about it." The Goldbergs corresponded with the C.O.'s widow for years sharing information.

It took seven years for their son to be declared KIA, allowing them to collect death insurance. Mr. Goldberg never lost hope. "As long as he lived he would not have been surprised if Bobby walked in 40 years later," Libby stated. "He'd say, 'I've been waiting for you.' He would not accept the finality of it."

Fraternity brothers and classmates Judson Creech and Jim Turner warmly remembered Bobby. Creech, a Pacific Marine veteran, said, "He was well liked on campus and interested in debating. Very conscientious, a very religious boy, one of the finest young men I ever met."[9] Fellow F4U pilot Turner added, "It was against every rule in the book to have a Jew in your fraternity. But Bobby was such a super guy that national headquarters was

---

[*] Goldberg and VMF-511 are memorialized in the World War II museum of the USS *Yorktown* (CV-12) at Patriot's Point, S.C.

petitioned for permission. Of all the guys to get killed, he would be the last on my list."[10]

Oscar Rockwell Jones and Aubrey A. Jones.[11] By September 1944, James D. and Nettie Sutton Jones of Greenville Sound Road "appeared to be the first family in New Hanover County to suffer two war casualties." Oscar died when his torpedoed LST-921 sank in the English Channel in August. Staff Sergeant Aubrey, 120th Infantry Regiment, 30th Division, was KIA on July 11 in France. Half-sister Peggy Jones, 8, remembered the family hearing about Oscar's death. "Mother and daddy crying and hollering—they were real upset, and it upset me. After they were killed, I thought that any minute they would come walking through the door. I thought someone was telling me a lie."

When the boys came home on leave, "Oscar put me up on his shoulders and sang *White Cliffs of Dover*." They kidded her and urged her to get them good-looking dates the next time they were home. The sons were Nettie's, then divorced from James, their father. Peggy went to tell Nettie nearby and when leaving heard her screaming. Aubrey is buried in the American Normandy Cemetery.

James Goodlet "Jimmy" Thornton, Jr. Captain Thornton, 26, a neighbor and 1941 graduate of The Citadel, broke his hip playing NHHS football and was exempted from combat. "But he wouldn't stand for it," sister Lucretia Thornton McDaniel recalled. "He could have had a desk job." First reported MIA, eleven months later he was confirmed KIA. "There's no telling what he would have accomplished had he lived." When the first telegram came, an upset Lucretia sat on the end of Johnny Mercer's pier and cried. Her mother sent a policeman to find her.[12]

Jimmy commanded Company B, 741st Tank Battalion, from Omaha Beach on D-Day into Germany.* "On September 14, 1944, the tank in which he was a crew member was hit by enemy artillery fire near Harspelt, Germany," an army letter stated. "Medical personnel discovered Captain Thornton, seriously wounded, lying a short distance from the tank. They began to evacuate him, but were forced to take cover....Captain Thornton disappeared and his remains were not recovered."[13] The battalion history recorded:

> We were almost through fighting for the day....Captain Thornton and I were in a position behind a small hill when a doughboy came up asking us to move up with our tanks to a crossroad beyond the pillboxes....There wasn't supposed to be anything out there....This time however Jerry had moved in....Captain Thornton's tank was hit and before we could get out

---

* "Thornton, Captain James G., Jr.: Physical Description: 5'4", 140, 26, medium complex, brown hair, grey eyes, shoe size 7½D, pants size 30W29L, shirt size 15x30." [Casualty Clearance Plan, Headquarters, 741st Tank Battalion, 30 August 1945]

of the line of fire it was hit again. Nothing we did seemed to stop the direct fire that the enemy was throwing at us. We maneuvered about and had almost gotten out of range, when another round sent the captain's tank up in flames....[14]

Bill Warnock remembered Jimmy "was standing in the commander's hatch of his tank when it was hit....One of the shots blew him from the tank, severing his left leg above the knee and wounding him in the left arm." The 109th Infantry placed a tourniquet on his leg. "He was last seen being taken into captivity by the Germans who presumably carried him to an aid station....I suspect that [he] died of his wounds while under German care and they buried him."[15] A Citadel classmate also found him. "He met his death like a soldier....He didn't whimper and when I told him that he could not be evacuated, that we were cut off by the Germans, he did not complain...."[16]

Before officials in 1945 confirmed his death, a casualty status report stated (partial):

> Location: "coordinates 888-757, Sheet #107, Houffalize, France and Belgium, 1:50,000. Occurred in vicinity of Stupbacherseif, Germany. Terrain rolling, consisting of alternating stretches of cleared and lightly wooded sections. Conclusion: No member of this organization has additional knowledge of the three missing members of this tank crew which would indicate that they either survived or perished....A presumption of survival can no longer be held. Recommendation:...that the status of Capt. Thornton...be changed from MIA on 14Sep44 to KIA 14Sep44."[17]

Thornton is memorialized as MIA in the U.S. cemetery in Luxembourg. In 1997 nephew Paul J. McDaniel asked the army to locate recoverable remains, but the army begged off resuming the search because of limited funds.*

Herman John Gerdes, Jr.[18] Mr. and Mrs. H. J. Gerdes of Brookwood "held out hope that their son was alive; a hope inspired when the Navy Department learned, following Japan's surrender," that four unidentified crewmen of the submarine USS *Robalo* (SS-273) had been taken prisoner. But the navy "failed...to produce evidence indicating that the four men had survived their imprisonment." *Robalo* and Ensign Gerdes, a 1943 Naval Academy graduate, failed to return from a mission off the Philippines in August 1944.

Clifford Davis "Cliff" McIver.[19] Ensign McIver served in Fighter Squadron 30 (VF-30) on the USS *Belleau Wood* (CVL-24) in the Western Pacific. Flying his F6F *Hellcat* fighter in March 1945 around Iwo Jima and Chichi Jima, he and another pilot damaged three freighters and downed a twin-engine patrol plane. "I got my first real sock in on the Japs a few days ago,"

---

* Wilmingtonian Jane Fonvielle wrote Jimmy's sister Frances Thornton Reynolds after visiting. "I could not believe that in all the cemeteries in the world I would see Thornton, James G., North Carolina....The place is kept perfect." [Fonvielle to Reynolds, June 3, 1984]

he wrote his brother Mack McIver, a navy chaplain, on March 5. About 130 miles from his task force, they made three passes and left the ships ablaze. "Both our planes got hit—but not bad. I got one side of my cockpit canopy knocked out and didn't get a scratch." Inbound, they attacked the patrol plane. "He was burning all over when I pulled away at 150 feet off the water. My wing man saw him hit the water and go right under...."

In May 1945 the navy declared him to be MIA after a March 18 raid on Tokyo. In December he posthumously received the Navy Cross and Distinguished Flying Cross. An NHHS '40 honors graduate, center Cliff was "one of the ten best football players in the state in 1940." The boys were sons of Mr. and Mrs. Malcolm Chester McIver, whose third son of four (the family also included five daughters), LaMar W. McIver, was a merchant marine warrant officer.

Ens. Clifford Davis "Cliff" McIver, Fighter Squadron 30 (VF-30), *first row on right*, was killed in action in March 1945.
Mildred Sneeden McIver

Mack officiated at Cliff's 1944 wedding. "Bette writes every day and I try to do the same....I don't see how I can love anyone as much as I love her," Cliff wrote. Mack recalled, unfortunately, "His wife was so upset after his death that she cut off all contact with us [family]. We don't know what happened to her." The conclusion: "His parents still are hoping that he is living and that in the not distant future Ensign McIver will come home from the wars...."

NHHS '42 Classmates

Members who died in uniform included James Edward Hill, James Borden "Jim" ("Jimmy") Lynch II, John Graham "Jack" Nall, Claude D. Orrell, Claude Clifford Owensby, Jr., Tony S. Reynolds, John Willard Smidt, Joseph Edward Starkey, and Samuel Thomas "Sammy" Tyler.

Orrell, a B-24 *Liberator* gunner, was KIA over the Ploesti, Rumania, oil fields on June 6, 1944. On his final mission he downed one enemy fighter with another "probable." Star athlete and Third Army cavalry soldier Owensby fought in France, Belgium, and Luxembourg before dying of wounds in March 1945.

Lieutenant Smidt, 22, died in a B-17 training accident in Tallahassee, Florida, in July 1944.[20] An ROTC captain and football player, he received a Wake Forest athletic scholarship but entered the air force in September 1942. Baseball player and Merchant Marine Academy cadet Tyler died at sea during convoy duty on February 3, 1943.

On his 41st mission, B-25 *Mitchell* bomber pilot Nall went down over Italy on July 6, 1944.[21] Stationed in Corsica with the 321st Bomb Group, Nall wrote classmate Mac Wilson six weeks earlier, "We are hitting the railroads and harbors in Southern Italy just above Rome." Gene Edwards, a pallbearer when he was re-interred in Oakdale in 1948, remembered, "He was my buddy. He was an awful good boy, but he was crazy—the first guy I remember in high school who swallowed goldfish—they were supposedly alive. His dad never knew he had been killed. The news had gotten out that Jack had died but they didn't want to tell him." Ironically, the same newspaper edition also announced the death of his father, John P. Nall, retired from the Atlantic Coast Line, on October 23, 1944.

Lynch. Numerous people who knew him have declared Jim was truly destined for stardom, governor at least. He stood above the rest. With the family strongly believing in his potential, nurturing and encouraging him, he excelled in school academically, socially, and in leadership. At St. James Episcopal he achieved Eagle Scout and crucifer, "an honor bestowed upon the outstanding boy in the senior class."[*]

Jim's mother, Jane Iredell Green Lynch, died before his 14th birthday, fostering a close bond with his father, Herbert A. Lynch.[22] He was their seventh child and fourth son. "Father wanted him to be a lawyer. Jim so intended," stated brother Thomas G. Lynch. "He was bright enough to be anything he wanted to be, and expressed himself well. He was a great son to my father. He had an amazing record for a young man."[23]

After finishing NHHS in 1942 as *The Wildcat* editor, ROTC commander, and National Honor Society president, he enrolled at the University of North Carolina to await the draft. Mac Wilson roomed with him. In November 1942 Jim wrote his father:

> Ever since the United States went to war...I have been waiting anxiously for the time when I could get into the fight....I have no illusions as to its glories. I don't want to fight because I think it is glamorous or a lot of fun. I know that it...has to be done before we can resume our normal

---

[*] Years ago St. James placed a marble memorial plaque on the sanctuary north wall, and the Parish Hall contains his crucifer photograph. Wet eyes and many memories come to Wilson on visits to St. James, the Hugh MacRae Park memorial, and the Oakdale Cemetery site.

lives....The first and most natural reason...is that I want to help my country....Behind this is a natural curiosity and a desire to know what war really is like....Someday the world will be ruled by my generation, and I think it's my duty to gain adequate experience to do my part....I shall never know whether I am capable or not until I have tested myself....I have no illusions that it will make the slightest difference to the world whether I live or not....[24]

However obsessed, until then Jim had not convinced his father he should volunteer. Almost 19, he enlisted one year after Pearl Harbor to become a fighter pilot, and Mac enlisted in the army. Jim's brothers already serving: army Captain Herbert A., Jr., army Major Charles E., and navy Lieutenant Thomas G., all eventually stationed overseas.

In March 1944 Jim received his wings and commission, and joined the 15th Air Force's 31st

Army air forces 1st Lt. James Borden "Jim" Lynch II, P-51 *Mustang* fighter pilot, killed returning to his Italy base on February 9, 1945, after his 31st mission.

Thomas G. Lynch

Fighter Group in Italy. "Thirty-one" would be unlucky. At night on February 9, 1945, when returning from his 31st combat mission "with fuel low and weather bad, he attempted to land his P-51 *Mustang*...at an alternate airfield along the shore of the Adriatic Sea near Bari." He crashed and died instantly.[25]

Thomas was at Ulithi (40 months overseas) when he received his father's letter. In the same mail was Jim's last letter, which he read first. "He loved flying; he loved what he was doing. It was the saddest thing that ever happened to our family. Father tried to keep him out of the service."[26] But, "his father could follow but one course—honor the pact [of consent to his enlistment]. He regretted it for every minute of the six years that he lived after Jim's death...."[27]

When the newspaper reported Jim's death on February 23, 1945, "there was an instant outpouring of love and sympathy....His father received many letters...expressing their admiration and love...." One read, "Jim was truly a Christian soldier. I know that many times on his missions he must have put out his hand and touched the hand of God."[28] Friend Robert Strange wrote, "This soldier typifies the finest things of youth—youth which we are realizing as never before is so very fine. He gave his life when this life filled with the love of life."[29]

A pensive Wilson warmly reminisced, "He was more of a patriot than I was." He had a photographic memory, hardly cracked a book and made A's, spent his time at UNC drinking beer, pledged a fraternity, didn't have girlfriends particularly, didn't play sports. "What he wanted to do in life—we never talked about that. I think he would have made an excellent lawyer. He was very quiet, easy to get along with."[30] Wilson wrote his own father in March 1945 from a foxhole in Germany:

> Your news of Jim's death gave me—without exception—the worst shock of my life!....Goes to show you "One never knows, does one." Have one more reason now—stronger than any of my others—to see this foul war to its bloody end. Wish you could read the letter I received from Ruth [Middleton] yesterday—one she wrote the night she received the news of Jim's death at Meredith. It'd break your heart, Dad. She begins by sayin': "Nearly every time I get a letter from home they write about someone I know gettin' killed! What good is this war going to do any of us?" Samighty [*sic*] hard question to answer, I think.[31]*

Jim, first buried near Bari, in 1948 returned home. He posthumously received the Bronze Star, Purple Heart, and Air Medal with two OLCs.

* * *

Other Boys Whose Lives Were Taken

Infantry First Lieutenant Oscar Nolan Sanford, mortally wounded in Belgium on January 12, 1945, became the first member of the Brigade Boys Club Senior Fraternity to die. "We will not say Nolan died for his country, but that he laid down his life...unselfishly for you and me," stated his pastor.[32] ● Army pilot Charles Graham Edwards, The Citadel graduate and brother of W. Eugene Edwards, died on a Panama training flight in April 1945. "He was my role model, a great athlete," said Norm Davis, whose father's Davis Grocery store building was owned by Edwards' father.[33] "My parents would never write me when I was overseas and tell me about the boys who were killed."[34]

Sergeant Allen Bowen Marshburn died of injuries received in an automobile accident while home on furlough in June 1942. ● Private First Class James Carr Saunders, Jr., 252nd Coast Artillery Battalion, drowned in Aruba in July 1942 trying to save a civilian. ● Tail gunner Charles H. "Charlie"

---

* Ruth's brother Jim Middleton was Mac's close friend. She knew Jim, but mostly "was expressing a feeling that many young people felt in those days." [Interview with Ruth Middleton Clayton, June 17, 2000]

Chapter Seventeen

Eldridge of Sunset Park, friend of Mike Michaelis, went down when his B-17's tail was shot off over Italy in July 1944. "I understand they never found his body."[35]

Rabbi Samuel Friedman of B'Nai Israel conducted funeral services for Sergeant Arthur B. Schwartz in August 1948. He had been killed in a plane crash off Ireland on December 17, 1943. ● Yeoman 3rd Class Olin H. White died "when the destroyer USS *Drexler* (DD-741) was sunk in a vicious 90-second attack by three Japanese suicide bombers off Okinawa on May 28, 1945." He was among 158 killed.[36] ● Army Captain Charles Dusham King, son of Mr. and Mrs. J. U. King, succumbed to meningitis in Italy in April 1944. ● A 1943 automobile accident in Arizona claimed the life of soldier Sammy A. Ammons.

Former shipyard worker Private William N. White, Jr., 18, was KIA in France. ● Air force Second Lieutenant William F. Pritchard, son of Stephen A. Pritchard, was KIA over Italy on June 13, 1944. ● First Lieutenant John Wessel Spooner of Winter Park, an 82nd Airborne paratrooper, was KIA in Germany on April 7, 1945. He had seen combat in North Africa, Sicily, Normandy, Southern France, and the Anzio beachhead. ● Wilmington lost a merchant sailor(s) in 1943 whose name(s) were either John William Lewis or James Woodrow Lewis. Newspaper items mentioned each but with different Wilmington mother(s). Likely they were two men.

Merchant marine Captain Horace R. Weaver, 29, went down when his ship was torpedoed in February 1943. ● North Africa veteran Navy Lieutenant (Junior Grade) Lloyd Dixon Hollingsworth, Jr., died in a plane crash off Massachusetts in June 1943. ● Private Archie L. Brown, formerly with Armour Packing Company, was mortally wounded in North Africa in 1943. ● In a November 1943 automobile accident in South Carolina while returning to their base, Lieutenant Ralph M. Rusher died and Sergeant William B. Best survived.

A member of my church, Major Francis Rivers Lawther, Kelly Field, Texas, chief of surgical services, died instantly as a passenger when a B-25 crashed in Arizona in January 1945. His widow and two sons lived there, and parents, Mr. and Mrs. Thomas A. Lawther, and two brothers and two aunts lived here. ● Technician 5th Herbert D. Massie, KIA in Italy in March 1944, left behind wife Edna Freeman Massie and two sons in Wilmington. ● Mrs. Wallace W. Sellers, Jr., presented two service flags to the Fifth Avenue Methodist Church honoring her son James William "Jim Billy" Craig, navy machinists mate second class, KIA in the Mediterranean in July 1944, and two more church members who were killed, G. Wakefield Parker, and William L. Dixon, Jr. Seventy (or 10 percent) of the congregation were serving in uniform. ● In October 1944 the Fourth Street Advent Christian Church held a memorial service for Soundman Second Class Owen Clanton Fillyaw, whose minesweeper, USS *Tide* (AM-125), blew up in the English Channel on June 7, 1944, during the Normandy invasion. His body was re-interred at the Wilmington National Cemetery in 1949.

Mrs. W. B. Mincey of Maffitt Village lost her only sons in 1944, Marine Corporal Thomas Jason Davis, KIA on Peleliu, and Marine Private First Class John P. Davis, KIA in the Marshalls. One report had their last name as Mincey. • Seven-year merchant seaman Charles Talley, Jr., was lost at sea in 1943. • Three days after he landed in France on July 5, 1944, First Lieutenant Porter Lee Hufham was KIA. A member of Wilmington-based Company I, 120th Infantry, he left a wife, Jessie Boudreau Hufham. • Private First Class Warren Stewart Pennington, Jr., 21, 26th Infantry Division, was KIA in Luxembourg of January 4, 1945. Wounded in November, he returned to duty five weeks later. NHHS established a scholarship in his name in 1945.

On June 10, 1945, Okinawa claimed the life of Hospital Apprentice First Class Ernest Ruben Mayhan, Jr., 19. A Marine corpsman, he posthumously received the Silver Star. The football and baseball player was "a familiar figure on campus." His father "Foots" Mayhan owned a grocery store at 1910 Castle Street next to his house.[37] • Fireman First Class Floyd Bagley Sneeden was lost when the USS *Quincy* (CA-71) sank in the Battle of Savo Island, Guadalcanal, on August 9, 1942.

P-47 *Thunderbolt* pilot Second Lieutenant John Heathcote, 413th Fighter Squadron, was hit during a raid over Formosa five days before Japan surrendered. No parachute being observed, it was concluded he went down with his aircraft. He trained at Bluethenthal Field. • Corporal Henry Gilbert Foard, Jr., had spent much of his life here as nephew of Mrs. Henry MacMillan and Mrs. Will Johnston, and grand-nephew of Mrs. William Latimer. The Yugoslav underground buried him after his plane crashed in April 1945.

Neighbor Marine Warrant Officer Harry L. Hundley, Jr., serving on Saipan with a 37mm-gun platoon in the 23rd Marines, 4th Marine Division, voluntarily charged an enemy rocket and machine gun position. A sniper's bullet killed him

Pvt. Herman E. Tyson, brother of my Forest Hills School and NHHS classmate Norman, KIA in Italy in 1944.
Norman Tyson

while he was directing fire from an exposed position. His father received the posthumous Silver Star at their Forest Hills home.

* * *

One might express the natural concern without expecting a response. Why did God take the best and brightest among all the rest, promising young men like Billy Brown, Jimmy Thornton, Joseph Taylor, Dick Garrabrant, Bobby Goldberg, and Jim Lynch in particular whose lives had been underway, or the young boys who never had a chance to start. "After Jim died," Mac Wilson lamented, "I kept asking myself, 'Why him and not me?'" He later would find the loss of his friend was only part of the wartime experience that would affect the rest of his life. "'As a generation, we had to mature in a hurry.'"[38]

Who knows what direction and to where Wilmington's future would have gone—and how quickly—had they all come home?

Appendix A

Wilmington, 1944–45[1]

Form of government—Council-manager

Population—Estimated 51,620 (inside city limits)

Area—6.5 square miles

Altitude—30 feet

Climate—Mean annual temperature 63, average rainfall 53"

Parks—6 with 298 acres

Assessed valuation—$39,032,000 with $1.35 per $100 tax rate (1943)

Bonded debt—$3,710,500

Financial data—1 bank and 3 trust companies with deposits of $72,206,000 (December 31, 1943), and total resources of $76,039.000

Postal receipts—$503,695 (1943)

Telephones in service—10,932

Building and construction—723 permits , $531,000 (1944)

Streets—Approximately 150 miles: 64 paved (11 miles paved brick), 962 street lights

Industry, city and surrounding territory—Manufacturing, retail and wholesale trade, and shipping. 110 manufacturing establishments employing 28,000 men and 6,000 women, paying wages of $23.6 million annually, products valued at $92 million annually (1942 estimate). Principal manufactured products: steel ships, fertilizers, bromine, creosoted products, lumber, sugar, tobacco products, petroleum products, and cotton goods.

Trade area—Retail area extends 75 miles inland with population of 275,000. Wholesale area 150 miles inland (385,000).

Newspapers—2 dailies: *Morning Star* (circulation 9,000), *News* (afternoon, 6,000); 1 Sunday *(Sunday Star-News)*; 2 weeklies *(Wilmington Post* and *Cape Fear Journal* [Negro])

Banks—People's Saving Bank & Trust Company (deposits $3.3 million); Wilmington Savings & Trust Company ($6.9); Morris Plan Bank ($1.4); Security National Bank ($15.1)

Building & Loan Associations—Carolina, Citizens, Cooperative, Hanover; total shares 95,304; white shareholders 7,853, Negro 2,266

Hotels—4 principal with 550 rooms: *Cape Fear Hotel, 202 rooms with bath; *Wilmington Hotel, 104 of which 79 have bath; Orton, 66 and 40 with bath; Brunswick, 50 rooms, 13 with bath.
*Fireproof [Orton burned down right after war]

Railroads—2: Atlantic Coast Line and Seaboard Air Line

Electric power—Tide Water Power Company

Airports—1 (administered by army)

Amusements—7 moving-picture theaters with seating capacity of 7,100; 2 golf courses.

Recreational facilities—Greenfield Lake, Pembroke Jones and Robert Strange Playgrounds, Brookwood and Hilton Parks, Legion Field, Thalian Hall

Hospitals—4 with approximately 600 beds: James Walker Memorial, public ward beds 109, private 56, bassinets 20; Bulluck's 0/38/3 (closed 1944); Community (Negro), 44/6/13; Babies, 10/25/3

Education—10 public schools including 2 senior high, 2 parochial. Pupils in public schools 13,000

Churches—city 35 white, 29 Negro

Radio—WMFD, serves area of 50–75 miles, 250 watts, 1400 KC

City statistics—Total street mileage 100 (62 paved). Miles of gas mains 75; sewers 70; water works capacity 7 million gallons; value of plant $2.264 million. Fire Department 68 men, 6 stations, 15 pieces of motor equipment ($192,000). Police Department 56 men, 1 station and 9 pieces of motor equipment equipped with FM radio.

Other Characteristics

Railroads. Atlantic Coast Line Railroad has track mileage of 5,101 serving the South Atlantic and other connections. Three separate lines link with ACL main track from Richmond, Va., to Jacksonville, Fla.; fourth line runs northeast to New Bern. Seaboard Air Line covers large territory of South Atlantic with one line connection into Wilmington. ACL and SAL tracks connect.

Fresh-water harbor 28 miles from the bar, channel to 30' at mean low water and Inland Waterway connecting to Miami and Boston. Second largest fertilizer and petroleum products port on Atlantic Seaboard; 75 percent of the state's petroleum passes through. Big exporter of molasses, lumber, tobacco, bromine, and petroleum. The Middle West and Panama Canal possibly in more direct communication via Wilmington than by any other South Atlantic port. Immense terminals can load 16 ocean-going ships simultaneously with 600,000 square feet of warehouse space. Two immense cotton presses and two marine railways.

City's principal stevedoring corporation holds the record for all South Atlantic ports for quick dispatch of cargo. American-Hawaiian Line maintains eastbound inter-coastal service with three arrivals per month. North Carolina Line and Norfolk, Baltimore & Carolina Line operate vessels in Atlantic Intra-coastal Waterway. Terminus of highways U.S. 117, 17, 421, 74, 76; State 87. Stevedores: Diamond Steamboat and Wrecking Company, Cape Fear Shipping Company, Southeastern Shipping Service, Tower Unloading Company. Steamship agencies: Heide & Company, C. D. Maffitt & Company, Cape Fear Shipping Company, Pryde Forwarding Agency, Southeastern Shipping Service.

Center of one of the country's greatest vegetable-producing districts and world's largest strawberry-growing and lettuce-growing districts. Produces nearly $18 million in early crops, bulbs, flowers and truck, with 250 annual growing days.

City of big payrolls, usually about $14 million, exclusive of shipyard payroll ($600,000 to $1 million monthly). Headquarters for ACL system employing 1,750 people locally, monthly payroll nearly $300,000. Enterprises: North Carolina Shipbuilding Company, several large fertilizer factories, Ethyl-Dow Chemical Company, North State Creosoting Company, Gulf States Creosoting Company, Taylor-Colquitt Company, American Molasses Company, Southland Manufacturing Company, Chilian Nitrates Company, Barrett Company, Nehi Bottling Company, Pepsi-Cola Bottling Company; these oil companies: Standard, Texas, Cities Service, Pure, National, Shell, Sinclair, and Republic; Atlantic Refining, and Gulf Refining.

Airport. Government has spent $4.7 million enlarging and improving it. Acres—547.5; hangars—1 wood, 1 metal; 2 repair shops; sod field; 3 runways 7000' each—1 concrete, 2 asphalt, can handle gross load of 120,000 pounds on 4-wheeled gear. Lighting adequate for any weather, beacon operating. Airport within 3.5 miles of city center, 10 minutes ride.

Four beaches (Wrightsville, Carolina, Kure's, Seabreeze) attract approximately 500,000 visitors every summer; one can drive directly there in an automobile. "There has never been a wind of destructive force in the Wilmington area in over 200 years."

Central business district. Extends east from river Front to 3rd, and south from Red Cross to Ann. Front, Market, Chestnut, and Princess are the main streets, and most of the office buildings and stores located here and on the intersecting streets from Front to 3rd. Security National Bank, Acme, Masonic, Tide Water Power Company, Murchison, and the Trust are the "largest and most up-to-date" buildings.

Appendix B

In Memoriam Compilation

New Hanover County Men Who Died
Serving Our Country, World War II (Partial)

KIA—Killed in action
MIA—Missing in action (unaccounted for)
DW—Died of battle wounds
DNB—Died of non-battle causes
A—Army
AF—Army Air Forces
N—Navy
MC—Marine Corps
MM—Merchant Marine
RCAF—Royal Canadian Air Force

Each name is included on the Hugh MacRae Park Memorial except those marked as follows:

+ New Hanover County man, not listed on Memorial
* Had direct County connection (wife or parent[s] living here, worked here, enlisted here, etc.), not listed on Memorial

Compilation Shows:

New Hanover County Men		Men with Direct County Connection	
KIA/DW/DNB	187	KIA/DW/DNB	44
MIA†	4	MIA†	13
	191		57

Aiken, Allen Henry	N KIA Guadalcanal, Solomons	15Oct42
Allen, Allison Graham	MC KIA Okinawa, Ryukyus	20Jun45
Allen, Emmett M.	A DNB South America	

† Probable dead

Allen, Fulton T.	AF DNB Florida	
Ammons, Sammy A.+	A DNB Tucson, Ariz.	Nov43
Arnold, Joseph H.+	KIA Southwest Pacific	31Mar43
Atkinson, Calder	N DNB Brazil	10May44
Autry, David	N KIA Pacific	1945
Avant, Edwin H.*		
Baldwin, Alfred L.	A KIA France	9Aug44
Batson, Charles Horace		
Batts, Daniel		
Bell, Marsden W., Jr.	A KIA France	1944
Bellamy, Preston B.	AF KIA Central Pacific	29May44
Bennett, Robert O.	A DNB	
Best, Jack Lyon	N KIA	1944
Best, William G.+		
Bolton, James B., Jr.	A KIA France	12Jul44
Boyd, Charles B., Jr.	A KIA Germany	1Apr45
Bradley, James C., Jr.	A KIA	
Bragaw, Henry Churchill*	A KIA Italy	22Jan44
Branch, J. W.*	MM MIA at sea	9Apr45
Brooks, Norwood Orrell*	A KIA France	5Nov44
Brown, Archie L.	A DW	
Brown, Boyd A.	A KIA Europe	Oct44
Brown, Chappelle A.	A DNB	
Brown, David Henry	MC KIA Okinawa, Ryukyus	15May45
Brown, Leroy M.	A KIA	
Brown, Vivian G.	A KIA Italy	30Jan44
Brown, William Albert, Jr.	A KIA Germany	24Mar45
Brymer, Floyd Anson, Jr.	N KIA	1944
Butler, LeRoy C.	KIA Italy	12Apr44
Butler, William R., Jr.*	AF KIA Germany	22Feb44
Byers, Horace Wellington+		
Campbell, Norman+		
Carney, Carlton Eugene	A KIA France	22Jun44
Carr, Irwin H.	KIA Mediterranean	Feb44
Cassell, William O.	A KIA	
Chavis, Joseph	A DNB	
Cherry, Julian Curtis*	KIA	11Feb45

Chiswell, Lawrence*	A KIA Italy	3Jun44
Clarke, Thomas Cole	N DW	
Cline, Edward F.		
Coker, John D.	A DW North Africa	1943
Coker, Thomas W., Jr.	A DW North Africa	Sep43
Combs, Seldon W.	MC KIA Cape Gloucester, New Britain	16Mar44
Cook, Claude H.*	A KIA Italy	29May44
Corbett, Linwood A.*		
Corbett, William (Wilbur) R.*	MIA Europe	1944
Coughenour, James A.	A KIA Philippines	Feb45
Crabb, John Calvin, Jr.	N KIA Guadalcanal, Solomons	1942
Craig, James William	N KIA Mediterranean	5May45
Cribbs, LaRue F.*	AF MIA Holland	7Jul44
Curtis, Luther Azle+	N MIA at sea	1942
Dail, William T.	AF KIA France	8Aug44
Dale, Floyd E.*		
Davenport, Ellon E.*		
Davis, John Kirby		
Davis, John P.	MC KIA Marshalls	18Feb44
Davis, Thomas J.	MC KIA Peleliu, Palaus	20Sep44
Deason, Lonnie D.	A DNB	
Dew, Robert L.	A KIA Europe	16Jan44
Dickson, Roy E.*	A Holland	
Dilazzero, Frank L.	A KIA Holland	10Oct44
Dixon, Richard Graham	A KIA Burma	4Jun44
Dixson, William L., Jr.*	A MIA Europe	Jun44
Dobson, Amos R., Jr.*	A KIA Belgium	2Jan45
Dobson, Morrison Calhoun	N DNB Narragansett Bay, R.I.	May43
Dobson, Norwood H.*	N DNB Cape Cod, Mass.	8May44
Duncan, Deward William, Jr.	N	1944
Dunham, William+		
Dusham, Charles King*	DNB Italy	13Apr44
Eakins, William David	AF KIA Europe	2Oct44
Edwards, Charles Graham	AF DNB Panama	21Apr45
Eldridge, Charles Hood	AF KIA Italy	22Jun44
Farrar, A. P. (Byng)*		
Fillyaw, Owen Clanton	N KIA English Channel	7Jun44

Fitzgerald, John J.*	MM DNB at sea	1945
Ford, George T.	A DNB	
Garrabrant, John Richard	A KIA Montebourg, France	10Jun44
George, Daniel Hand*		Oct43
Gerdes, Herman John	N KIA Philippines	Aug44
Giddens, Ralph	KIA	
Gillette, Douglas Wiley	N KIA Santa Cruz, Solomons	26Oct42
Godbold, Harold	A KIA New Guinea	31Jul44
Goins, John J., Jr.	A DNB Ft. Crook, Neb.	14Nov43
Goldberg, Robert Aaron, Jr.	MC KIA Ryukyus	27May45
Grubb, Edward Dwight	A DNB Camp Shelby, Miss.	Nov42
Halyburton, William D., Jr.+	N KIA Okinawa, Ryukyus	10May45
Hamilton, Maurice W.	A KIA Germany	23Sep44
Hardison, Charles Preston	N KIA Philippines	6Jan45
Harrelson, Homer S.*	KIA Asia	1945
Harvin, George Washington		
Hatch, Robert Rhodes	AF KIA New Guinea	10Jan43
Hatch, Samuel George	A KIA Germany	3Dec44
Hayes, Clarence H.+		
Heathcote, John*	AF KIA Formosa	9Aug45
Heins, James Bell*	A KIA Belgium	4Jan45
Herzberg, James	A KIA	
Heustess, Talbert J.	KIA	
Hewett, James W.+	A Luzon, Philippines	19May45
Hewett, Lester L.+	MIA	22Dec44
Hobbs, Graham K.+	AF DNB Tennessee	Aug44
Hobbs, Jesse*	A MIA France	20Jan45
Hocutt, William Ivon	N DNB Local accident	26Sep44
Holden, Homer G.+		
Hollingsworth, Lloyd Dixon	N DNB Rockport, Mass.	15Jun43
Horrell, Harvey Howard	N KIA Pearl Harbor, Hi.	7Dec41
Houston, Herbert C.	AF DNB Shaw Field, S.C.	Jan44
Howard, David W.+		
Hudson, James C.		
Hufham, Porter Lee	A KIA France	8Jul44
Hughes, Carroll E.*	KIA Mediterranean	Feb44
Hundley, Harry L.+	MC KIA Saipan, Marianas	1944

Israel, Joseph	KIA	Aug43
Ivey, Winston P.*	MIA Mediterranean	Feb44
Jackson, Arthur Wiley	A KIA France	20Nov44
Jackson, James+	N DNB Port Chicago, Cal.	18Jul44
Johnson, Frank L., Jr.+		
Jones, Aubrey A.	A KIA France	11Jul44
Jones, Carlayne	N KIA Atlantic	19Jun44
Jones, Oscar Rockwell	N KIA English Channel	14Aug44
Jones, William Lee*	KIA France	27Jan45
Jordan, John T., Jr.	A KIA Germany	17Nov44
Justice, W. D.+		
Kennedy, R. Van, Jr.*	RCAF DNB England	28Feb43
King, Charles Dusham+	DNB Italy	13Apr44
King, George B., Jr.	A DNB	
Lane, James Kennedy+	N KIA Pacific	Sep42
Lawther, Francis Rivers	A DNB Arizona	20Jan45
Lennon, David O.	A DNB	
Lennon, Woodrow W.*	A MIA France	10Jan45
Lewis, James Woodrow+	MM KIA	Feb43
Lewis, John William*	MM MIA	Feb43
Long, Roscoe S.*		
Lord, Eric W. T.	AF DNB Helena, Ark.	Jul43
Loren, Jesse Nathan	A KIA France	16Feb45
Lynch, James Borden II	AF KIA Italy	9Feb45
MacMillan(iam), H. D., Jr.	A DNB	
Manning, James W.+	A KIA	
McCaskill, Ralph R.	A KIA	
McCormick, Robert L.	A KIA	
McIlwinen, John H.*	A KIA Europe	13Dec44
McIver, Clifford Davis	N KIA Western Pacific	8Mar45
Marshburn, Allen B.	A DNB Locally	14Jun42
Marshburn, Clarence Empie+		
Massie, Herbert B.*	A KIA Italy	Mar44
Mayers, William H.*		
Mayhan, Ernest Ruben, Jr.	N KIA Okinawa, Ryukyus	10Jun45
Melton, Herbert Franklin*	N KIA Pearl Harbor, Hi.	7Dec41
Melton, James B.	A KIA France	12Jul44

Mercer, Jasper C.	A DW	
Mercer, Robert V.*		
Miller, Raymond M.	A DW	
Mintz, Victor Lee	AF DNB England	1944
Moore, Albert E.		
Moore, Clyde Carson	N KIA Pearl Harbor, Hi.	7Dec41
Morris, Hardy R.+	A MIA Luxembourg	24Dec44
Mosley, Gilbert	A KIA	
Mosley, Harry (Henry) H.	A KIA	
Murrell, Jack A.*	MIA Holland	16Sep44
Musselwhite, Mitchell A.	A KIA France	8Aug44
Nall, John Graham	AF KIA Italy	6Jul44
Nealey, Joseph E.	A KIA Italy	7Mar45
Newton, Walter H.+	MM KIA Caribbean	Aug42
Nixon, Clifton I.	A DNB	
Nixon, James Henry+	N DNB Port Chicago, Calif.	18Jul44
Noland, Oscar Sanford	A DW Belgium	
Oates, William*	MM KIA Gibraltar	21Dec42
Orrell, Claude D.	AF KIA Romania	6Jun44
Owensby, Claude Clifford, Jr.	A DW Luxembourg	3Mar45
Padrick, Oscar Owen*	N	
Page, Lloyd Griffith	AF KIA Europe	Jun44
Pardy, Jack G.*		
Parker, G. Wakefield+		
Pate, Roy+	AF DNB	1943
Patterson, Harold L.*		
Peiffer, Carl David	N KIA Midway	4Jun42
Pennington, Warren S., Jr.	A KIA Luxembourg	4Jan45
Penny, Lewis E.	A DNB	
Perry, John W.*		
Peschau, Ernest F., Jr.	AF KIA Central Pacific	29May44
Peterson, John H.	A DNB	
Phillips, Renwick*	A MIA Normandy, France	14Aug44
Pittman, Paul T.*		
Polites, Nicholas	A DNB Europe	8Nov45
Potter, Douglas Fairbanks	AF DNB Kansas	4Oct43
Pound, Henry T.*		

Powell, Carson Franklin	N KIA	Oct43
Pridgen, Alex Houston	A KIA France	6Jun44
Pritchard, William Frank	AF KIA Italy	13Jun44
Raynor, John+		
Reynolds, Tony Sherwood	N KIA	9Aug44
Riley, Malcolm D.+	A KIA	
Robbins, Bruce C.*		
Robertson, LeRoy Compton, Jr.	A DNB Surinam	17May43
Rogers, Ernest Linwood	A DNB Germany	26May45
Ross, Isaac W.	A DNB	
Rusher, Ralph N.	A DNB South Carolina	Nov43
Russell, Rodger Purnell, Jr.	A DW Germany	24Nov44
Sanford, Oscar Nolan	A DW Belgium	15Jan45
Sanford, Tebe D., Jr.	N KIA at sea off China	24Oct44
Saunders, James Carr, Jr.	A DNB Aruba	Jul42
Schulken, Arthur	A KIA	24Jun44
Schwartz, Arthur B.+	A DNB Ireland	17Dec43
Scott, Charley L.	A DNB	
Shepard, Graham Wood	A DNB France	26Jul45
Shepherd, Elmore W.	A KIA	
Simon, Robert N.	A DNB	
Slayton, Robert Wesley*	N MIA	1944
Smallbones, John Wells	A KIA North Africa	13Oct44
Smidt, John Willard	AF DNB Florida	30Jul44
Smith, John Thomas*	MIA Germany	16Dec44
Smith, John W.+	AF DNB Florida	30Jul44
Sneeden, Floyd Bagley	N KIA Savo Island, Solomons	9Aug42
Southerland, William W., Jr.	A KIA	1945
Soverel, Ralph Waldo, Jr.	AF DNB California	28Mar43
Spencer, William A.	AF KIA Germany	11Sep44
Spooner, John Wessel	A KIA Germany	7Apr45
Starkey, Joseph Edward	N DW Pacific	12Apr45
Stefano, John W. Richard	A DNB Local accident	1944
Strayhorn, William D.*	MIA Europe	Aug43
Sturdivant, James D.*	A KIA Leyte, Philippines	31Dec44
Swanger, John M.	A KIA Mediterranean	Jun44
Talley, Charles, Jr.+	MM MIA	Apr43

Tant, Kenneth*		
Tate, Andrew J.*	MIA	1945
Taylor, Joseph D.	A DNB New Guinea	Mar44
Thornton, James G., Jr.	A KIA Germany	14Sep44
Tyler, Samuel Thomas+	MM KIA North Atlantic	3Feb43
Tyson, Herman E.	A KIA Italy	4Feb44
Vause, James Edward*	A MIA North Africa	14Feb43
Wadsworth, Forest*		
Walker, George Herman, Jr.	AF DNB Panama	13May42
Walton, James L.	A DNB France	1Sep44
Ward, Alonzo George	N KIA submarine	29Apr43
Watson, Grover D.	A KIA England	16Jan45
Watters, William S., Jr.	AF DNB Asia	9Apr43
Weaver, Horace R.+	MM KIA at sea	Feb43
Weber, James A.	MC KIA	Jun44
White, Olin Hughes	N KIA Okinawa, Ryukyus	28May45
White, William N., Jr.	A KIA France	Oct44
Whitfield, Morris E.		
Wilkes, Robert Archie	N KIA	Jun42
Willett, James Marvin	N DW Sicily	4Aug43
Williams, Linwood E.*	MIA	1945
Winn, C. G.*	AF Austria	27Dec44
Worley, Ray C.*		
Zeigler, James H.	A KIA Germany	14Dec44

Principal Sources: Hugh MacRae Park War Memorial; *Wilmington Star-News*, 1941–48; American Legion Post 10 Wartime Scrapbooks; various interviews and personal papers

Notes

CHAPTER 1

1. Interview with George H. McEachern, March 8, 2000.
2. Interview with Tabitha H. McEachern, March 8, 2000.
3. *Wilmington Morning Star*, November 2, 1944, and December 3, 1944; hereafter cited as *Star*. That same night the Cape Fear Loan Office at 12 South Front Street was robbed of $1,000 in jewelry.
4. Interview with Patty Southerland Seitter, April 27, 2000.
5. Tabitha McEachern interview.
6. Interview with Clara Copeland, May 28, 1999.
7. Interview with Blanche Stanley Sneeden, January 13, 1999.
8. Interview with Sam T. Gresham, Jr., and Mary Emma Gresham, September 23, 1998.
9. Interview with Richard V. Hanson, April 1, 1999.
10. *Wilmington Sunday Star-News*, January 21, 1945; *Star*, January 24, 1945.
11. Interview with Rae West, July 29, 1998.
12. Interview with Mary Belle Ormond, August 25, 1999.
13. Interview with Harold P. Laing, July 20, 1999.
14. Ibid.
15. Interview with Perida Roland, January 15, 1999.
16. Interview with Elizabeth Allsbrook, June 16, 1999.
17. Tabitha McEachern interview.
18. Interview with Thurston Eugene "Gene" Edwards, February 10, 1999.
19. Interview with Lucretia Thornton McDaniel, February 15, 1999.
20. *Star*, February 28 and 29, 1944; Interview with Ronald G. "Ronnie" Phelps, January 27, 1999.
21. Interview with Joseph H. "Joe" Johnson, Jr., June 30, 1999.
22. Ibid.
23. Interview with Bertha Buck, May 12, 1999.
24. Interview with Betty Buck Page, May 12, 1999.
25. Ibid.
26. Interview with Willie Stanford Leiner, January 28, 1999.
27. Johnson interview.
28. Phelps interview.
29. Johnson interview.

30. Phelps interview.
31. Interview with George Rountree III, April 14, 1999.
32. Interview with Catherine Russell Stribling, October 28, 1998.
33. Interviews with Joseph C. "Joe" Knox, Jr., May 21, 1999, and January 23, 2000.
34. Interview with Betty Bugg Crouch, January 28, 1999.

CHAPTER 2

1. Interview with Cornelia Nelliemae "Nealie" Haggins Campbell, June 16, 1999.
2. Interview with George N. Norman, November 18, 1998.
3. Interview with Robert F. "Bobby" Cameron, January 11, 1999.
4. Ibid.
5. Roddy Cameron survey, November 6, 1998.
6. Interview with Norman E. "Norm" Davis, May 20, 1999.
7. Interview with Lee Lewis Davis, May 20, 1999.
8. Interview with William Nathan "Bill" Kingoff, June 1, 1999.
9. Interview with Frances Coughenour Dinsmore, June 29, 2000.
10. Interview with James Otis Sampson, Jr., March 9, 1999.
11. Interview with Derick G. S. Davis, November 17, 1998.
12. Bernard Rabunsky to author, July 9, 1999.
13. Interview with Bernard Rabunsky, July 8, 1999.
14. Interview with Janet Rabunsky Evenson, July 8, 1999.
15. Interview with James Whitted, October 8, 1998.
16. *Wilmington Morning Star*, December 1, 1943. Hereafter cited as *Star*.
17. Whitted interview.
18. Interview with Lottie "Clara" Marshburn Welker, October 2, 1998.
19. Interview with Caroline Newbold Swails, November 12, 1998.
20. Interview with James B. "Jim" Stokley, February 16, 1999.
21. Swails interview.
22. Interview with Millard James "Jim" Fountain, March 2, 2000.
23. Interview with John Frederick "Mike" Michaelis, May 19, 1999.
24. Interview with Haskell S. Rhett, Jr., May 11, 1999.
25. Ibid.
26. Interview with Betty Buck Page, May 12, 1999.

CHAPTER 3

1. *Wilmington Morning Star*, June 24, 1944. Hereafter cited as *Star*.
2. *Star*, January 9, 1945.
3. *Star*, January 29, 1944.
4. James G. Thornton quoted in *Star*, October 4, 1944.
5. *Star*, February 12, 1944; *Sunday Star-News,* February 13, 1944. Hereafter cited as *Star-News.*
6. C. H. Casteen quoted in *Star*, April 9, 1943; *Star*, June 24 and July 7, 1943; Sankey Lee Blanton quoted in *Star*, July 8, 1943.
7. *Star*, February 1, 1943.
8. *Star*, February 13 and March 15, 1943.
9. *Star*, July 9 and 23, November 27, and December 4, 1943; *Star-News*, July 18, 1943; interviews with Margaret Tiencken Hewlett and Ann Hewlett Hutteman, September 14, 1998.

10. Interview with Vince Norako, January 15, 1999.

11. Interview with Muriel Williamson, October 5, 1998.

12. *Star*, January 3, 1944.

13. William Crowe, Jr., quoted in *Star*, October 21, 1943.

14. Barbara Frey Waxman, ed., "1898-1998 B'Nai Israel: The First Hundred Years," 1998.

15. Interview with Daniel D. "Dan" Retchin, May 27, 1999.

16. Interview with William "Bill" Schwartz, September 25, 1998.

17. Peggy Mae Warren Longmire Survey, September 2, 1998.

18. Longmire Survey, September 2, 1998; Peggy Mae Warren Longmire interview with J. V. "Pat" Warren, September 1998.

19. Interview with Jean McKoy Graham, May 6, 1999.

20. *Star*, May 2, 1942.

21. Interview with James Madison "Jim" Lee, June 21, 1999.

22. *Star*, May 26, 1943.

23. *Star*, June 12, 1943.

24. *Star-News*, October 15, 1942.

25. Interview with Leon Stein, May 27, 1999.

26. Interview with Heyward C. Bellamy, March 31, 1999.

27. *Star*, January 21, 1943.

28. *Star*, June 24, 1943.

29. Associated Press item in *Star*, January 29, 1945.

30. *Star*, January 15, 1944.

31. *Star-News*, September 25, 1945; Interviews with Marcus E. Hobbs, July 24, 2002; Isaac Hobbs and Jane Hobbs McPhaul, July 29, 2002.

CHAPTER 4

1. Robert C. Cantwell III memoir.

2. Hugh MacRae quoted in *Wilmington Morning Star*, December 11, 1941. Hereafter cited as *Star*.

3. *Wilmington Sunday Star-News*, February 7, 1943. Hereafter cited as *Star-News*.

4. *Star*, February 25, 1943.

5. *Star*, February 4, 1943.

6. *Star-News*, February 7, 1943.

7. *Star*, August 12, 1943.

8. *Star*, September 2, 1943.

9. *Star*, December 28, 1943.

10. *Star*, December 19, 1944.

11. Interview with Mitchell Saleeby, Jr., February 24, 1999.

12. Interview with Richard V. Hanson, April 1, 1999.

13. Interview with Catherine Ann Solomon, April 6, 1999.

14. Interview with Heyward C. Bellamy, March 31, 1999.

15. *Star-News*, February 7, 1943.

16. Interviews with Robert C. "Bob" Cantwell III and Betty Garrabrant Cantwell, July 30, 1998.

17. Interview with Stanley Rehder, October 29, 1998.

18. Interview with Betty Bugg Crouch, January 28, 1999.

19. Interview with Gladys Brown, December 2, 1998.

20. Interview with William "Bill" Schwartz, September 25, 1998.
21. *Cape Fear Journal,* November 28, 1942.
22. Interview with Hannah Block, July 22, 1998.
23. *Star-News,* February 17, 1946.
24. Interviews with George T. Fokakis and Nichalos T. Fokakis, June 12, 2000.
25. *Star-News,* February 7, 1943.
26. *Star,* January 6, 1944.
27. *Star-News,* January 23, 1944.
28. *Star,* January 24, 1945.
29. *Star-News,* July 4, 1943.
30. Interviews with Catherine Black, Cecelia Black Corbett, D. J. "Jackie" Black II, and R. E. Corbett, Jr., October 6, 1998.
31. *Star,* July 9, 1945.
32. *Star,* June 29, 1945.
33. *Star,* July 25, 1945.
34. *Star,* August 7, 1945.
35. *Star,* December 24, 1945.

CHAPTER 5

1. Alonzo L. Jones quoted in *Wilmington Morning Star*, May 26, 1945. Hereafter cited as *Star.*
2. *Star,* September 1, 1944.
3. *Star,* December 11, 1941.
4. *Star,* December 30, 1942.
5. *Star,* July 12, 1944.
6. *Star,* January 10, 1946.
7. William G. "Billy" Broadfoot, Jr., to his parents, May 14, 1944.
8. Jesse Helms quoted in *Star,* June 8, 1942.
9. *Star,* July 13, 1942.
10. Robert C. Cantwell III memoir.
11. Interview with James Otis Sampson, Jr., March 8, 1999.
12. Interviews with William F. "Bill" McIlwain, July 6 and August 2, 1999; Dave Koonce quoted in *Star,* July 26, 1944.
13. Interview with W. T. "Bill" Childs, October 28, 1998.
14. Interview with Clayton Smith, May 21, 1999.
15. *Cape Fear Journal,* November 29, 1942.
16. Interview with McCulloch B. "Mac" Wilson, Jr., March 1, 2000.
17. Cantwell Memoir.
18. Interview with Joseph Roy "Joe" Reaves, March 10, 1999.
19. Interview with Richard B. "Dick" Jones, May 27, 2000.
20. Interview with Herman Hartis, February 22, 1999.
21. Interview with John W. "Bill" Walton, Jr., August 19, 1998.
22. Interview with Martin S. Willard, Jr., May 19, 1999; Willard memoir.
23. Interviews with John J. Burney, Jr., October 20, 1998, and February 3, 1999.
24. Robert C. Ruark, Jr. quoted in *Lower Cape Fear Historical Society Bulletin*, October 1999.
25. Lillian M. George quoted in *Wilmington Star-News*, March 18, 1945.
26. Interview with Henry Von Oesen, January 19, 1999.
27. George Bethell quoted in *Star,* December 25, 1942.

28. Interview with Mark D. Venters, Jr., May 10, 1999; Venters to Mrs. M. D. Venters, Sr., February 1, 1944.

29. Interview with Emerson Willard, April 22, 1999.

30. Interviews with Daniel David "Dan" Cameron, February 1 and July 28, 1999; Interview with Bruce B. Cameron, April 28, 1999.

31. *Star*, May 19, 1945.

32. Ralph Buckner Barden quoted in *Star*, October 25, 1945.

33. *Star*, June 19 and 21, 1945.

34. Interview with Nichalos T. Fokakis, June 12, 2000; T. T. Hamilton, Jr., undated letter (believed June 1943).

35. Blanche Stewart quoted in *Star*, December 16, 1941.

36. Garland "Jack" Suggs quoted in *Star*, August 29, 1942.

37. *The American Jewish Times,* undated (believed January 1944).

CHAPTER 6

1. *Wilmington Morning Star*, July 15, 1943. Hereafter cited as *Star.*

2. *Star*, March 11, 1943.

3. *Star*, April 1, 1943.

4. *Wilmington Sunday Star-News*, June 7, 1942. Hereafter cited as *Star-News*.

5. *Star*, July 9, 1942.

6. *Star*, June 8 and June 19, 1944.

7. Sarah McCulloch Lemmon, *North Carolina's Role in World War II* (Raleigh: State Department of Archives and History, 1964), 50–51.

8. Ibid.

9. Associated Press item quoted in *Star-News*, April 16, 1944.

10. *Star*, June 8, 1943.

11. *Star,* July 6, 1993.

12. Interview with Peggy Moore Perdew, March 18, 1999.

13. Earl M. Page memoir.

14. *Star*, January 30, 1945.

15. Frances J. Wagner to author, April 18, 1999.

16. *Star*, February 17, 1943.

CHAPTER 7

1. Interviews with William G. "Billy" Broadfoot, Jr., and Mary Bason Broadfoot, February 24, 1999.

2. William G. "Billy" Broadfoot, Jr., to his parents, August 24, 1944.

3. *Wilmington Sunday Star-News*, April 1, 1945. Hereafter cited as *Star-News*.

4. Broadfoot to parents, December 3, 1943.

5. Broadfoot to parents, December 17, 1943.

6. Broadfoot to parents, January 21, 1944.

7. Broadfoot to parents, May 16, 1944.

8. Broadfoot to parents, April 3, 1945.

9. Broadfoot to parents, April 7, 1945.

10. *Star*, November 10 and December 25, 1944.

11. Interview with Dorothy Ames "Dotty" Harriss Weathersbee, July 22, 1999.

12. T. L. Roach to Thelma Merritt, November 19, 1943.

13. Charles James, Jr., to Cornelia Haggins, September 18 [believed 1944].
14. *Star*, April 21, 1945.
15. *Star-News*, October 10, 1943.
16. *Star*, September 17, 1943.
17. Interview with Fuller Sistrunk, Jr., August 19, 1999.
18. Interview with Aline Hufham Hartis, February 22 and April 1, 1999; Interview with Gurney J. "Jack" Hufham, July 27, 1999.
19. *Star-News*, September 25, 1945.
20. Interviews with Addie Lee Gaylord and Mary Daniel Carr Fox, June 1, 1999.
21. U.S. Second Armored Division history book, undated [believed 1944].
22. Rodger P. Russell, Jr., to Barbara Allen, [believed] December 1943.
23. Russell to Allen, [believed] January 1944.
24. Russell to his parents, October 12, 1943, in *Star*, December 7, 1943.
25. Russell letter [believed August 1944] in *Star*, August 14, 1944.
26. Wilmington newspaper, [believed] December 9, 1944.
27. Interview with Isabell Adelaide Russell Gore, June 18, 1999.
28. Jane Ellen Baldwin Yates memoir.
29. Interview with Thurston Eugene "Gene" Edwards, June 19, 2000.
30. Interviews with Eleanor "Elkie" Burgwin Fick, June 22 and 23, 2000.
31. Marie Burgwin Sanborn to author, June 26, 2000.
32. Interview with Frances Coughenour Dinsmore, June 29, 2000.
33. *The Hanoverian*, New Hanover High School, 1942.

CHAPTER 8

1. *Wilmington Sunday Star-News*, December 21, 1941. Hereafter cited as *Star-News*.
2. Interview with Herman G. Alberti, November 4, 1998.
3. Martha E. Vann quoted in David A. Stallman, *A History of Camp Davis* (Hampstead, N.C.: Hampstead Services, 1990), 21.
4. Interview with Janet Rabunsky Evenson, July 8, 1999.
5. Interview with Justin Raphael, February 8, 1999.
6. *Wilmington Morning Star*, February 2, 1944. Hereafter cited as *Star*.
7. *Star*, February 8, 1944.
8. Brigadier General Bryan A. Milburn quoted in *Star*, May 13, 1944.
9. *Star*, July 28 and 29, 1944.
10. *The State: A Weekly Survey of North Carolina*, August 19, 1944.
11. Colonel Adam E. Potts quoted in *Star*, August 25, 1944.
12. Camp Davis *AA Barrage*, September 2, 1944, quoted Stallman, 16.
13. *Star*, September 7, 1944.
14. *Star*, December 28, 1944.
15. *Star*, December 29, 1944.
16. *Star*, December 29, 1944.
17. *Star*, January 10, 1945.
18. *AA Barrage*, May 6, 1945, quoted in, 17.
19. *Star*, July 5, 1945.
20. *Star*, July 7, 1945.
21. *Star*, July 17, 1945.

22. *Star*, July 21, 1945.
23. *Star*, August 8, 1945.
24. *Star-News*, January 13, 1946.
25. *Star-News*, February 17, 1946.
26. *Star*, March 16, 1946.
27. *Star*, May 24, 1946.
28. Interviews with James C. "Skinny" Pennington and Anna Feenstra Pennington, February 23, 1999.
29. Interview with Muriel Williamson, October 5, 1998.
30. *Star-News*, April 25, 1943; *Star*, May 20, 1943.
31. Interview with Peggy Moore Perdew, March 18, 1999.
32. *Star*, November 16, 1946.
33. *Star*, April 5, 1946.
34. F. H. Jeter in *Star*, May 22, 1944.
35. James T. Hayes quoted in *Star*, May 25, 1944.
36. *Star*, July 24, 1945.
37. *Star-News*, July 30, 1944.
38. Earl M. Page memoir.
39. Various *Star* and *Star-News*, 1941–46, 1984; Alberti interview; Stallman; Everard H. Smith, *Victory on the Home Front* (1998); *The State: A Weekly Survey of North Carolina*, 1941–44.
40. Interviews with Claude and Mary Daughtry, October 8, 1998.

CHAPTER 9

1. Interview with John J. Burney, Jr., February 3, 1999.
2. Ibid.
3. Interview with William "Bill" Schwartz, September 25, 1998.
4. Interview with James B. "Jim" Stokley, February 16, 1999.
5. Interview with Carl Welker, October 2, 1998.
6. Peggy Warren Longmire interview with J. V. "Pat" Warren, September 1998.
7. Peggy Warren Longmire Survey, September 2, 1998; Warren interview.
8. Burney interview.
9. Ibid.
10. Interviews with George Burrell Byers and Katharine Harriss Byers, May 10, 1999.
11. Item of November 1944 in American Legion Post 10 Wartime Scrapbooks, Randall Library, University of North Carolina at Wilmington; George Burrell Byers to Katharine Harris, November 15 and 26, 1943.
12. Interview with Haskell S. Rhett, Jr., May 11, 1999.
13. Interview with Thurston Eugene "Gene" Edwards, February 10, 1999.
14. Ibid.
15. Interview with Mitchell Saleeby, Jr., February 24, 1999.
16. Interview with Leonard Gleason Allen, April 2, 1999.
17. Interview with Heyward C. Bellamy, March 31, 1999.
18. Robert H. Hollis quoted in *Wilmington Morning Star*, June 14, 1945.

CHAPTER 10

1. James B. "Jim" Stokley memoir.
2. Interview with Betty Henderson Cameron, July 28, 1999.

3. Interview with L. W. "Billy" Humphrey, Jr., September 7, 1998.
4. Interview with H. G. Bryant, August 19, 1999.
5. Interview with John Mintz, April 7, 1999.
6. Interview with Emerson Willard, April 22, 1999.
7. Interview with Fred N. Day, May 4, 1999.
8. Philip "Phil" Dresser Memoir, April 1996.
9. Robert S. "Rob" Pollock survey, October 20, 1998.
10. Earl M. Page Memoir.
11. Interview with Clayton Smith, May 21, 1999.
12. Interview with Ray Funderburk, May 24, 1999.
13. Interview with Jack F. Hart, September 2, 1998.
14. Interview with Bertha Buck, May 12, 1999.
15. "Five Years of North Carolina Shipbuilding," North Carolina Shipbuilding Company (Wilmington, N.C.: May 1, 1946).
16. Interview with H. G. Bryant, August 19, 1999.
17. Interview with Cornelia Nelliemae Haggins Campbell, June 16, 1999.
18. *Wilmington Morning Star*, August 19, 1942. Hereafter cited as *Star*.
19. *Star*, August 22, 1942.
20. Willard interview.
21. Interview with James Whitted, October 8, 1998.
22. Interview with Elizabeth Bell Day, May 4, 1999.
23. *Star*, April 3, 1943.
24. *Star*, April 3, 1943.
25. Interview with Robert S. "Rob" Pollock, October 29, 1998.
26. Smith interview.
27. Ibid.
28. *The North Carolina Shipbuilder*, North Carolina Shipbuilding Company, April 1, 1945.
29. *Star*, September 26, 1944.
30. *North Carolina Shipbuilder*, January 1, 1944.
31. Jake Wade of the *Charlotte Observer* quoted in *North Carolina Shipbuilder*, September 1, 1945.
32. L. A. Sawyer and W. H. Mitchell, *The Liberty Ships: The History of the 'Emergency' Type Cargo Ships Constructed in the United States During the Second World War, Second Edition* (New York: Lloyds of London Press, 1985), 109.
33. *Star*, March 5, 1943.
34. *Star*, March 6, 1943. No one I interviewed spoke about such absenteeism where they worked, indicating only intense schedules.
35. *Star*, March 23, 1943.
36. *Wilmington Sunday Star-News*, September 5, 1943. Hereafter cited as *Star-News*.
37. Smith interview.
38. *Star-News*, September 5, 1943.
39. *Star*, January 20, 1944.
40. *Star-News*, August 18, 1946; *Star*, December 3, 1946.
41. "Five Years of North Carolina Shipbuilding."
42. Page Memoir.
43. Sawyer and Mitchell.
44. *Tidewater Magazine*, January 1985.

CHAPTER 11

1. H. Winfield Smith quoted in *Wilmington Morning Star*, August 2, 1944. Hereafter cited as *Star.*
2. *Star*, August 28 and 31, 1943; *Wilmington Sunday Star-News*, August 29, 1943. Hereafter cited as *Star-News*.
3. *Star*, August 4, 1942.
4. *Star*, May 11 and 13, 1944; *Star-News*, May 28, 1944.
5. *Star*, April 20 and 22, 1944.
6. *Star*, November 30, 1944.
7. *Star*, May 14, 1943.
8. *Star*, June 26 and September 2, 1943.
9. *Star*, November 20, 1943.
10. *Star*, May 20, 1943.
11. *Star-News*, August 29, 1943.
12. *Star*, October 3, 1944.
13. *Star-News*, March 19, 1944; *Star*, May 18, 1944.
14. *Star*, December 26, 1941.
15. *Star*, September 21 and October 8, 1943.
16. *Star*, May 25 and June 15, 1943.
17. Smith quoted in *Star*, January 26, 1944.
18. *Star*, April 8, 1944.
19. *Star*, March 30 and April 1, 1944; Mrs. Bruce Ludlum and Alton Lennon quoted in *Star-News*, April 2, 1944.
20. *Star*, September 28, 1944.
21. *Star-News*, August 13, 1944; *Star*, February 9, 1945.
22. *Star*, September 7, 1944.
23. *Star*, June 18, 1943.
24. *Star*, August 12, 1943.
25. *Star-News*, April 16, 1944; *Star*, April 19, 1944.
26. *Star*, June 30 and July 19, 1944.
27. *Star*, February 15, 1943.
28. *Star*, April 28, 1944.
29. *Star*, February 1, 1945.
30. *Wilmington News*, December 2, 1942.
31. *Star*, July 19, 1945.
32. *Star*, August 6, 1942.
33. *Star*, April 3, 1943.
34. *Star*, May 5, 1943.
35. *Star*, July 8, 1943.
36. *Star*, December 28, 1943.
37. *Star*, September 9, 1944.
38. *Star*, January 28, 1946.
39. *Star*, November 4 and 7, 1944; *Star-News*, November 5, 1944.
40. *Star*, January 10, 1945.
41. *Star*, October 27, 1943.
42. *Star-News*, January 9 and 23, July 30, September 24, 1944; *Star*, October 4, November 9, 16 and 17, 1944.

CHAPTER 12

1. Interviews with R. Thomas "Tom" Sinclair and Myrtle Reynolds Sinclair, August 10, 1999; "That Men May Live: The Story of the Medical Service—ETO," pamphlet, 1945; Official Report, "History of the 51st Field Hospital, 10 September 1943 to April 1945."

2. *Wilmington Morning Star*, June 10, 1942. Hereafter cited as *Star*.

3. *Wilmington Sunday Star-News*, November 1, 1942. Hereafter cited as *Star-News*.

4. Walter H. Meshaw quoted in *Star*, November 20, 1942.

5. *Star-News*, June 21, 1942.

6. *Star-News*, January 2, 1944; *Star,* February 11, 1944.

7. Kenneth L. Dixon in *Star*, January 28, 1944.

8. Pelton W. "Mickey" Ellis quoted in *Star*, August 24, 1944.

9. *Star*, July 6, 1944.

10. *Star*, August 26, 1944.

11. S. Davis Polvogt quoted in *Star*, April 14, 1944.

12. Interview with Clifford Cohen "Cliff" Morris, Jr., May 11, 1999; *Wilmington News,* March 30, 1945.

13. Interview with Frederick B. Sternberger, May 25, 1999.

14. James B. Stokley to his parents, March 2 [believed April], 1945.

15. *Star*, September 29, 1945.

16. John J. Burney, Jr., to father, John J. Burney, December 21, 1944.

17. Burney to parents, January 12, 1945.

18. Burney to mother, January 1945.

19. Burney to father, April 28, 1945.

20. Interviews with George T. Fokakis and Nichalos T. Fokakis, June 12, 2000.

21. George Fokakis interview.

22. John A. Gorman quoted in *Star-News*, June 25, 1944.

23. *The North Carolina Shipbuilder*, North Carolina Shipbuilding Company, September 1, 1945.

24. Jack F. Hart handwritten notes.

25. *Star*, October 6, 1943.

26. *Star*, June 4, 1942.

27. *The Park City Daily News*, Bowling Green, Ky., March 22, 1942.

28. *Star*, February 2, 1945.

29. Associated Press item in *Star*, January 27, 1944.

30. Albert B. Haynes quoted in Associated Press item in *Star*, March 15, 1944.

31. *Star-News*, June 13, 1946; Hugh Morton to author, October 25, 2004.

32. *Star*, December 13, 1944.

33. Interview with Gurney J. "Jack" Hufham, July 27, 1999.

34. Interview with Leon Stein, May 27, 1999.

35. *Star*, March 1987.

36. Interviews with James C. "Skinny" Pennington and Anna Feenstra Pennington, February, 23, 1999.

37. Interview with John Van B. "Johnny" Metts, April 12, 1999.

38. Carl J. Cunningham to Howard Pierce, August 11, 1942, quoted in *Star*, September 24, 1942.

39. L. B. Harper quoted in *Star*, October 2, 1943.

40. Allan Taylor Strange memoir; Interview with Strange, June 17, 1999.

41. Interview with Simpson Fuller Sistrunk, Jr., August 18, 1999; *Star-News*, October 8, 1944.

42. James H. Morse quoted in *Star*, May 17, 1945.

43. *Star*, May 18, 1945.

44. Interviews with William G. "Billy" Broadfoot, Jr., February 24, 1999 and January 26, 2000; James M. Fielder, *495th Fighter Squadron: The Twin Dragons, C.B.I., 1943–1945; A History*, self-published 1993; *Ex-CBI Roundup* Magazine, January 1999.

45. Broadfoot to parents, May 16, 1944.

46. Broadfoot to parents, February 5, 1944.

47. Broadfoot to parents, May 8, 1944.

CHAPTER 13

1. *Wilmington Morning Star*, December 12, 1941. Hereafter cited as *Star*.

2. *Star*, August 14, 1942.

3. *Star*, July 23 and 25, 1943.

4. *Star*, August 24, 1943.

5. *Star*, September 14, 1943.

6. *Star*, May 5 and 6, 1943.

7. *Wilmington Sunday Star-News*, January 16, 1944. Hereafter cited as *Star-News*.

8. *Star*, December 31, 1942.

9. *Star*, September 28, 1944.

10. *Star*, March 24, 1945.

11. *Star*, August 9, 1943.

12. *Star*, June 9, 1944.

13. *Star*, March 19, 1943.

14. *Star*, July 8, 1943.

15. *Star*, December 29, 1942.

16. *Star-News*, November 29, 1942.

17. *Star*, February 23, 1943.

18. *Star-News*, January 10, 1943.

19. *Star*, March 17, 1944.

20. *Star*, January 12, 1943.

21. Interviews with Eloise B. Humphrey and L. W. "Billy" Humphrey, Jr., September 7, 1998.

22. Interview with Harold P. Laing, July 20, 1999.

23. *Lower Cape Fear Historical Society Bulletin*, May 1999.

24. Mildred Harris in *Lower Cape Fear Historical Society Bulletin*, May 1999.

25. *Star*, June 9, 1942.

26. *Star-News*, January 26, 1946.

27. *Star*, January 25, 1944.

28. *Star*, August 11 and 22, September 16, 1944.

29. *Star*, April 4, 1945.

30. *Star*, February 25, 1943.

31. *Star-News*, May 7, 1944.

32. *Star-News*, May 21 and June 4, 1944; *Star*, May 26, 1944.

33. *Star*, June 19 and July 13, 1943.

34. *Star*, January 1, 1946.

35. *Star*, February 18 and April 14, 1944; July 27, and July 31, 1945; *Star-News*, February 20, 1944.

36. *Star*, May 12, 1944.
37. *Star,* May 17, 1944.
38. *Star-News*, March 5, 1944.
39. *Star*, June 17, 1943.
40. *Star*, June 19, 1943.
41. *Star*, October 28, 1943.
42. *Star*, June 6, 1944.
43. *Star*, January 27, 1944.

CHAPTER 14

1. *Wilmington Morning Star*, February 4, 1944. Hereafter cited as *Star*.
2. Interview with Lottie (Clara) Marshburn Welker, October 2, 1998.
3. *Wilmington Sunday Star-News*, March 28, 1943. Hereafter cited as *Star-News*.
4. *Star-News*, June 18, 1944.
5. Interview with Emma Worth Mitchell Wilcox, February 25, 1999.
6. Interviews with John E. Clayton, Jr., and Percy Hedquist, July 28, 1999.
7. *Star*, May 2, 1942.
8. Interview with Mary Belle Ormond, August 25, 1999.
9. Interview with Justin Raphael, February 8, 1999.
10. Camp Davis *AA Barrage*, July 22, 1944.
11. *Star*, September 19, 1944.
12. Everard H. Smith, "The Wilmington USO Building and Community Arts Center," flyer, 1998.
13. *Star*, February 19, 1944.
14. Interview with Millard James "Jim" Fountain and Pearl Winner Fountain, March 2, 2000.
15. Interview with John D. "Jack" McCarley III, August 25, 1999.
16. Interview with Catherine Ann Solomon, April 6, 1999.
17. Frances J. Wagner to author, April 18, 1999.
18. Interview with Eva Sanders Cross, June 11, 1999.
19. Interview with Harold P. Laing, July 20, 1999.
20. Interview with Sylvester "Buddy" Adkins, October 28, 1998.
21. Interviews with Virginia Harriss Holland and Raymond H. Holland, Jr., May 5, 1999.
22. Interview with Harry Mann, March 8, 2000.
23. *Star*, January 8, 1944.
24. *Star*, May 12, 1944.
25. Augustus "Shuney" Brittain quoted in William F. "Bill" McIlwain in *Star*, May 3, 1944.
26. Interview with Frederick B. Sternberger, May 25, 1999.
27. Interview with Joseph Roy "Joe" Reaves, March 10, 1999.
28. Interview with Isabell Russell Gore, June 18, 1999.
29. Interview with Manette Allen Dixon Mintz and John Mintz, April 7, 1999.
30. *Barrage*, June 24, 1944.
31. *Star*, February 1, 1944.

CHAPTER 15

1. "Teachers' Bulletin," New Hanover County Public Schools, 1943–44.
2. *Wilmington Morning Star*, August 28, 1942. Hereafter cited as *Star.*
3. James Brandon in *Star*, August 27, 1942.

4. Kenneth R. Murphy to author, May 30, 1999.
5. Evelyn Bergen Loftin to author, June 6, 1999.
6. Interview with Joseph C. "Joe" Knox Jr, May 21, 1999.
7. Interview with William Charles "Bill" Leeuwenburg, May 28, 1999.
8. Interview with Ronald G. "Ronnie" Phelps, January 27, 1999.
9. George Dudley Humphrey Survey, November 5, 1998.
10. Interview with Bertha Buck and Betty Buck Page, May 12, 1999.
11. Interview with George Rountree III, April 14, 1999.
12. Interview with Edward Swart, August 23, 1999.
13. *Star*, October 27, 1944.
14. Interview with Ann Williams Johnson, June 30, 1999.
15. Nancy West Jones Survey, November 13, 1998.
16. *Star*, July 5, 1943.
17. *Star*, July 3, 1945.
18. *Star*, July 10, 1942.
19. J. W. Grise quoted in *Star*, July 25, 1944.
20. H. M. Roland quoted in *Star*, May 7, 1943.
21. *Star*, December 14, 1942.
22. *Star*, October 19, 1943.
23. *Star*, October 19, 1943.
24. Interview with Janet Rabunsky Evenson, July 8, 1999.
25. Interview with Donald P. "Don" Blake, May 5, 1999.
26. Interview with Norman E. "Norm" Davis, May 20, 1999.
27. Interview with Frederick B. "Fred" Sternberger, May 25, 1999.
28. Interview with James Madison "Jim" Lee, June 21, 1999.
29. Interview with John Frederick "Mike" Michaelis, May 19, 1999.
30. Interview with Catherine Russell Stribling, October 28, 1998.
31. Interview with William F. "Bill" McIlwain, July 6, 1999.
32. Interview with Gurney J. "Jack" Hufham, July 27, 1999.
33. Interview with Richard B. "Dick" Jones, May 27, 2000.
34. Interview with John D. "Jack" McCarley III, August 25, 1999.
35. *Star*, March 15, 1946.
36. *Star*, June 11, 1946.
37. "Teachers' Bulletin"; *Star*, March 20 and April 7, 1943.
38. *The Hanoverian*, New Hanover High School, 1943.

CHAPTER 16

1. *Wilmington Morning Star*, December 7, 1942. Hereafter cited as *Star*.
2. *Wilmington Sunday Star-News*, September 27, 1942. Hereafter cited as *Star-News*.
3. Interview with Laura Roe Fonvielle, August 19, 1999.
4. *Star*, January 8, 1943.
5. *Star*, January 12, 1943; J. Frank Hackler quoted in *Star*, January 12, 1943.
6. *Star*, January 12, 1943.
7. *Star*, January 15, 1943.
8. *Star*, April 7, 1944.
9. *Star*, March 15, 1944.

10. *Star*, February 22, 1943.
11. *Star*, January 22, 1943.
12. *Star*, March 21, 1943.
13. *Star*, July 1, 1944.
14. *Star*, April 15, 1943.
15. *Star*, February 9, 1943.
16. *Star-News*, February 21, 1943.
17. *Star*, February 25, 1943.
18. *Star*, April 8, 1943.
19. *Star*, January 19, 1944.
20. *Star*, January 20, 1944.
21. Forest Hills School PTA Scrapbook, 1943–44, with undated articles (ca. 1944) from Wilmington newspapers.
22. *Star*, October 19, 1943.
23. *Star*, November 24, 1945.
24. Star, June 12, 1945.
25. Dan Herring quoted in *Star*, June 20, 1945.
26. *Star*, April 23, 1943.
27. Kenneth R. Murphy to author, May 30, 1999.
28. *Star*, March 6, 1943.
29. *Star*, April 28, 1945.
30. *Star*, February 24, 1944.
31. *Star-News*, July 30, 1944; *Star*, August 1, 1945.
32. *Star-News*, December 6, 1942.
33. Earl M. Page Survey, June 1, 1999; Page Memoir.

CHAPTER 17

1. Interview with Harold Fussell, June 22, 1999.
2. *Wilmington Morning Star*, December 8, 1942; Hereafter cited as Star; *Sunday Star-News*, December 13, 1942; Hereafter cited as *Star-News*; Jack Coggins, *The Campaign for Guadalcanal: A Battle That Made History* (New York: Doubleday & Company, 1962), 99.
3. *Star*, July 18, August 19, December 15 and 16, 1944; Interviews with Margey Garrabrant, November 2, 2000, and William "Bill" Garrabrant, May 7, 2004.
4. *Star*, August 9 and 17, 1944; Interview with Manette Allen Dixon Mintz and John Mintz, April 7, 1999; American Legion Post 10 Wartime Scrapbooks, Randall Library, University of North Carolina at Wilmington.
5. *Star*, January 24, 1944.
6. *Star*, April 11, 1945; Daniel Page letter, April 19, 1945, in *Star,* April 20, 1945.
7. *Star*, January 17, 1945; *Star-News*, June 24, 1945.
8. Interview with Frances Goldberg Walker and Libby Goldberg O'Quinn, April 21, 1999.
9. Interview with Judson Y. Creech, June 16, 2000.
10. Interview with Jim Turner, June 18, 2000.
11. Interview with Peggy Jones Kearney, June 12, 2000; *Star*, September 1, 1944; *Star-News,* November 18, 1944.
12. Interview with Lucretia Thornton McDaniel, February 15, 1999.
13. Lieutenant Colonel Robert B. Steward, Department of the Army, to Paul J. McDaniel, October 23, 1997.
14. Unmarked, undated pamphlet dedicated to Captain James Goodlet Thornton, Jr.

15. Bill Warnock to Paul McDaniel, July 29, 1997.
16. Charles R. Thomas to J. G. Thornton, June 8, 1945.
17. Lieutenant Colonel Preston R. Bishop in Casualty Clearance Plan, Headquarters, 741st Tank Battalion, 30 August 1945.
18. *Star,* February 1, 1946.
19. Clifford Davis McIver to Malcolm C. "Mac" McIver, Jr., March 5, 1945; Interview with Malcolm C. McIver, Jr., July 25, 2000; Wilmington newspaper, May 1945; *Star-News*, December 2, 1945.
20. Interview with Norman E. "Norm" Davis, May 20, 1999.
21. Interviews with Thurston Eugene "Gene" Edwards, June 19, 2000, and McCulloch B. "Mac" Wilson, Jr., March 1, 2000; *Star*, October 24, 1944, and December 8, 1948; John Graham "Jack" Nall to McCulloch B. "Mac" Wilson, Jr., May 17, 1944.
22. *The Grapevine* Newsletter, St. James Parish Episcopal Church, Wilmington, N.C., May 1997.
23. Interview with Thomas G. Lynch, July 22, 1999.
24. James Borden Lynch II to his father, November 21, 1942.
25. Lynch Family undated biographical sketch of James Borden Lynch II.
26. Thomas Lynch Interview.
27. Lynch Family sketch.
28. William Borden Cobb, Jr., letter quoted in Lynch Family sketch.
29. Robert Strange letter in *Star-News*, February 25, 1945.
30. Wilson interview.
31. Wilson to his father, March 16, 1945.
32. J. O. Walton quoted in *Star*, April 17, 1945.
33. Davis interview.
34. Ibid.
35. Interview with John Frederick "Mike" Michaelis, May 19, 1999; *Star*, October 25, 1944.
36. Item of August 11, 1945, in American Legion Post 10 Scrapbooks; *Star*, August 13, 1945.
37. Interview with Ronald G. "Ronnie" Phelps, May 20, 2000; *Star*, June 19, 1945, and July 18, 1946.
38. Wilson quoted in Tracy Rose in *Star-News*, May 28, 1995.

APPENDIX A

1. OCO *Hill's City Directory, Wilmington and New Hanover County, N.C., Vol. 26, 1944–45* (Richmond, Va.: Hill Directory Co., 1944); "Wilmington: The Leading Port City of North Carolina, Statistical Review" (Greater Wilmington Chamber of Commerce, 1941).

Glossary

A-bomb—Atomic bombs dropped on Hiroshima and Nagasaki, Japan, August 6 and 9, 1945

AA—Antiaircraft

AAA—Antiaircraft artillery

AAF (USAAF)—(U.S.) Army Air Forces

ABC—Alcoholic Beverage Control (state agency)

a/c—Aircraft

ACL—Atlantic Coast Line Railroad

AE—Navy ammunition ship

AEF—American Expeditionary Force

AKA/aka—Attack cargo ship (C-2 hull); also known as

AME—African Methodist Episcopal church

AP—Associated Press

Armed Forces—The U.S. military and naval establishment, including army (and army air forces), navy, Marine Corps, Coast Guard

ASF—Army Service Forces

ASW—Antisubmarine warfare

A&T—North Carolina Agricultural and Technical College (Negro), Greensboro.

AWOL—Absent without leave (from military)

AWS—Aircraft Warning Service (Corps)

(the) bomb—See A-bomb

BAAB—Bluethenthal (Field) Army Air Base

BB—Navy battleship

BOQ—Bachelor officers quarters

CA—Coast artillery; navy heavy cruiser

CAP—Civil Air Patrol

CBS—Columbia Broadcasting System

CD—Civilian defense

C.O.—Commanding officer

Coast Line—See ACL

colored—See Negro

CV—Navy aircraft carrier

CVE—Navy escort carrier

CVL—Navy light carrier

Davis—Camp Davis

DD—Navy destroyer

D-Day—Date of an amphibious landing; at Normandy, France, June 6, 1944

D+2—The second day after D-Day

dinner—Southern for noon meal (lunch)

DFC—Distinguished Flying Cross

DNB—Died from non-battle causes

DSC—Distinguished Service Cross (army)

duration—Until the war is over

EWT—Eastern war time

FBI—Federal Bureau of Investigation

FDR—President Franklin Delano Roosevelt

4-F—Rejected for military service for physical or mental incapacity

GI—Nickname for army/army air forces soldiers; also generic name for armed forces personnel

GMC—General Motors Corporation (truck)

grammar school—(then grades 1-8) Today's elementary school

gyrene—United States Marine nickname

HACOW—Housing Authority of the City of Wilmington

here—Wilmington and New Hanover County area

"hot-bunking (bedding)"—Use of the same bed in a rooming house by defense shift workers

HRO—Housing Registration Office

(the) Hut—Woodrow Wilson Hut Servicemen's club

IJN—Imperial Japanese Navy (ship)

Inland Waterway—Now Intracoastal Waterway

Japs—Slang name for Japanese enemy

Jerry—Slang name for German enemy

jukebox—Commercial record-playing machine

JWMH (James Walker)—James Walker Memorial Hospital

KIA—Killed in action

KP—Kitchen police duty

liberty—Navy and Marine term for authorized free time away from duty station

Liberty ship—Cargo merchant ship (C-1 hull) built in Wilmington for the Maritime Commission

LST—Navy landing ship, tank

Lumina—The Lumina pavilion, Wrightsville Beach

MIA—Missing in action

military—Usually the army (soldiers), but sometimes means armed forces in general

MM—U.S. Merchant Marine

MP—Military police

(the) newspaper—*Wilmington Morning Star/News/Sunday Star-News* (same publisher, one a.m., one p.m., one Sunday)

NBC—National Broadcasting Company

NCO—Noncommissioned officer (military)

NCSC—North Carolina Shipbuilding Company

Negro—African American/black, also colored

Negress—Female Negro

NHHS—New Hanover High School (also New Hanover)

NYA—National Youth Administration

OCD—Office of Civilian Defense (New Hanover County)

OCS—Officer candidate school

OLC—Oak Leaf Cluster (for multiple awards of same decoration)

OPA—U.S. Office of Price Administration

party line—Operator-dialed phone service serving multiple customers; you waited your turn, or listened in

PFC—Private first class

piccolo joint—Jukebox, beer, and snack hangout

POW(s)/PW—Prisoner(s) of war

PT boats—U.S. patrol torpedo boats

PX—Military post exchange (store)

(the) railroad—See ACL

ROTC—Reserve Officers Training Corps

R&R—Rest and relaxation

SAL/Seaboard—Seaboard Air Line Railroad

(the) shipyard—See NCSC

SS—Navy submarine

Star-News—See (the) newspaper

States/Stateside—Back in the continental United States

supper—Southern for evening meal

TB—Tuberculosis

TWPC—Tide Water Power Company

U-boat—German submarine

UNC—University of North Carolina (Chapel Hill)

USA—U.S. Army; United States of America

USCGC—U.S. Coast Guard cutter

USMC—United States Marine Corps

USN—United States Navy

USO—United Service Organizations

(the) USO—Any USO club; specifically the one at 2nd and Orange Streets

USES—U.S. Employment Service

USS—United States Ship

V-E Day—Victory in Europe, May 8, 1945

VF—Navy fighter squadron

V-J Day—Victory over Japan, August 14, 1945 (U.S. time) (some historians cite September 2, the day the peace treaty was signed)

VMF—Marine Corps fighter squadron

WAAC—Women's Army Auxiliary Corps (forerunner to WAC)

WAAFs—Members of the Women's Auxiliary Air Force of the Royal Air Force (Britain)

WAC—Women's Army Corps

WAR—Wilmington Air Region

WASPs—Women's Airforce Service Pilots

WAVES—Women Accepted for Volunteer Service (navy)

WC—Women's College of the UNC, Greensboro

WFD—Wilmington Fire Department

WHC—War Housing Center (Wilmington)

Williston—See WIS

WIS—Williston Industrial (High) School

WLI—Wilmington Light Infantry

wolf whistles—sharp, short lip whistle blasts by a male on seeing an attractive female nearby

WPB—U.S. War Production Board

WPD—Wilmington Police Department

Wrens (WRNS)—Members of the Women's Royal Naval Service of the Royal Navy (Britain).

YMCA—Young Men's Christian Association

YMS—Navy small minesweeper

YP—Navy patrol craft

YWCA—Young Women's Christian Association

Bibliography

Interviews

Adkins, Sylvester "Buddy"

Adkins, Carrie Congleton

Alberti, Herman G.

Alexius, Harold D.

Allen, Leonard Gleason

Allsbrook, Elizabeth

Andrews, Richard C. "Dick"

Banck, Margaret

Bellamy, Heyward C.

Bellamy, Mary Cameron Dixon

Benton, Hulon

Black, Catherine

Black, D. J. II "Jack"

Blake, Donald P. "Don"

Block, Hannah (Mrs. Charles)

Boylan, George S.

Boylan, Louise Washburn

Broadfoot, Mary Bason

Broadfoot, William G., Jr., "Billy"

Brown, Gladys

Bryant, H. G.

Buck, Bertha

Burnett, Gilbert

Burney, John J., Jr.

Burney, Louis A.

Byers, George Burrell

Byers, Katharine Harriss

Cameron, Bruce B.

Cameron, Daniel David "Dan"

Cameron, Robert F. "Bobby"

Cameron, Suwanna Elizabeth Henderson "Betty"

Campbell, Cornelia Nelliemae Haggins "Nealie"

Cantwell, Betty Garrabrant

Cantwell, Robert C. III "Bob"

Chavers, James D.

Childs, W. T. "Bill"

Clayton, John E., Jr.

Clayton, Ruth Middleton

Copeland, Clara

Corbett, Cecelia Black

Corbett, R. E., Jr.

Crawford, Sally Josey

Creech, Judson Y.

Cross, Eva Sanders

Crouch, Betty Bugg

Daughtry, Claude

Daughtry, Mary

Davis, Derick G. S.

Davis, Lee Lewis

Davis, Norman E.

Day, Elizabeth Bell

Day, Fred N. III

Debnam, John H.

229

Dickinson, Sarah
Dibble, Dorothy Bunn
Doetsch, Robert "Bob"
Eason, Frank Delane
Edwards, Estelle Owens
Edwards, Thurston Eugene "Gene"
Edwards, W. Eugene "Gene"
Evenson, Janet Rabunsky
Fick, Eleanor Burgwin "Elkie"
Fokakis, George T.
Fokakis, Nichalos T. "Nick"
Fonvielle, Laura Roe
Fountain, Millard James "Jim"
Fountain, Pearl Winner
Fox, Mary Daniel Carr
Funderburk, Ray
Fussell, Harold
Garniss, Elizabeth Jones "Lib"
Garrabrant, Margey
Garrabrant, William "Bill"
Gaylord, Addie Lee
George, Edward "Ed," "Pat"
George, Parthenia
Gideon, J. C.
Gigax, Vernon
Glover, Lucy Ann Carney
Gordon, Diane Snakenburg
Gordon, Frank
Gore, Isabell Russell
Graham, Jean McKoy
Grant, Oscar
Gresham, Mary Emma
Gresham, Sam T., Jr.
Hanson, Richard V. "Dick"
Hardy, Gladys
Hart, Jack E.
Hart, Joy
Hartis, Aline Hufham Spencer
Hartis, Herman

Hedquist, Percy
Hewlett, Margaret Tiencken
Higgins, Glendy Willard "Glenn"
Higgins, Miles C.
Holland, Virginia Harriss
Holland, Raymond H., Jr.
Hood, Mary Elizabeth
Horton, Ralph T.
Hufham, Gurney J. "Jack"
Humphrey, Eloise B.
Humphrey, L. W. "Billy," Jr.
Hutteman, Ann Hewlett
Johnson, Ann Williams
Johnson, Joseph H., Jr., "Joe"
Jones, Richard B. "Dick"
Kearney, Peggy Jones
Kingoff, William Nathan "Bill"
Knox, Joseph C., Jr., "Joe"
Laing, Harold P.
Lee, James Madison "Jim"
Leeuwenburg, Carol Bunch
Leeuwenburg, William Charles "Bill"
Leiner, Willie Stanford
Lynch, Thomas
McCarley, John D. III "Jack"
McDaniel, Lucretia Thornton
McEachern, George H.
McEachern, Tabitha H.
McFadden, Leroy
McIlwain, William F. "Bill"
McIver, Malcolm C. "Mack"
McRee, Fred
Mann, Harry
May, Aaron
May, Norma
Meier, Tanky
Metts, John Van B. "Johnny"
Michaelis, John Frederick "Mike"
Mintz, John

Mintz, Manette Allen Dixon
Morris, Clifford Cohen, Jr., "Cliff"
Morris, Evelyn Volk
Murray, Charles P. Jr., "Chuck"
Norako, Vincent "Vince"
Norako, Dorothy
Norman, George N.
O'Quinn, Libby Goldberg
Ormand, Mary Belle
Page, Betty Buck
Pennington, Anna Feenstra
Pennington, James C. "Skinny"
Perdew, Peggy Moore
Phelps, Ronald G. "Ronnie"
Pollock, Robert S. "Rob"
Rabunsky, Bernard
Raphael, Justin
Raphael, Shirley Berger
Reaves, Joseph Roy "Joe"
Rehder, Stanley
Renstrom, Keith
Retchin, Daniel D. "Dan"
Reynolds, Frances Thornton
Rhett, Haskell S., Jr.
Rogers, Margaret Sampson
Roland, Perida (Mrs. H. M.)
Rountree, George III
Saleeby, Mitchell, Jr., "Mitch"
Sampson, James Otis, Jr.
Schwartz, Bernice
Schwartz, William "Bill"
Seitter, Patty Southerland
Simmons, Helen Swart
Sinclair, Myrtle Reynolds
Sinclair, R. T. Jr. "Tom"
Sistrunk, Simpson Fuller, Jr.
Smith, Clayton
Sneeden, Blanche Stanley
Solomon, Catherine Ann
Somersett, Kathleen

Starnes, James R.
Stein, Leon
Sternberger, Frederick B. "Fred"
Stokley, James B. "Jim"
Stovall, Harry
Strange, Allan Taylor
Strange, Jocelyn Peck
Stribling, Catherine Russell
Sutton, Billy
Swails, Caroline Newbold
Swart, Bessie Burton
Swart, Bettye Rivenbark
Swart, James Edward
Swart, Robert S. "Bob"
Taylor, Victor G.
Turner, Jim
Tyson, Norman E.
Venters, Mark D., Jr.
Von Oesen, Henry
Walker, Benjamin D. III
Walker, Frances Goldberg
Walton, John W. Jr. "Bill"
Weathersbee, Dorothy Ames Harriss "Dotty"
Welker, Carl
Welker, Lottie Marshburn "Clara"
West, Rae
Whitted, James E.
Whitted, Joseph W.
Whitted, Lucilla White
Wilcox, Emma Worth Mitchell
Willard, Emerson
Willard, Gibbs Holmes
Willard, Martin S., Jr.
Williams, Christine W.
Williams, Evalina Campbell
Williamson, Muriel
Wilson, McCulloch B., Jr. "Mac"
Woodbury, Louie E. III
Wychel, Ellen Gilliard

Wartime Letters

William G. Broadfoot, Jr.

John J. Burney, Jr.

George Burrell Byers

Cornelia Nelliemae Haggins Campbell

Mary Daniel Carr Fox

Jack F. Hart

John D. McCarley Collection of German POW Letters

William F. McIlwain, Jr.

Malcolm C. McIver

James B. Stokley

Allan T. Strange

Martin S. Willard

Memoirs

Thelma Kelly Canady

R. C. Cantwell III

Joe Cross

Fred N. Day

Philip Dresser

Elizabeth Jones Garniss

George H. Garniss

Jack F. Hart

Peggy Mae Warren Longmire

Vincent Norako

Earl M. Page

Robert S. Pollock

Margaret Sampson Rogers

James B. Stokley

Allan T. Strange

Catherine Russell Stribling

Martin S. Willard

Doris Dickens Wilson

Jane Ellen Baldwin Yates

Books, Monographs, Pamphlets, Papers

Allegood, Jimmy. "Down Exchange Alley: The 50-Year History of Exchange Club of Wilmington, North Carolina, 1924–1974," 1974.

Benson, Rupert L., and Helen S. Benson. *Historical Narrative 1841–1972 of Wrightsville Beach, N.C.* Wilmington: Carolina Printing and Stamp Co., 1972.

Cashman, Diane Cobb. *Champions: The History of the Cornelia Nixon Davis Health Care Center at Porters Neck, Wilmington, N.C., 1966–1991.* Wilmington: Wilmington Printing Co., 1991.

Al Derecho Creations. "The Poetry of a Man: The Life and Poetry of Percy C. West." Mesa, Ariz., 1993.

Dickinson, Lieutenant Clarence E., USN. *The Flying Guns: Cockpit Record of a Naval Pilot from Pearl Harbor through Midway.* New York: Charles Scribner's Sons, 1942.

Fielder, James M. *495th Fighter Squadron: The Twin Dragons, CBI, 1943–1945; A History,* 1993.

The Hanoverian. Yearbooks of New Hanover High School, Wilmington, N.C., 1938–47.

Hickman, Homer H., Jr. *Torpedo Junction: U-Boat War Off America's East Coast, 1942.* Annapolis, Md.: Naval Institute Press, 1989.

Hill's City Directory, Wilmington and New Hanover County, North Carolina, Vol. 25, 1943. Richmond, Va.: Hill Directory Co., 1943.

Hill's City Directory, Wilmington and New Hanover County, North Carolina, Vol. 26, 1944–45. Richmond, Va.: Hill Directory Co., 1945.

"History of Forest Hills School and PTA," undated paper.

Hoffman, Glenn, and Richard E., eds. *Building a Great Railroad: A History of the Atlantic Coast Line Railroad Company.* CSX Corporation, 1998.

"Industrial Survey of Wilmington and New Hanover County, N.C." Wilmington Industrial Commission, 1941.

"Introducing Camp Davis," undated monograph (believed 1944), by Fourth Service Command, Camp Davis, N.C.

Lee, Clark. *They Call It Pacific: An Eyewitness Story of our War against Japan from Bataan to the Solomons.* New York: Viking Press, 1943.

Lemmon, Sarah McCulloh. *North Carolina's Role in World War II.* Raleigh: State Department of Archives and History, 1964.

"North Carolina Manual 1943." Raleigh: Secretary of State, 1943.

Reaves, William M., and Beverley Tetterton, ed. *Strength Through Struggle: The Chronological and Historical Record of the African-American Community in Wilmington, North Carolina 1865–1950.* Wilmington: New Hanover County Public Library, 1998.

Sawyer, L. A., and W. H. Mitchell. *The Liberty Ships, Second Edition.* New York: Lloyds of London Press, 1985.

Scrapbooks of the Forest Hills School PTA, 1943–45.

"Seabreeze: A Heritage Renewed." Wilmington: New Hanover County Planning Department, 1988.

"The Sinking of the SS *John D. Gill.*" Undated paper, Southport (N.C.) Historical Society.

Smith, Everard H. *Victory on the Home Front: The USO in New Hanover County, N.C., 1941–1946,* monograph, 1998.

Stallman, David D. *A History of Camp Davis.* Hampstead, N.C.: Hampstead Services, 1990.

Tillman, Barrett. *SBD Dauntless Units of World War II.* Oxford, England: Osprey Publishing, 1998.

"1948 update to Sanborn Insurance Maps," "Insurance Maps of Wilmington." New York: Sanborn Map Co., 1915, updated.

Watson, Alan D. *Wilmington: Port of North Carolina.* Columbia: University of South Carolina Press, 1992.

"We Ripened Fast: Unofficial History of the Seventy-Sixth Infantry Division." Undated.

Willcox, George W., and Bruce Barclay Cameron. *The Camerons of Wilmington.* 1994.

"Wilmington Unit, American Legion Auxiliary to Wilmington Post No. 10, Department of North Carolina, Year Book 1945–46."

Newspapers and Periodicals (Partial)

AA Barrage newspaper, Camp Davis, N.C., 1943–44.

The American Jewish Times, undated (believed 1944).

Cape Fear Journal, Wilmington, N.C., November 29, 1942.

David W. Carnell in *Wilmington Morning Star,* July 31, 1998.

Evening Post, Wilmington, N.C., various 1944–45.

Ex-CBI Roundup, January 1999.

Gab newspaper, 1942.

Globe, Camp Lejeune, N.C., newspaper, various 1944.

Lower Cape Fear Historical Society Bulletins, Wilmington, N.C., May, July, October 1999.

Morning Star, Wilmington, N.C., 1941–46, and later years.

News, Wilmington, N.C., various 1941–45.

News & Courier, Charleston, S.C., 1943.

The North Carolina Shipbuilder, Wilmington, N.C., 1942–45.

The Park City Daily News. Bowling Green, Ky., March 22, 1942.

"Sixth District Soundings," U.S. Coast Guard Auxiliary, Charleston, S.C., 1943–45.

"Southeastern North Carolina in World War II," *Wilmington Star-News* Supplement, 1992.

The State: A Weekly Survey of North Carolina magazine, 1944.

Ben Steelman in *Wilmington Sunday Star-News,* February 4, 2001.

Sunday Star-News, Wilmington, N.C., 1941–46, and later years.

Tidewater magazine, January 1985.

Waves and Currents, Cape Fear Museum, Wilmington, N.C., May 1999.

The Wildcat, New Hanover High School, Wilmington, N.C., 1941–45.

Wilmington (N.C.) Telephone Directory, March 1945.

Woman's Home Companion, February 1945.

Surveys

Roddy Cameron

Claude Daughtry

Irving T. Glover

Mary B. Walton Hawkinson

Sandra Kinlaw Huddle
George Dudley Humphrey
Jeannine Stanley Jones
Nancy West Jones
Peggy Mae Warren Longmire
Earl M. Page
Robert S. Pollock
Margaret Sampson Rogers
Marie Burgwin Sanborn
Blanche Stanley Sneeden

Correspondence to Author (Partial)

Captain Luciano Callini, Italian Navy, to Leonard Kiesel, January 1995
David W. Carnell, May 29 and October 24, 2000
Harriett Harrington Connolly, October 25, 1998
Thelma Barclift Crowder, November 3, 1998
Claude and Mary Daughtry, October 9, 1998
Dorothy Bunn Dibble, August 28, 1999
Mary Fisher Eason, January 5, 2000
George J. Green, October 1, 1998
John R. Hicks, September 9, 1998
George F. Hunt, Jr., 1999
Viola M. Jones to George and Jo Chadwick, August 12, 1969
Adrian L. Lawson, July 27, 1999
Evelyn Bergen Loftin, November 6, 1998, and June 6, 1999
Kenneth R. Murphy, May 30, 1999
Arvel Harrison Perryman, June 5, 1999
Bernard Rabunsky, July 9, 1999
Catherine Crowe Ragland, October 31, 2001
Marie Burgwin Sanborn, October 28, 1998, and June 26, 2000
Clayton Smith, May 23, 1999
Frances J. Wagner, April 18, 1999
Jane Baldwin Yates, December 11, 1999

Miscellaneous (Partial)

American Legion Post 10 Wartime Scrapbooks, MS Accession #70. William Madison Randall Library, University of North Carolina at Wilmington.

Bronze Star Citation, 5th Marine Division, FMF [1945]. Private First Class Mitchell N. Saleeby, Jr., USMCR.

"Five Years of North Carolina Shipbuilding," North Carolina Shipbuilding Company, Wilmington, N.C., May 1, 1946.

"Greetings from Camp Davis, N.C." Post card folder, Service News Co., Wilmington, N.C.

Headquarters, Armed Forces Induction Station, Fort Bragg, N.C., 3 August 1943. Special Orders Number 184.

Elizabeth Davis Kinlaw, song 1944, *The Victory Ship*. © Elizabeth Davis Kinlaw.

Miscellaneous ship, aviation, and personnel records of the Naval Historical Center, Washington, D.C.

"New Hanover County Public Schools Teachers' Bulletin, 1943–44."

North Carolina Shipbuilding Company *Wartime Plant Protection Bulletin No. 4*, "Air Raid Warnings and Blackouts," December 20, 1941.

Notes from presentations given during "An Afternoon of Sharing: World War II and African-Americans," August 22, 1999, at Chestnut St. Presbyterian Church: Cornelia Haggins Campbell, Peggy Pridgen, Bertha Todd, George E. Norman.

Lieutenant General G. S. Patton, Jr,, commanding Third U.S. Army, 16 April 45, to Commanding General, 95th Infantry Division.

Program of "Shipyard Days, 1999," Wartime Wilmington Commemoration, 1999, North Carolina State Ports Authority.

Program for the unveiling of the Commemorative Marker to be placed Shipyard Boulevard and Carolina Beach Road for North Carolina Shipbuilding Company, 1941–1946, on October 1, 1992.

"Report: History of 51st Field Hospital, 10 September 1943 to April 1945."

"Reunion Yearbook," New Hanover High School Class of 1942 (50th, June 5–6, 1992).

Lieutenant General W. H. Simpson, commanding Ninth U.S. Army, to Major General Harry L. Twaddle, 95th Infantry Division, 6 May 45.

Dr. Everard H. Smith, "The Wilmington USO Building and Community Arts Center" flyer, 1998.

"Souvenir Program of the First (and maybe last) Musical Revue, 366th Fighter Group, Monday November 15th [1945], Base Theater, Army Air Base, Bluethenthal Field, Wilmington, N.C." Provided by Hannah Block.

Temple of Israel Bulletin, Wilmington, N.C., April 5, 1944. Provided by New Hanover County Public Library.

J. V. "Pat" Warren interview by Peggy Mae Warren Longmire, September 1998.

Dr. Barbara Frey Waxman, ed., "1898–1998 B'Nai Israel: The First Hundred Years," 1998, Wilmington, N.C.

Index

Photographs are in **_bold italics_**

Forest Hills School (wartime), xxvi, 6, 7, 56,
164, 166, 173, 177, 193
activities, 164, 166
5th grade class/schoolmates, *165*, 184, 193
Parent-Teachers Association/teachers, 164,
177, 178
Formosa, 193
Fort Benning, Georgia, xviii
Fort Bliss, Texas, 43
Fort Bragg, North Carolina, 58, 67, 91, 156,
158, 159, 182
Fort Campbell, Kentucky, 70
Fort Caswell, North Carolina, xxiii
Fort Caswell Naval Station, North Carolina,
inshore-warfare patrol (antisubmarine
warfare) base, xxiii
Fort Crook, Nebraska, 95
Fort Dix, New Jersey, 114
Fort Fisher, North Carolina, 29, 54, 64, 180
as advanced anti-aircraft artillery (AAA)
training base, xxiii, 79, 80, 83, 87
business/residents/social life, 87, 153, 155,
156, 158
Fort Screvin, Georgia, 136
Fountain, Millard James, Jr. "Jim," 22, 156,
157
Fountain, Pearl (Winner). *See* Winner, Carl,
Jr. family
Fountain Oil Co., 192
Fountain, W. G., 157
Fowler, George A., 127
Foy, N. L., 150
Fox, Joe B., 50
Foxtown neighborhood, 6, 16
Fraley, E. B., 115
France, Campaign in, xxv, 20, 45, 50–52, 72,
95, 110, 112, 123, 125, 128–31, 133,
134, 136, 182, 184–86, 189, 192, 193,
201, 203, 205
Aix-la-Chappelle, 136
Anthera, 127
Benwihr, Alsace, 52
Colleville-sur-Mer. *See* Normandy, France,
Campaign in/invasion/Battle of
Colmar Pocket. *See* Colmar Pocket, Battle of
Dijon, 50
French Army, 51
French (people), 129
Houffalize, 187
Jebsheim, Battle of, 129
Le Havre, 50, 112, 135
Marseilles, 50, 52
Metz, 134
Montebourg. *See* Normandy, France,
Campaign in/invasion/Battle of

Mortain. *See* Normandy, France, Campaign
in/invasion/Battle of
Nantes, 136
Normandy. *See* Normandy, Campaign in/
invasion/Battle of
Paris, 51, 53
St. Lo. *See* Normandy, Campaign in/
invasion/Battle of
Southern France (the South of France), 51,
55, 127, 131, 184, 192
Vosges Mountains, 52
Franklin, Mal, 117
Franks, Jack, 166
Frazier, Glenn, 59
Freed, Walter B., 29
Freeman, Jere, Jr., 5
Freeman's Shoe Store, 41
Friedman, Samuel, 29, 192
Funderburk, Banks, 118
Funderburk, Ray, 21, 103
Fussell, Harold, xix, 181
Fussell, J. H., Jr., 150
Futrelle's Drug Store, 1

G

Galphin, Robert W., 143
Gardner, Harry L., 32, 143
Garey, George A., 14, 150
Garey, Robert Ranor, 14, 57
Garniss, George Hubbard, xxiii, 3
Garniss, Viola Elizabeth Jones. *See* Jones,
Wilbur D. family
Garrabrant family, 182–84
Betty Garrabrant Cantwell. *See* Cantwell,
Betty Garrabrant
Edgar Cornelius Garrabrant (senior), *183*
Mr. & Mrs. Edgar Cornelius Garrabrant,
182
Edgar Garrabrant (child), 182, *183*
John Richard "Dick" Garrabrant, xvii, 14,
182, *183*, 184, 194, 202
Margey Garrabrant, xvii, 182, 183
William "Bill" Garrabrant, 12, 182, *183*, 184
Garrison, Mabel, 152
Gaylor family, 54
Gaylord family
Addie Lee Gaylord, 70
Mrs. Gaylord, 70
Robert Lee Gaylord, 70
George, Daniel Hand, 202
George, Lillian M., 53
Georgia, 67, 90, 92, 96, 126, 136, 169
Augusta Military Academy, 169
Atlanta, 67
federal prison, 46, 65